Living Sideways

"Spilyay/Coyote and the Stars," by Roxanne Chinook (Wasco). Reproduced by permission of the artist.

Living Sideways

Tricksters in
American Indian Oral Traditions

Franchot Ballinger

UNIVERSITY OF OKLAHOMA PRESS : NORMAN

A version of chapter 3 appeared in *American Indian Quarterly* 13.1 (winter 1989): 15–30, © 1989 by the University of Nebraska Press. A version of chapter 4 appeared in *Studies in American Indian Literatures* 12.4 (winter 2000): 15–39. A version of chapter 5 appeared in *MELUS* 17.1 (spring 1991–92): 21–39. Copyright information for the trickster stories included in this volume can be found at the end of each story.

This book is published with the generous assistance of The McCasland Foundation, Duncan, Oklahoma.

Library of Congress Cataloging-in-Publication Data

Ballinger, Franchot.
  Living sideways : tricksters in American Indian oral traditions / Franchot Ballinger.
    p.   cm.
  Includes bibliographical references and index.
  ISBN 0-8061-3632-4 (cloth)
  ISBN-13 : 978-0-8061-3796-4 (paper)
  ISBN-10 : 0-8061-3796-7 (paper)
    1. Indian mythology—North America. 2. Legends—North America. 3. Tricksters—North America. I. Title.

E98.R3B234 1998
398.2'089'97—dc22

                                           2004046091

To the tribal people of North America, whose stories these are and whose gifts to me personally have been immeasurable.

Contents

Preface

This book started as a research and writing project in the 1983 National Endowment for the Humanities Summer Seminar on American Indian Literatures directed by A. LaVonne Ruoff. I chose American Indian tricksters as my project for purely practical and self-serving reasons: I wanted to attend the seminar, and so I chose a topic that I thought would improve my chances of being accepted. Even at that relatively early point in my study of American Indian oral traditions and literatures, I could see that tricksters were ever popular with those interested in Indian cultures, both general readers and academic specialists. My specific seminar topic was a study of American Indian tricksters in relation to European picaros, with whom the indigenous tricksters have been compared. My seminar paper became a presentation at the Midwestern Modern Language Association in November 1983 and then grew into an essay, "Ambigere: The Euro-American Picaro and the American Indian Trickster," published in *MELUS,* the journal of The Society for the Study of the Multi-Ethnic Literature of the United States. My reading that summer convinced me that I had chosen a subject of such diversity and complexity as to occupy me for some time.

As I continued studying tricksters, I saw three major problems in the literature. First, there had been relatively little effort to consider North American Indian tricksters in relation to each other. I knew that some generalizations about American Indians are possible, but I also knew that their cultural diversity makes generalizing risky. I wondered to what degree such issues extended to tricksters. My second concern was that some of the best known and most influential essays about North American tricksters were too seldom grounded in American Indian oral traditions and culture. Finally, there were few book-length studies of American Indian tricksters. For years, the only book (aside from a few collections of stories) was Paul Radin's *The Trickster* (1927). While it is a seminal work in trickster studies, Radin's book focuses narrowly on the Winnebago trickster in the context of Winnebago culture, with brief summaries of Assiniboine and Tlingit myths. Essays by Kerènyi and Jung included in *The Trickster* are cross-cultural at best, with no attention paid to the particulars of American Indian cultures. In 1993 William Bright's *A Coyote Reader* was published. Bright's book is essentially an anthology of trickster stories, with relatively brief commentary on tricksters. Many of the stories are from California, Oregon, and Washington, and a few are not even American Indian.

Living Sideways: Tricksters in American Indian Oral Traditions is my effort to confront some of these issues. My intention is to examine tricksters in all their roles and dimensions (acknowledging their diversity as necessary): their frequent sacred powers and their roles as story characters, social critics, teachers, buffoons, transformers, mediators between humanity and gods and humanity and nature, outlaws, headmen, fathers or mothers, husbands, and so forth. Whenever possible I highlight germane facts about American Indian cultures and points of view, thereby hoping to present tricksters as less reflective of non-Native perceptions than is often the case. My goal throughout has been to foreground the tricksters of North American tribal oral traditions, not Euro-American scholarly theories. However, this book is not a definitive analysis of tricksters; it is, rather, an introduction to the mysteries and delights of this most popular of oral-tradition personages. Nor, as I discuss in the introduction, does it claim to offer the definitive Indian view on tricksters. I welcome the possibility that this book's inevitable shortcomings will encourage more American Indian scholars and creative writers to acquaint us with the tricksters of their own communities' oral "critical" traditions.

While the book is one non-Native's effort to step beyond accepted academic criticism, I have not abandoned non-Native scholarship. After all, most of the sources I draw upon exist because of Euro-American scholarship. Like any book with scholarly pretensions, this one would not have been possible without the foundation laid by many who have preceded me in trickster studies. I am grateful for their contributions even when I do not agree with them, and I trust that my documentation throughout demonstrates the extent of my debt.

I am also grateful to the peer reviewers and editors of *American Indian Quarterly, American Indian Culture and Research Journal, MELUS,* and *Studies in American Indian Literatures* for publishing my articles on tricksters. Significant portions of this book are based on some of those essays.

There are individuals who merit special thanks. Let me begin with Bob and Jeanne Foskett. In addition to their long-standing friendship, I am grateful for their reading recommendations in the early days of my interest in American Indian cultures. From this seed, a significant part of my academic career grew. Furthermore, studying American Indian cultures led me to search in my own traditions for evidence of social and spiritual values that might, in their own way, reflect what I admire in American Indian traditions. More recently, Bob and Jeanne encouraged me during the process of submitting my manuscript and, in fact, were instrumental in my screwing up my courage to submit it to the University of Oklahoma Press.

Like many others in the discipline of American Indian studies, I am indebted in numerous ways to A. Lavonne Ruoff, in whose NEH seminar I first studied tricksters. I am grateful as well to the National Endowment for the Humanities for making my participation possible. This seminar also brought me a new friend in Roger Dunsmore, who, at different times over the years of our long-distance friendship, has encouraged and challenged me from his own deep understanding of American Indian oral traditions and contemporary writing. Colleagues in the Association for the Study of American Indian Literatures have been important to me, in particular Paula Gunn Allen, Bob Nelson, John Purdy, Jarold Ramsey, Carter Revard, Jim Ruppert, Susan Scarberry-Garcia, Brian Swann, and Andrew Wiget. They might be surprised to see their names here, but each at some time has provided me an important opportunity to grow in the discipline or has encouraged me in ways that he or she might not even remember.

Thanks to my erstwhile dean and department head, John Bryan and Janet Reed, for support in the form of released time and academic leave. I am also grateful to Marvin Garrett, colleague, ex-office partner, and friend. More than once in the past, Marvin's faith in my teaching and writing buoyed me up when I might otherwise have sunk.

John Biederman provided valuable, time-saving computer help. Rich James provided last-minute research help. John Bierhorst made significant criticisms and recommendations during the review process at the University of Oklahoma Press. Many at the Press are responsible for all that is good in this book. Acquisitions Editor Jo Ann Reece kept me informed about my manuscript's progress through the review process and, once the book was accepted, patiently answered my neophyte's questions and provided other essential guidance. Sarah Nestor's skillful copyediting created clarity where there was none, led to greater accuracy, and improved the prose style. Jennifer Cunningham smoothed my way through the final stages of the editorial process and more. She, too, patiently answered my frequent questions.

I am particularly grateful to Wasco artist Roxanne Chinook and Lakota artist S. D. Nelson for having enough faith in this book to let me use their work as illustrations for it.

Of course, I must acknowledge the American Indians whose stories are the subject of this book. I cannot personally thank the individuals who told the stories, so in appreciation of all American Indian people, my royalties for this book are being directed to the American Indian College fund.

Finally, and most important to me, I acknowledge with loving gratitude Henrietta, my wife, whose many sacrifices over the years have made my work possible.

Living Sideways

Ojibwe Creation

Taiya Nanabush! He was really afraid!
Oh! then he remembered Mushrat [*sic*].
"Hey, you dive."
"Alright, I'll get wet."
"Ey! Muskrat, be careful."
Taiya Muskrat lifted his tail,
then kwack! It sounded like that.
Oh! Muskrat swam around,
soon he came in sight of trees and
he hadn't drowned yet . . .
then he got halfway down the trees and
on the bottom he went unconscious
but not before he had taken some earth in his mouth,
and some in his hands holding tight,
and some around his stiff poker.
All the while Nanabush was watching for him.
Taiya! he saw a ball of fur floating on the water
and he picked it up
and for no reason he opened up the hand.
Taiya he held earth clasped in his hand!
And again, in the other hand he held earth tight
and there on his poker he looked.
Still more earth!
and there down his throat was lots more.
And so Nanabush blew on him and again Muskrat lived.
Nanabush dried the earth,

"Now I will complete the earth."
Nanabush blew on it.
Kuniginin, a little island floated there!
And already the *manidoog* came out of the water. He spoke to them,
"Slowly! Later when the earth is bigger you will come out!"
Again he blew, a great island floated there,
and then where he blew was much earth.
And more life stirred the *manidoog.*
Again he blew on the earth.
He spoke to the one of swift flight, Falcon,
"Let's go, fly around the earth, find out how large it is."
For some time he was gone,
then he arrived back and said,
"It is not so very large."
Again Nanabush breathed on it,
a long time he breathed on it,
Again he spoke,
"Let's go, you, Raven, learn how large is the earth."
Sure enough Raven started out.
It is uncertain how many months Raven was gone.
Later he returned.
"I wasn't able to learn how large is the earth,
I ran out of earth."
So Nanabush spoke to Raven,
"So that you will be proud I will create you,
how would you be proud?"
"Make me as the blue sky on a clear day Nanabush."
So sure enough Nanabush touched him blue,
and this now is Raven,
created by Nanabush.

Kim Echlin, "Ojibwe Creation," originally published in *Studies in American Indian Literatures* 8, no. 2 (1984). Reprinted by permission of Kim Echlin. General notes for each trickster story can be found in the notes section.

Introduction

No other figure in the verbal art of American Indian oral traditions has garnered so much attention as tricksters in all of their guises, the best known of the family being Coyote. Since the last third of the nineteenth century, thousands of North American trickster stories have been recorded and retold by anthropologists, ethnographers, missionaries, tourists, and explorers, as well as sundry literary types. Accompanying or proceeding from these have been numerous commentaries on tricksters, most of them essay length. One obvious reason for all of this attention is the prominence of tricksters in the mythologies of many American Indian tribes. Another reason is the fact that contemporary writers, Native and non-Native alike, have made the wayward trickster, usually in the form of Coyote, something of a celebrity among many readers. Poet Gary Snyder is probably the most prominent among non-Native writers to have appropriated Coyote. American Indian writers who draw on trickster traditions—their own or those of other tribes—are numerous. Probably best known among these are: Simon Ortiz and Leslie Marmon Silko, for whom Coyote is, among other things, emblematic of the survival of American Indian traditions (as he is for many other Native writers); Louise Erdrich, who draws upon the Anishinaabe (Ojibwe/Chippewa) trickster for characters in her fiction (for instance, Gerry Nanabush in *Love Medicine*) and for the figure of Old Man Potchikoo in her poetry; and Peter Blue Cloud, whose contemporary Coyote is as ribald and wily as any of his North American tribal precursors.[1] Yet another reason for tricksters' popularity is the fact that from the beginning of academics' acquaintance with them, tricksters have challenged the dominant culture's understanding as a conundrum—but one, all seemed certain, ultimately amenable to Euro-American scholarship. This optimism has given rise to a long line of questions and answers, many of them quite imaginative. However, in spite of such inventiveness, the scholarship sometimes seems to navigate waters different from those of the American Indian oral traditions in which we find the tricksters.

Of course, non-Indians cannot hope to experience tricksters as do those raised in the traditions, nor can we hope to convey "meaning" with the same understanding. What do we really know about tricksters if we view them through Euro-American and not tribal eyes? How do we even begin to understand tricksters given the impossibility of our experiencing a Native vision? Most of us are, as Arnold Krupat says, "unwilling to speak for the Indian, and unable to speak as an Indian,"[2] and so we should be mindful of Greg Sarris's indictment of white scholars writing about American Indian culture: "what all these scholars do not seem to see is that while purportedly defending Indians and enlightening others about them, they replicate in practice that which characterizes not only certain non-Indian editors' manner of dealing with Indians but also that of an entire European and Euro-American populace of which these editors and scholars are a part. The Indians are absent or they are strategically removed from the territory, made safe, intelligible on the colonizer's terms."[3]

To keep the American Indian present in studies such as this, one must make earnest efforts to convey the American Indian view of trickster whenever possible. But, of course, even earnest intentions are fraught with difficulties, not the least of them being the attempt to define what the American Indian view is.[4] One's hope lies in Robert Pelton's assurance that "the knotty logic of the trickster is best unraveled by keeping him firmly situated within the cultural context."[5] Those who have not known as participants the cultural contexts in which trickster stories were and are told must rely on the observations of others, Native and non-Native. Unfortunately, there have been few extended commentaries on tricksters and their role in their cultures by American Indians themselves;

most have come to us filtered through the voices of dominant-culture researchers.

Additionally, trying to reach some sort of understanding about what añ individual story might mean to a Native audience is a daunting task. One obvious difficulty is that of interpreting the experiences and ideas of one culture to another. How does one negotiate the differences, and what about apparent similarities? How far can one rely on seeming correspondences between one's own culture and an American Indian culture?[6] Is it really likely, for example, that the American Indian trickster shares significant qualities and experiences with the European picaro, as has been claimed? Accepting purported similarities can lead to serious misconceptions. Irving Goldman warns that a representation of people's thinking in a different culture is suspect if it sounds familiar to "the western academic mind."[7] Certainly, Christian missionaries have been known to report trickster stories in ways more reflective of their cultural biases than of American Indian perspectives. Franz Boas reports that missionaries who recorded tales of the Thompson Indians of British Columbia gave more emphasis to trickster as an altruistic culture hero than the Indian storytellers he was working with intended.[8] Did such emphasis reflect the missionaries' cultural assumptions about what a cosmic creator or an earthly hero should be like? Possibly. The Reverend E. Ahenakew might have allowed his own world and moral views to intrude into his transcriptions of Cree trickster stories, for even while the Cree sequence he published contains a number of episodes that are cognates of other tribes' trickster stories, it is singularly lacking in the bawdy trickster so common in many other American Indian oral traditions. Moreover, in the opening episode, his rendering of a woman who becomes infatuated with snakes and her husband's curse on them has a familiar Judeo-Christian ring.[9]

Another important question is: What can a single telling of a story reveal to us about its culture? Individuals know that generalizations about their own culture are often unreliable, yet we persist in generalizing about others' cultures. This book, like many that have preceded it in American Indian Studies, makes assertions about cultural attitudes the stories dramatize. Such assertions must be read with qualification and with the

understanding that one telling of a story may be an insufficient foundation for broad assertions. To say that a story conveys this or that cultural
outlook is to ignore the dynamics of that story's life in its community.
Such a declaration is also problematic because it assumes a collective
Indian and fails to take into account the possible role of an individual
storyteller's style or artistry, to say nothing of the prospect that the story
version under consideration may well be—unknown to us—a response
to a particular social or historical event.[10] Craig Thompson explicates
this problem in "Gender Representation in Two Clackamas Myths." In
his analysis of stories recorded and interpreted by Melville Jacobs,
Thompson's understanding of culture leads him to interpret the myths
differently from Jacobs. Thompson argues that a culture is not composed
of a single group; rather, it comprises "an amalgamation of groups."
Further, groups and individuals within them are not objects embodying
"cultural meaning"; they generate such meaning. It is not accurate to
claim that a myth projects a society's "real" attitude about anything.
Instead, it is probably true that "in the actual context of performance,
there were a variety of audiences which a single 'univocal' reading doesn't
account for." Stories are part of a "continual social discourse"; that is,
meaning lies in "reactions to the tales and in the effect that the tale had
on intertribal relations."[11] Similarly, Kathleen Sands, writing of the collaborative nature of American Indian texts, says, "Each is in some measure
communal in origin and on-going performance: each expresses cultural
and individual sensibilities in varying degrees over time, and no single
voice can claim authority to speak for some essential tribal way of experiencing and articulating culture."[12]

Another obvious obstacle to our grasping American tribal tricksters
is the fact that the texts most of us read are translations. This cannot be
helped, but our experience and understanding will suffer from relying
on translations just as they do when we read any world literature in
translation. We who are acquainted with the stories only in translation
must accept that we actually know very little about them, certainly lacking
the intimacy that the word *know* suggests. We experience only one of a
story's many surfaces and probably little of its depths. Stories are more
than information vehicles. They are, as Sam D. Gill tells us,

complex symbols, networks of sounds, odors, forms, colors, temperatures, and rhythms. All of these nonverbal features and many more create the patterns through which reality is perceived. They create the moods and goals that give orientation to life. They provide a presence in which actions take on value. Consequently, any story, any song, any prayer is a stimulus that frees strings of associated images, emotions, and patterns. To ask what they mean and expect a translatable message is often to ask an inappropriate question. Their significance is inseparable from the whole field of symbols they evoke.[13]

Even if we had absolutely precise translations that manage to convey all the meanings and nuances of the tale's original language, the text's transformation from orality to print and the absence of both social and performative context would diminish our experience of the story. Archie Phinney, Nez Perce ethnographer, makes clear that a printed text is but a faint whisper of its performed self when he laments "the loss of spirit [in a printed text]. . . . When I read my story mechanically, I find only the cold corpse."[14]

Given such difficulties, a non-Indian's pursuit of American Indian tricksters may seem like arrogance or folly; but tricksters are a challenge, and few people can resist a puzzle. There is solace in knowing that American Indian authors also find tricksters to be an enigma. Mohawk poet Maurice Kenny says, "I'm not sure that you're supposed to understand coyote [sic]. If you were to ask Peter [Blue Cloud], who's written several books now on coyote, does he completely understand him? He'd be the first person to say 'No Way! that's why I write stories about him.'"[15] And perhaps I can also plead, "that's why I write about him."

ON MYTH, LITERATURE, AND MEANING

Understanding how trickster stories fit into American Indian oral traditions is essential to understanding trickster stories themselves. To begin, I should clarify my use of the word *myth*, a frequently troublesome term in the study of cultural traditions. As used in this book (and such studies generally), *myth* is not a judgment of a story's truth or lack thereof. We commonly denigrate another culture's beliefs or some mistaken belief in our own culture as "pure myth." That certainly is how the word has been applied by European and white American observers of alien, and particularly indigenous, religious beliefs and practices—in other words, as an ethnocentric verdict. In fact, for most in a culture, a myth is in some sense true. Jarold Ramsey's definition is both precise and conventional: "Myths are sacred traditional stories whose shaping function is to tell the people who know them who they are; how, through what origins and transformations, they have come to possess their particular world; and how they should live in that world, and with each other."[16] What John W. Roberts says of folklore in general is true of myth: Its "creation should contribute to culture building by serving as a means of transmitting the values on which a group's ideal image itself is based." Melville Jacobs made a similar point about Clackamas myths when he said that their emphasis is on people and relationships and on confirming the worth of the tribe's cultural heritage and system of values.[17] Ramsey's and Roberts's points are as relevant for trickster stories as for any other American Indian stories.

Claude Levi-Strauss says about myth: "Whatever our ignorance of the language and the culture of the people where it originated, a myth is still felt as a myth by any reader anywhere in the world. Its substance does not lie in its style, its original music, or its syntax, but in the story which it tells. Myth is langauge [sic], functioning on an especially high level where meaning succeeds practically at 'taking off' from the linguistic ground on which it keeps rolling."[18] There is something to this, but to minimize the role of style, and so forth, in a culture's experience of a story is to deny any uniqueness to the story itself. Storytellers—oral or literate—and poets know that style is as much a part of a story's significance as content itself. Frequently, a well-told American Indian story is not only entertainment; it might be essential to a healing or other ceremony or it might be a teaching opportunity, both uses being well grounded in the American Indian belief in the power of the word. Regardless of occasion and purpose, the telling of a story may reveal the touch of a master artist in his or her culture's tradition.

As we might guess, American Indian trickster stories are often told by accomplished American Indian raconteurs with all of the stylistic flourishes that characterize good storytelling in any culture: gestures, dramatic pacing, voice changes for different characters, and so forth. For example, in some traditions Coyote always speaks in a high-pitched, whining manner.[19] Few early researchers probed American Indian aesthetics beyond these obvious traits. Past translations of American Indian stories often aimed to convey only literal content and cultural context without considering how the storyteller might have shaped the story artistically. This approach led not only to dreary translations but also to translations that largely ignored American Indian storytelling aesthetics. Thus Alan Dundes argues that "folkloristic structure is independent of language."[20] Dundes in *The Morphology of North American Indian Folktales*, Stith Thompson in *The Folktale*, and Polly Pope in "Toward a Structural Analysis of North American Trickster Tales" base their structural analyses on types, combinations, and repetitions of actions and events in stories.

Some writers continue to describe formal characteristics of trickster stories in terms of content with some observations regarding style. Andrew Wiget categorizes trickster stories into two types by subject matter. One type criticizes social structure by focusing on cultural experience and suggests humans' inability to live up to their social roles and positions. The second dramatizes humanity's innate imperfection. In addition, however, Wiget makes important observations about form and style: "Trickster narratives may be presented as brief anecdotes that compress encounters with burlesque simplicity, as developed tales with exchanges of dialogue and scene shifts, or as cycles that weave together many tales into a narrative lasting an hour or so." Further, trickster stories are commonly "marked by recurrent formal features, which provide a background of expectations." In particular, tales are usually ahistorical (appropriate enough for stories generally classified as myths) and only occasionally set in an identifiable location (and in those few instances, usually for purposes of verisimilitude only).[21]

Other scholars have identified common types of trickster stories for specific cultures. For example, Galen Buller identifies the four most common kinds of Comanche Coyote stories in terms of subject matter: Coyote's attempts to imitate other animals, his relationships with people, his predicaments in circumstances involving white people, and his attempts to manage twentieth-century problems. Further, Buller says, there are two types of trickery story: those in which Coyote tries to trick other animals (relatively few, and even fewer stories in which he is successful) and those in which he tricks people (at which he is generally more successful, especially when he practices his wiles on whites).[22]

American Indians classify stories quite differently from Euro-American scholars. Commonly, American Indian oral traditions divide stories into two categories, one containing what we would call myths and another comprising stories we might call legends and/or historical stories. Different tribal traditions have specific names for each class; for example, an Inupiaq storyteller has classified stories as *unipkaaq* and *quliaqtuaq,* the former being myths and the latter stories in which people have names and stories about encounters with ghosts, about history, and so forth.[23] The Winnebagos distinguish between *waikan* ("what is sacred") and *worak* ("what is recounted").[24] As a rule, traditions place trickster stories specifically in one such category or another. The Gros Ventres distinguish between myth (*hanta'antya*) and tales (*waantsea*), with tales about the trickster Nix'ant being among the former.[25] Some storytelling traditions classify stories according to the era with which a story deals. Wichita history, for instance, consists of four eras: the creation; the transformation; an era following a deluge, the present; and finally, the end of the world. Coyote stories are of the transformation era.[26] Wind River medicine men and others with visionary gifts distinguish types of narrative by the kind of protagonist, as well as by entertainment value and "fictive historical" sequence. Story categories include cannibalistic forest and mountain trolls, turtle-dove stories, buffalo tales, hero stories, white men's tales, and Coyote stories. The latter are especially important because Coyote was the head of all animals.[27] Among the Pawnees stories are either true or fictional, the latter being those created especially by old men to express some moral precept or convey a warning. Trickster tales fall into the latter group.[28]

In the last thirty years or so, scholars have made a serious study of American Indian oral-tradition aesthetics. Scholars such as Dell Hymes,

Ekkehart Malotki, Anthony Mattina, Dennis Tedlock, and Barre Toelken, as well as the generation of scholars that these men have trained or influenced, regularly advance our understanding of the formal, stylistic characteristics of American Indian stories with translations that more nearly approximate the formal traits of the stories in their original languages. Such translations are particularly attentive to linguistic structure and culturally specific storytelling techniques. The particulars of these scholars' works are too complex to deal with here; however, a few brief examples from trickster stories will illustrate these qualities.

Trickster stories may be marked by specific linguistic and structural qualities. Toelken tells us that Navajo Ma'i stories are told slowly so that "key actions and words are stylistically foregrounded."[29] Paul Zolbrod points out that in one Ma'i story, the conniving Coyote's sentence structures and sentence lengths vary, while a chary prairie-dog character uses paired, often parallel sentences.[30]

Another formal trait of trickster stories that merits attention is their formulaic openings. Many stories from American Indian oral traditions—mythic or otherwise—begin with a formulaic phrase, that is, a set phrase that marks the beginning of the story and perhaps even alerts the audience members to the kind of story they are about to hear. Euro-Americans know that "once upon a time" usually signals entry into a world of make-believe. Similarly, nonmythic Zuni stories open with the word *son'ahchi,* a word used only in this context and which cannot be translated into English.[31] Northwest Sahaptin myths open with a phrase rendered by Melville Jacobs as "There was *ani.*"[32] Among the Delawares formulaic openings to stories include phrases such as "Many snows ago," "Long ago when the Lenape people lived in the east," and "My story camps."[33]

Trickster stories, too, often begin with formulaic phrases that translate as "Coyote was going there," "Coyote was traveling along," or some similar phrase reminding us that tricksters are ever peripatetic. Toelken and Tacheeni Scott's translation of the formulaic opening to Navajo Coyote stories is "Ma'i was trotting along [having always done so]." They explain in a note that the Navajo wording is complex and refers to this story as one of a series of repeated actions: "The closest English equivalent . . .

would be 'in one of these episodes.' . . . Yellowman [the storyteller] here limits himself to one incident in Coyote's career, but opens the narration in such a way as to remind his listeners of the whole fabric of Coyote legend."[34] In some traditions there are formulaic conclusions as well. Among the Dakotas, stories about the trickster Ikto traditionally ended with "And from then on, who knows where Ikto went next?"[35]

Toelken and Scott's use of the phrase "the whole fabric of Coyote legend" raises the important issue of whether American Indian trickster stories were/are understood in their traditions as a linear series, as Paul Radin implies for the Winnebago stories.[36] Radin argues that the trickster Wakdjunkaga progresses from being an undifferentiated, unsocialized psyche to being a socialized, responsible, knowingly benevolent individual. Seeing trickster episodes as a linear progression is essential to this thematic perception of the trickster's pilgrim's progress. Certainly, the commonly applied term *cycle* encourages us to look for a discernible pattern of thematic organization, for some sort of development from one identifiable condition to another; but Radin's (and others') use of the term *cycle* seems mostly a matter of applying a traditional Euro-American literary-folklore term to collections of trickster stories.

We do not know with any certainty that Radin's contention accurately reflects Winnebago tradition. Claims similar to his theory are made for a few other trickster traditions. For example, Melville Jacobs says that the Clackamas Coyote progresses from a libertine's irresponsibility to responsibility.[37] Buller maintains that Comanche trickster stories, if read in a series, show Coyote changing from being a bungler and imitator to being a leader, in control of his environment.[38] On the other hand, Buller is clearly much influenced by Jung's discussion of tricksters and by Radin's sense of organization in the Winnebago cycle.

Radin might have supposed that Winnebago storytellers and audiences experience the stories about Wakdjunkaga as—or at least understand them to be—serially arranged. Perhaps he collected the stories thus, but that does not mean sequential, linear tellings were routine. In many American Indian communities tricksters stories have always been told episodically and not in anything like chronological, serial order, and while many listeners were no doubt acquainted with the whole of the trickster tradition, we have no reason to believe that contextualizing an episode sequentially mattered for an audience's imaginative encounter with the story. Certainly, there seems to be precious little evidence that it mattered for the audience's perception of a trickster.

In reality the evidence may indicate that nothing about most trickster episodes implies a structure that linearly represents a trickster's psychic progression to individuation and benevolence, as Radin's version asserts. Robert Brightman, for example, tells us that among the Crees "there exists no canonical order of trickster stories," although some Cree story-tellers have "sequence designs" of their own for certain stories.[39] In general it seems that trickster episodes can be told sequentially or picked up at any point in a trickster's career. This is appropriate for the kind of indeterminacy that tricksters represent. In short, little in most other trickster traditions bears out Radin's thematic analysis. Nevertheless, some academics have used his work in *The Trickster* as a critical prototype and have interpreted trickster stories accordingly.

It does not appear that the *meaning* (what in a literature class we might call *theme*) of trickster stories resides for most American Indians in any particular order of telling. Our common understanding of another aspect of meaning in mythic trickster stories may be faulty also—that is, the assumption that trickster myths are etiological. Certainly, many myths contain etiological elements, and it is probably true that some storytellers narrate stories as a way of explaining the cause of certain natural phenomena. However, in an old study T. T. Watermann argues that the so-called etiological elements in myths are not present as explanation of anything but rather are confirmation of the authenticity of the story.[40] Hence, a story's plot is not intended to explain how skunk got its stripes; rather, the fact that skunks have stripes is verification of the story's truth.[41] Levi-Strauss has argued that it is a mistake "to think that natural phenomena are what myths seek to explain, when they are rather the medium through which myths try to explain facts which are themselves not of a natural but a logical order."[42]

Clearly, we will mistake the purpose and import of myth if we see it only as a way of teaching about origins. To begin with, in traditional American Indian communities explanation as teaching often tends to be much more indirect than the tacked-on explanatory elements of myths suggest.[43] There is, similarly, an indirection to meaning in American Indian stories. An example of such indirection and the validity of Levi-Strauss's suggestion can be seen in an anecdote Toelken recounts from his experience among the Navajos. One evening, the Navajo storyteller Little Wagon tells a visiting boy a story

> about an ancestor who had found a piece of beautiful burning material, had guarded it carefully for several months until some spirits . . . came to reclaim it . . . [he] asked then that the spirits allow him to retain a piece of it. This they would not allow, but they would see what they could do for him. In the meantime he was to perform a number of complicated and dedicated tasks to test his endurance. Finally, the spirits told him that in return for his fine behavior they would throw all the ashes from their own fireplace down into Montezuma Canyon each year when they cleaned house."

Later, after the boy has misunderstood the story as being about the cause of snow in Montezuma Canyon, Little Wagon explains to Toelken that the story was not at all about the origin of snow in the canyon: "rather, if the story was 'about' anything, it was about moral values, about the deportment of a young protagonist whose actions showed a properly reciprocal relationship between himself and nature."[44]

Not only is meaning in traditional myths governed by much indirection; it is also, writes Paula Gunn Allen, multiple, or as Ramsey would have it, "myths . . . may in fact be structured to 'perform' a number of functions all at once, and in concert."[45] One brief example of this will suffice. The following episode is from the Gros Ventre oral tradition but can be found in other versions among other tribes as well.

"Nix'ant was travelling. As he went, he heard the noise of a sundance." Searching about for the source of the sounds, he discovers mice holding a dance in an elk skull. Commanding the hole through which he looks to enlarge, he puts his head in the skull, scattering the mice in the process, and becomes stuck in the skull. Unable to see, he stumbles off, bumping into trees (which identify themselves for him, thereby revealing that he is getting closer to the river) until he falls into the river. As he floats toward a camp, he frightens swimmers who think that he is *bax'aan,* that is, a water monster. When Nix'ant says, "I allow only girls to get me," two girls wade in, catch the skull by the horns, and pull him to shore. He grabs one of the girls and begins to have sex with her. Now aware of his identity, everyone else runs back to camp spreading the word that Nix'ant is raping a virgin. The girl's mother runs to where the trickster is violating the girl and begins pummeling him with a club. He merely laughs, proclaiming that the blows make him thrust into the girl more vigorously and that "the place where you can kill me is in the middle of my head." The woman strikes there, breaking the skull. Nix'ant runs off pursued by all the women.[46] In this single episode, Nix'ant—consciously and unconsciously—accomplishes the following:

> points up the moral that there are limitations to what a person can do and that some behavior is not appropriate for a person (a large person should not stick his head into a small hole);
> warns against abusing one's powers for inappropriate and idle ends;
> as a buffoon able to wield magic, blurs the boundaries between profane behavior and a shaman's sacred powers (a circumstance which can be its own kind of sacredness, as in the behavior of ceremonial clowns);
> teaches some natural history regarding water-loving trees;
> ridicules human gullibility;
> takes advantage of human belief to indulge his inordinate sexuality;
> burlesques stories of sexual union between mythic creatures and humans;
> parodies ritualistic and other restrictions placed on human contact with spirits;
> reminds us by inversion that the mythic world interpenetrates the world of human experience;
> and, of course, amuses us.

Such an array of meanings is certainly consistent with the many-sided nature of reality as manifested in the trickster himself. Much in this book will illustrate the fact that when it comes to tricksters, experience, indeed, has many sides and is a mosaic of values, not all of which fit the others quite neatly enough to satisfy the Euro-American way of looking at the world.

CHAPTER ONE

On Scholars and Wandering

A number of North American indigenous tricksters fit Robert Lowie's characterization of Old Man Coyote: one minute benevolent transformer and founder of tribal traditions, the next, trickster or humiliated dupe.[1] How can it be that a creative, transforming personage—apparently of more than mortal stature—is simultaneously buffoon, rogue, and hero or even deity? Comprehending and then explaining such paradoxes have been the concerns of many Euro-American scholars as they have with much difficulty attempted to straighten the twisted, spiraling trail of American Indian tricksters. One of the earliest scholarly responses was Daniel Brinton's *Myths of the New World*, in which Brinton conjectured that the Algonquian trickster, Manabozho, was a character degenerated from a "God of Light."[2] James Mooney claimed that the Algonquian tribal name for the trickster, *wabos,* was confused with the word for "dawn," *waban,* so that "the Great White Rabbit is really the incarnation of the eastern dawn that brings light and life and drives away the dark shadows which have held the world in chains."[3] Boas, on the other hand, argued that culture heroes and deities develop from shapeless and ambiguous types like the American Indian tricksters. In addition he argued that "wherever [a protagonist's altruism] is brought out most clearly, the tales of the trickster are ascribed to a different being," a culture hero.[4]

In the first book-length examination of tricksters, *The Trickster* (1927), Paul Radin depicted the Winnebago trickster Wakdjunkaga as evidence of a figure evolving from an archaic primal type, but he gave this trickster a Jungian spin by representing him as first an undifferentiated, unsocialized psyche, who becomes a socialized, responsible, knowingly benevolent individual, conscious at the end of his story cycle of the great moral-social task to which he has been assigned by Earthmaker. *The Trickster* included C. G. Jung's essay "On the Psychology of the Trickster Figure," in which the great psychologist applies his framework of archetypes and theory of individuation to tricksters of all cultures. Trickster, he says,

> haunts the mythology of all ages . . . obviously a "psychologem," an archetypal psychic structure of extreme antiquity. . . . He is a faithful copy of an absolutely undifferentiated human conscious-ness, corresponding to a psyche that has hardly left the animal level. . . . The trickster is a primitive "cosmic" being of divine-animal nature, on the one hand superior to man because of his super-human qualities, and on the other hand inferior to him because of his unreason and unconsciousness. He is no match for the animals either, because of his extra-ordinary clumsiness and lack of instinct. . . . The trickster is a collective shadow figure, an epitome of all the inferior traits of character in individuals.[5]

Jung also saw trickster myths as "the reflection of an earlier, rudimen-tary stage of consciousness," a view of humanity that came "when the attainment of a newer and higher level of consciousness enabled [humans] to look back on a lower and inferior state" (201–2).[6]

Aside from the ethnocentrism in Jung's observation, a significant difficulty with his characterization is that American Indian oral tradi-tions do not seem to bear out some of its most important assertions and assumptions. For instance his diminution of tricksters' humanity ignores the fact that a trickster's human foibles are the object of ridi-cule in numerous tribal episodes. Moreover, many American Indian tricksters do, indeed, prove a match for animals, even though their own clumsiness, envy, and extravagance (that is to say, their humanity) repeatedly undo whatever successes they might otherwise have achieved.

Such shortcomings in the study's theoretical undergirding notwith-standing, Radin wrote what many regard as the seminal description of the American Indian trickster (or so the frequency of citations suggests). While acknowledging that Trickster has "no well-defined and fixed form," Radin says that "as found among North American Indians, Trickster is at one and the same time creator and destroyer, giver and negator, he who dupes others and who is always duped himself. He wills nothing consciously. At all times he is constrained to behave as he does from impulses over which he has no control. He knows neither good nor evil yet he is responsible for both. He possesses no values, moral or social, is at the mercy of his passions and appetites, yet through his actions all values come into being."[7] Most that Radin says is true enough, yet his point of view as a whole is askew because it is too governed by Euro-American categorization, too reliant on Western dualistic perception to present a really accurate image of American Indian tricksters.

Almost forty years later, in "The North American Trickster," Mac-Linscott Ricketts's solution to the puzzle of tricksters was to argue that all tricksters are to some degree "culture heroes." Moreover, he argues, "in the most archaic hunting cultures of North America the trickster and hero roles are always combined in the same figure."[8] Ricketts dis-misses the dualistic ambiguity that scholars have puzzled over as no puzzle at all; rather, he posits that "the trickster/transformer culture hero is in origin a unitary figure despite his complexity."[9] Trickster, he argues, is "Man himself, while his actions as related in the myths disclose man transcending himself."[10] He is "a symbol of [unconquerable and immortal] mankind."[11] Finally, Ricketts argues that many trickster stories—particularly Bungling Host and Eye Juggler stories—satirize shamans. In a later essay, "The Shaman and the Trickster," Ricketts qualifies this assertion by stating that the stories "may be viewed as mockery of shamans and all others who think they can get higher powers from animal spirits."[12] While Ricketts's essays refer in a broad fashion to various common American Indian trickster episodes, he deals more in general-ities than in specifics. Witness his more recent claim that Trickster, "apparently, sees no need to have powers other than those with which he is naturally endowed: his wits and his wit. These suffice for him to cope successfully with all the problems he encounters," a claim that seems to contradict his treatment of tricksters in Bungling Host stories.[13] Most people familiar with American Indian trickster stories could probably refute Ricketts's assertions by citing at least a dozen stories about a trickster's repeated efforts to possess powers that are not rightfully his. Nevertheless, among discussions of tricksters in the last half of the twentieth and the early twenty-first centuries, Ricketts's essay continued to be influential, even though it seems more infused with Euro-American humanism than American Indian thought. Ricketts retains a humanistic approach to American Indian tricksters in "The Shaman and the Trickster": "[T]he trickster, then, is the symbol of the self-transcending mind of humankind and of the human quest for knowledge and the power that knowledge brings. Unlike the shaman, the priest, and the devotee of supernaturalistic religion, the trickster looks to no 'power' outside himself, but sets out to subdue the world by his wits and his wit. In other words, as I see him, the trickster is a symbolic embodiment of the attitude today represented by the humanist."[14]

Ricketts goes on to identify the trickster as "an outsider whose attitude toward [the shaman's] world of superhuman powers is a negative one. He has no friends in that other world, and for him it is a realm opposed entirely to the will of human beings."[15] This is a curious statement considering that American Indian tricksters themselves often embody the creative and transformative powers of the spiritual world and that tricksters often mediate between animal, spiritual forces and humans.

Another scholar whose work continues to influence trickster studies and for whom the trickster's mediating role is especially significant is Claude Levi-Strauss. Levi-Strauss deals with trickster's putative paradoxes by naming him a mediator, who, because he "occupies a position halfway between . . . polar terms [life and death, agriculture and hunting/ warfare, herbivores and carnivores], must retain something of that duality— namely an ambiguous and equivocal character."[16] Unfortunately, Levi-Strauss's treatment of tricksters rests on his questionable assumption that coyotes and ravens are primarily carrion eaters. Nevertheless, his structural analysis makes clear that an American Indian trickster story is not to be approached as a simple folktale of an unsophisticated people. In the introduction to the 1972 edition of Radin's study, Stanley Diamond says that the trickster is a personification grown from "primitive perceptions."[17] This ethnocentric attribution obviously implies a level and quality of thinking inferior to ours because it is nonlogical and nonscientific. In contrast, Levi-Strauss argues that the thought of the distant, aboriginal past is not inferior to that in the present: "the kind of logic in mythical thought is just as rigorous as that of modern science. . . . [T]he difference lies not in the quality of the intellectual process, but in the nature of the things to which it is applied. . . . [T]he same logical processes operate in myth as in science, and . . . man has always been thinking equally well; the improvement lies, not in an alleged progress of man's mind, but in the discovery of new areas to which it may apply its unchanged and unchanging powers."[18]

Perhaps the most influential of all recent trickster scholarship is Barbara Babcock-Abrahams's essay, "A 'Tolerated Margin of Mess': The Trickster and His Tales Reconsidered." Drawing critical context, concepts, and vocabulary from Mary Douglas, Victor Turner, Laura Makarius, and others, Babcock-Abrahams defines Trickster as belonging to "the comic modality of marginality," *marginality* meaning, in her use, *outside or between the boundaries of dominant groups.*[19] A "situation of 'marginality' exists," she writes, "whenever commonly held boundaries [of the social structure, of law and custom, of kinship, family structure, and sexuality, of the human person, or of nature] are violated"[20]—all breaches of which American Indian tricksters stand guilty. However, it is in the disorder of such violations that, she argues, order is validated; that is, the rules are defined and emphasized in their violation. The antistructure of rule breaking defines structure.

Trickster's powers are "derived from his ability to live interstitially [in the cracks, betwixt and between, marginally], to confuse and to escape the structures of society and the order of cultural things."[21] The explanation of this scandalous buffoon's creativity, then, is in his marginality, for the "'sacred' is precisely the result of the violation of taboo," just as creativity springs forth when the imagination is freed from the constraints of, say, conventional social roles.[22] Trickster's contraventions place him at the margins of society or even beyond the social pale. From such a vantage point he radically reorients our perceptions, liberating humans from conventional social-moral boundaries and dramatizing new ways of perceiving and the possibility of new orders but also leading us to the "rediscovery of essential truths, a transvaluation of values, and the affirmation of a primal order."[23]

There is an essential validity in Babcock-Abrahams's view that tricksters confuse, release, and create through their transgressions. However, she applies her metaphor of marginality inconsistently. Indeed, the term itself, appropriate to Turner's theories of liminality but not here, obscures the particulars and uniqueness of the American Indian tricksters in favor of fitting them into critical theory and a more generic, cross-cultural characterization.[24]

Significant assertions by Babcock-Abrahams about American Indian tricksters simply are tenuously grounded in Indian oral traditions. At one point in her essay she lists sixteen characteristics of tricksters. A few are obviously traits of some American Indian tricksters—for example, the fact that tricksters might possess both animal and human characteristics. A few of her assertions are at best partial truths about American Indian tricksters, such as "their creative/destructive dualism . . . ambiguously situat[ing] them . . . between good and evil." About half of Babcock-Abrahams's claims lack specific support in American Indian oral traditions.[25]

Finally, in *Reading the Fire: Essays in the Traditional Indian Literatures of the Far West* Jarold Ramsey applies to Indian tricksters Levi-Strauss's concept of a "bricoleur . . . someone who works with his hands and uses devious means compared to those of a craftsman."[26] In Ramsey's use this figure becomes "a sort of mythic handyman who 'cobbles' reality in the form of a bricolage out of the available material, and with something distinctly less transcendent than a divine plan or teleology to guide him—namely his own impressionable, wayward, avid mind."[27] The paradoxical world that Trickster creates, then, is "the world as we have it," known and accepted by American Indians for what it is.[28] Tricksters further signify "both the persistence in us of the unconstructed Id, and the sheer avid amoral persistence of the human race itself."[29]

Ramsey's trickster is also a mediator, not of "polar terms" as in Levi-Strauss, but between the child's and the adult's consciousness.[30] This trickster, too, shapes perception (but differently from the way Babcock-Abrahams's trickster does so) as "sources of a kind of tribal historical perspective: 'Here's how uncouth and infantile it was around here at the beginning.'"[31] In spite of my reservations about Ramsey's use of the term *bricoleur,* his chapter on tricksters in *Reading the Fire* is (with Wiget's "His Life in His Tail") the most responsive to the facts of American Indian oral traditions, even while he draws upon Euro-American thought. At times in Ramsey's essay we see evidence of Turner, Radin, Jung, and Ricketts, but his use of these sources never obscures our view of the indigenous trickster.

None of the above criticisms are intended to deny the usefulness of many trickster studies. Some offer valuable insights into American Indian tricksters; others are salutary challenges to intellectual inertia. Throughout this book, readers will see evidence of influence by even those I have criticized. Such influence notwithstanding, the assumptions of some of the most influential trickster scholarship are questionable. Consider, for example, Babcock-Abrahams's analysis of the Sam Blowsnake version of the Winnebago trickster cycle as presented by Radin. Babcock-Abrahams claims that "the 'peripatetic,' 'marginal', and antistructural character of Trickster is reiterated in the episodic, serial quality and linear simplicity of the narrative."[32] Privileging Radin's assumption that Winnebago trickster stories are a "cycle" and assigning it a "serial quality and linear simplicity," Babcock-Abrahams's analysis becomes problematic for reasons I have already discussed in this book's introduction.

Without a doubt Babcock-Abrahams and others have created useful insights into some aspects of American Indian tricksters, and perhaps there are elements in trickster narratives that justify limited application of the metaphors they invent. Trickster's inveterate wandering, for example, seems to confirm the metaphor of marginality. Just as he has not bonded to place, so he seems not to have bonded to humanity. As he wends his disreputable way through the Native world and from self-indulgence to self-indulgence, scorning established social constraints, it is tempting to say with Babcock-Abrahams that he lives in the cracks of society or betwixt and between.[33] Furthermore, his behavior so isolates him morally, as a frequently ludicrous but still dangerous criminal, that it is easy to call him an outsider. But we forget too quickly that the terms we apply are metaphors and not facts. Then, the metaphors—useful though they may be—obscure other significant perspectives on tricksters, perspectives occasionally noted but seldom pursued analytically. Or we may become so enamored of the metaphor that we fail to see how or when it breaks down.[34] For instance it is not really accurate to say that American Indian tricksters live in the cracks of society. Huck Finn lives in the cracks, but Coyote or Raven or Iktomi does not. We do not find American tribal tricksters living in the equivalent of Huck's river, between society's Scylla and Charybdis. Nor do tricksters fall into the cracks of a dark underworld, as do so many Euro-American picaroons.[35] The language of marginality obscures a Trickster's real status in society, which is generally something like a fish bone stuck in the throat.

All in all, the remoteness of some critical vocabulary and arguments from American Indian Oral traditions in trickster studies is troublesome. As the dramatization of what can go wrong in the greater social order when individuals try to live as a society of one and as figures deserving the ridicule heaped on them, American Indian tricksters receive, at best, passing glances, after which we avert our eyes back to the Euro-American stereotype of Trickster as the creative breaker of taboos represented in Ricketts, Babcock-Abrahams et al. We make nodding recognition at Ramsey's description of Indian societies as "sternly normative"[36] and then return to our delight in the comically rebellious Trickster, glorying in him as a release from social repression. This antinomian trickster seems to have become a culture hero for the literary establishment, even if he is not for some American Indians. Viewed from the context of the dominant culture's glorification of individualism, tricksters may, indeed, appear to be kindred souls to several Euro-American heroes. While there is no doubt that tricksters are often creative transformers or that some of their creativity is consequent to their violating taboos, these tricksters are very much in danger of finding themselves the adopted brothers of various Euro-American picaros or romantic overreachers and of losing their real identity by literary acculturation.

Commenting on Ricketts's trickster, Ann Doueihi makes this point when she writes that the trickster "becomes a Faustian rebel, an idealized and heroic figure and not the sort of character who would almost drown in his own feces, as Trickster does."[37] The truth of the matter is that the putative American Indian tricksters that we read about in much contemporary writing may be largely the creation of dominant-culture scholars and writers tailored to academic fashion rather than the character American Indian peoples have known.[38]

It is understandable that we non-Natives redefine tricksters through our own eyes. They seem so fluid, so malleable in our analytical hands. While he was probably referring to worldwide trickster traditions, not only American Indian ones, Radin may have implied other reasons for this: "every generation occupies itself with interpreting Trickster anew. No generation understands him fully but *no generation can do without him. Each had to include him* in all its theologies, in all its cosmogonies, *despite the fact that it realized that he did not fit* properly into any of them. . . . And so he became and remained everything to every man [emphasis added]."[39] Perhaps we sense in American Indian trickster stories ways of experiencing and understanding life that are missing from much of our own culture.

The Euro-American mind finds paradox and that which is not clearly categorized to be intellectually discomfiting, labeling such experiences as ambiguous. Indeed, in the European-Christian tradition, with its roots in Judaism, the whole of Creation is in distinct categories, defined and ordered and not to be confused.[49] Moreover, much of traditional Christianity's conception of history—individual and cosmic—as a struggle against the evil empire demands such definition. Stanley Diamond argues that two works central to the Christian and European worldview, the book of Job and Plato's *Republic,* are bent "upon denying human ambivalence and social ambiguity."[41] Contrasting the more integrative worldviews of most in the world with "the matter/spirit dichotomy of the Indo-European worldview," Karl Luckert explains how the dichotomy is codified in language so that "speakers of that language will thenceforth have great difficulty thinking about that which once was an un-divided whole."[42] It may be such cultural predilections that have caused so many scholars and others, looking for the relief of certainty, to pursue this enigmatic creature down the highways and byways of Euro-American scholarship.

Quite possibly, dualistic Western consciousness has created the scholarly quandary over the apparent indeterminacy of American Indian tricksters. On occasion, efforts to comprehend tricksters have been couched in the classificatory terms of dualism. Radin, for instance, trying to delineate the multifarious personality and role of the Winnebago trickster, is finally reduced to simply listing dualisms: "He became and remained everything to every man—god, animal, human being, hero, buffoon, he who was before good and evil, denier, affirmer, destroyer and creator."[43] In a well-known characterization of tricksters, Levi-Strauss adopts a different strategy in which he attempts to accommodate the ambiguous to the dualistic when he calls Coyote a mediator who "occupies a position halfway between two polar terms" and who therefore "must retain something of that duality—namely an ambiguous and equivocal character."[44]

To be sure, some American Indians themselves have expressed confusion about one or another trickster character, but at least some of these had been influenced by Euro-American thinking. Among the Klamaths, elderly consultants who were practicing Christians displayed bewilderment about trickster-heroes, just as they were uncertain about accepting the half-animal, half-human depiction of some mythic personages.[45] Apparently, Christian Klamaths held more dualistic conceptions of supernaturals than traditionals did. Some Klamaths did not see the trickster as a deity, while some even saw him as Satan.[46] Similarly, in *Crashing Thunder: The Autobiography of an American Indian,* a peyote follower draws morals from trickster tales and identifies the trickster as Satan.[47]

Nevertheless, most American Indians have had less difficulty with this character that Babcock-Abrahams appropriately calls "paradox personified."[48] It appears that for many American Indians, tricksters' perceived ambiguities and paradoxes, which have given rise to all of this Sisyphean scholarly effort, are much less knotty than for non-Natives.

Many have traditionally regarded tricksters with mixed awe and amusement.[49] In most tribal traditions the fuss over the nature of tricksters is probably irrelevant, for there is no conflict of the Stupid Innocent with heroic or godlike qualities in Trickster. For example, Toelken says that the Navajos do not distinguish among the various Coyotes (Ma'i): the animal coyote, "the personification of Coyote power in all coyotes," the trickster/clown/transformer, and the mythic purveyor of disorder. "Ma'i," he writes, "is not a composite but a complex; a Navajo would see no reason to distinguish between separate aspects."[50] Melville Jacobs notes, "Elements that feel contradictory in Western civilization were fused in normal Chinook personalities."[51]

American Indian thought, although anything but relativistic, seems capable of accepting the world and humanity's experience in terms other than a totally black-and-white moral taxonomy.[52] Indian cultures, including their oral traditions, are full of examples. For instance after the Hopi emergence into this world, a witchlike person who came up with the people undetected insists that he has a role to play in this world. His special knowledge allows him to teach the people "how to make the sun, moon, and stars and to loft them into the sky to make the world light," and so he is allowed to stay.[53] Katherine Spencer distinguishes between two classes of thought among the Navajos: existential, which explains the *what* and *how* of existence; and *normative*, which is concerned with what ought to be, with norms of taste, propriety, and ethical rightness. But even though these classes exist, they are seldom held as separate; rather, they interpenetrate and blend. Navajo myths contain ideas with both "normative and existential components."[54] Clearly, these components are also present in stories of the Navajo trickster Ma'i. Why not in the character himself as well? And why not also in other tricksters?

Understanding tricksters' refusal to be pigeonholed or fixed is essential to understanding their powers. Babcock-Abrahams argues against such pigeonholing by stating that Trickster derives his power from his "ability to live interstitially."[55] Whether we accept Babcock-Abrahams's vocabulary or not, such a description reminds us that Trickster is the derelict of codified and conventionalized experience. For tricksters there can never be resolution, no matter how many scholars put their shoulders to the wheel. Like subatomic particles, tricksters never allow a final definition of time, place, and character. They never settle or shape themselves so as to allow closure, either fictional or moral. We may believe that we have somehow secured a trickster in place at one moment, but if we look from another angle, he is gone. If we ask a different question, we get a different answer, which—we must confess—is coterminous with the first. Tricksters elude all attempts to place them within the categories of definition and classification, especially in "either/or" or "both" terms.[56] At most we can say only that tricksters are, in fact, neither/nor, either/and, and both. Most American Indian traditions seem to accept this state of affairs.

Rather than asserting that a trickster derives both ambiguity and power from his "ability to live interstitially," it may be closer to the truth to say that the source of his power is his wandering through paradoxical-vagrant reality. Between villages, in the nonhuman realm throughout the wilderness—many an American Indian trickster is the quintessential wanderer. Understanding tricksters must begin with this fact. The dominant culture's customary use of "ambiguity" refers to something with two or more meanings, which, we generally believe, must be resolved or "mediated." When we non–American Indians write and talk of tricksters' ambiguity, it might be well to remember—paradoxical though it seems—the term's English etymology: *ambigere,* from the Latin, *to wander about.* Tricksters wander beyond conventional order *and* among the many poles of the real world. In their norm-defying travels, they swallow all—classifications and cracks—in their ravenous and extravagant appetite for life. Wherever tricksters wander, there is a mosaic of values and truths to experience, just as Navajo patients' symbolic journey in a sing exposes them to the sources of complex universal healing and spiritual powers. It is best to think of tricksters not as those who mediate dualism or "bivalence" (any stay-at-home can do this) but rather as those whose wanderings reveal to us "polyvalence," the many-sidedness of what is, in all of its perplexing dynamics.[57] Moreover, as in chemistry, Trickster's polyvalence is a characteristic of how he mixes/reacts in various contexts. American Indian tricksters reveal to us an openness to life's multiplicity and paradoxes largely missing from modern Euro-American moral tradition.

Finally, non-American Indian culture has so insulated us from experiencing life head-on that many of us are bemused by its complexities and prefer a clearly scripted reality such as television and modern politicians offer. But American Indian tricksters are not following the script when they revel in the comic in the midst of the sacred. These figures remain difficult for many, perhaps, because the dominant culture denies the sacred a place in our "ordinary" experience. When Vine Deloria tells us that among American Indians "every factor of human experience is seen in a religious light as part of the meaning of life," he provides the best explanation yet of why and how a trickster can be a sacred as well as a comic figure.[58] The final truth of the matter is that tricksters roam across all levels of experience in ways that the dominant culture will not recognize.[59] As they roam, many tricksters transform themselves and the realities around them, thereby reinforcing their roles as the image of life's many-sidedness *and* its source, even while acting the fool.

Coyote and Eagle Part.
Coyote Kills the Swallowing Monster
and a Soft Basket Person

1. There was Coyote, there was his friend Eagle. He (Eagle) would go about for deer, he would shoot deer. There was an old woman, she had a girl, a niece. (2) She told her, "Go! There is a chief. Go there!" The girl went to that place, she reached there. Coyote saw a woman had come, and he said to her, "So you have come here, sister-in-law! My older brother has gone hunting for deer." (3) The woman said to him, "Yes! My grandmother said to me, 'Go!' And so I have come." The woman went and dug white camas, she roasted the white camas in ashes underground, she gave them to Coyote, and Coyote ate the white camas.

2. Eagle came along, he brought meat with him, he reached there. The woman was at the house. He said to her, "When did you

arrive, my wife?" That is how Eagle spoke to the woman. (2) The woman replied, "My grandmother said to me, 'Go to where there is a man!' And so I came." That is how she spoke to him. (3) Eagle replied, "Very good! It is well that you have come, my wife." That is how Eagle spoke to the woman.

3. Coyote spoke, "I will leave you, brother! I will go away, my older brother, I will leave you." That is how Coyote spoke to Eagle. Eagle said to him, "Very well! You may go. It is well that I shall be alone. (2) I too shall plan how all sorts of things are to be in this land." That is how his older brother Eagle spoke to Coyote. (3) He (Coyote) said to him, "I shall go as far as there is land. I shall go so far, until where I die. The people coming are nearby now. (4) I shall make over whatever there is now here that is not right. I shall fix it properly, and then it will be a different land, (with) different people." (5) That is how Coyote spoke to his older brother Eagle. Coyote said to him, "Never again will you be as you are, or I as I am. The people will be different now." That is how he spoke to his older brother Eagle. (6) "I am leaving you now, I am parting from you forever. You will not plan as much as I shall plan about all sorts of things that are to be done here. (7) A different land will come (to be) here, there will be different people now, because of my ruling (that it be so)." Eagle said to him, "Very well! You may go." Coyote went away. He went far, far away.

4. He arrived at, "There is a dangerous being here at this place in the river." He turned aside there at a rock. He called out, "Oh! Let us contend and swallow each other!" (2) The dangerous being did not give him (much) thought. "Let him be there! It is Coyote." He knew it was Coyote. "Let him be!" (3) Coyote went out of sight, made himself different in appearance, and came again to that very same place. He shouted, "Ah! Let us swallow each other!" He saw it was Coyote. (4) "Let him be!" (But) he thought of him silently. Coyote went away, again he made himself different, he came back to the very same place again, he appeared in view in different guise, though it was still he. (5)

He shouted differently, "Let us swallow each other." He saw it was Coyote. "Let him be!" He went away, again he made himself different. That was how he treated the dangerous being, five times.

5. The dangerous being became tired of it. "I will gulp that damn fellow Coyote, he is a nuisance!" He (Coyote) appeared by the rocks. "Let us contend and gulp each other." He thought him a nuisance. (2) He gulped down Coyote, at that place (inside) sat (Coyote). He saw, "What can this be, dangling here?" He took a bag for carrying flints, took out a flint, and cut it through. (3) "What can this be dangling? It must be the heart of the dangerous being." He cut through it, cut if clear off! The dangerous being gave a gasp a . . . , la . . . , out came whatever the dangerous being had swallowed. (4) He gasped out all of them, everything that is in this country. Those people were there, and they all came out. There Coyote laughed, "Huhuhu, huhuhu." (5) This dangerous being had been a person who swallowed things. ["]At no place will it be like that, the people coming are nearby now. Although people will go along in canoes, you may only frighten them, but you may not swallow them. (6) Nowhere will you do it like that. The people coming are nearby now." Coyote made over all the people. Those became people who had been swallowed by the dangerous being. (7) That place is named "person-who-swallows," it was in the (Columbia). Coyote completed it all. And then he went on.

6. "I shall go as far away as there is land, to the sunrise. Now I shall go." Coyote went away. He reached there, there was a different dangerous being. (2) She sat at that place on the side of the river, there sat the Soft Basket Person, the dangerous person. Coyote went down to the waterside at that place, and said to her, "How are you, sister-in-law? How might I get across, sister-in-law?" (3) The Soft Basket Person burst into laughter, "Huhuhuhu. Yes indeed, brother-in-law, come across!" "With what could I cross?" (4) She said to him, "Oh, yes! Over there at that place is my husband, he has a canoe to cross with there, you may cross over there at that place."

7. Coyote went there, he reached there. On the other side Crane
was making a canoe. Coyote called out to him, "Come across to
me, old man! I want to cross over. Come across to me!" (2) The
old man extended his legs across the river. He said to him,
"Cross over on them there!" Coyote replied, "Oh no, I might
fall in." (3) That is how Coyote replied to him. He said to him,
"Not at all! Come across!" They talked back and forth at each
other for a long time. In vain did he say to him, "Come across!"
(4) Coyote replied, "I will certainly not cross. I might fall in."
He said to him, "Not at all! Come across!"—"No! I shall make a
canoe also, I shall cross with that." (5) That is how he replied to
him. The latter (Crane) belonged to the Soft Basket Person, he
was not her husband at all, he merely killed people for (her)
food. (6) If anyone did cross over, Crane would draw up his
legs, they would fall into the water, he would seize them, give
them to the Soft Basket Person, and the Soft Basket Person
would eat them. That is how she wished to do it to Coyote. (7)
But Coyote played smart too, he would not cross over at all.
Coyote also knew (what was what) there. So he went away, he
made a canoe. "I'll cross over now." Coyote crossed over, he
went on, he reached the Soft Basket Person's place.

8. He said, "That is not your husband, by no means did he cross
over to me. I called him in vain." That is how he spoke to the
Soft Basket Person. (2) She said to him, "You did not want to
cross." That is how she spoke to him. "But very well, brother-
in-law, you have come now. You are my brother-in-law."

9. In this manner the Soft Basket Person spoke to Coyote. "How is
it that you have become white?" Coyote replied to her, "Yes
indeed! I heated rocks, and when the rocks were hot, I put pitch
all over myself at that place, and I threw myself on the hot
rocks there. (2) That is how I became white. I burned myself
with the pitch. That is how I became like that." That Soft Basket
Person said to him, "Oh dear! Now I could be white like that
also. I want to be like that too." (3) He said to her, "Well, prepare

pitch, while I heat Rocks! You will get the pitch ready meanwhile." The Soft Basket Person replied, "Very well. I shall get the pitch."

10. She went to obtain pitch, she prepared a lot of pitch. Coyote heated the rocks. The Soft Basket Person brought the pitch, and said to him, "I shall strip off all my clothes." "Very well." (2) So she became like that (stripped), the Soft Basket Person stripped completely. Coyote said to her, "I shall put pitch on you." (3) He rubbed pitch all over her, and said to her, "Throw yourself onto the fire. The rocks are already hot." The Soft Basket Person almost cast herself into the fire. (4) "Oh dear! I might burn." Coyote said to her, "You would not burn at all!" That is how the Soft Basket Person told him, five times. She would make as if to. At length he convinced her. (5) Then the Soft Basket Person cast herself into the fire. The pitch blazed up. "Ow!" (said) the Soft Basket Person, "I am burning." Coyote took a stick, he held her down in it, and the Soft Basket Person burned up. Coyote roasted the Soft Basket Person there.

11. He covered her over, and said, "Nowhere will you be a dangerous being. The people coming are nearby now. You will not be like that! You will (not) eat people, not like that! (2) When the people are here, if a child should cry they will speak like this, 'The Soft Basket Person will hear you.' That is how a child will be told. The child will be frightened immediately. (3) But you will never really eat them!" That is how Coyote spoke to the Soft Basket Person. Then the aforementioned person became Crane, he never again made canoes, Crane quit. That is how Coyote completed it (there). He left. He had killed the Soft Basket Person.

Melville Jacobs, *Northwest Sahaptin Texts,* 64–68. Copyright © 1934, reprinted by permission of Columbia University Press.

CHAPTER TWO

A Trickster by Any Other Name

Overwhelmed by his own appetites, preoccupied with the orifices of his own and everyone else's bodies, suffering from such severe dissociation that his right hand often indeed does not know what his left hand is doing, proclaiming his irresponsibility in word and deed and relishing it despite all costs, here is a fool fit to discombobulate the self-important servants of status and the status quo. Trotting, skulking, whining, lurking, ranting, leering, laughing, always hungry, never satisfied, he is an animate principle of disruption, about to precipitate chaos and humor through sacrilege, self-indulgence, and scatology. He wanders through the dark field of the liminal imagination until he arrives to summon into play the force at work in some dimly lit social scene. There for a few moments he exercises his trickery, displays his foolishness, sparks some sure flash of imagination and insight. Then he departs the circled light into the surrounding darkness almost as suddenly as he arrived, still oversexed, underfed, dissatisfied, and on the move....

And while it is important to know that he can change his external appearance at will and manipulate his body in marvelous ways, it is more important to know that the name and the visage mask several personae. He may appear, in one instance, to be an absolute fool, bumbling into social situations from which his disposition or ignorance makes it impossible to escape without punishment. In another story, the same name and mask may be endowed with a high sense of mission and tremendous powers in order to accomplish tasks beneficial to mankind. And in yet another tale, he will appear deceitful, vain, and selfish, and bend all his talents toward the satisfaction of his own desires. This ambiguity at once horrifies and fascinates us. It also creates real problems of interpretation, often exacerbated by the sketchiness with which some of the stories are told.[1]

Often in trickster scholarship and other writing, we talk about tricksters as if there were a generic figure, *an* American Indian Trickster—one encapsulating all such personages. Even while we pay lip service to the diversity among Native peoples' cultures, we generalize a Trickster into existence.[2] To be sure, American Indian tricksters do often share traits. Wiget's description above is valid in many ways. Nevertheless, generalizing is in part responsible for the ambiguities we attribute to tricksters. We invent a generic figure comprising all that we think we see and all that we want to see. It may also be a reason that some writers' tricksters seem to correspond to Euro-American literary figures. Coquelle anthropologist George Wasson implies as much when he says he tries

> to avoid the use of the term "Trickster" in describing, or mentioning "Old Man Coyote" (Talapus, in Chinook Jargon) as it is a purely Anglo-European concept. Coyote does NOT play tricks on others as the old European tricksters have/do in their stories, he is funny, humorous, devious, etc, but the "tricks," "jokes" or other antics nearly always turn back on him, not others.
>
> I've not yet adopted a descriptive term for him, but could easily call Coyote a "Reverend Rascal" or something close to that.[3]

Unfortunately, the tendency to treat American Indian tricksters generically has been reinforced by some writers—among them William Bright and Barry Lopez—who have focused on Coyote as if he is the only American Indian trickster. Certainly, there is truth in Bright's contention that Coyote is the dominant trickster of the West Coast, the Plateau and Great Basin areas, as well as the Southwest and the Southern Plains.[4] However, this range still omits half of the North American continent and disregards other western American tricksters, thereby obscuring the diversity of American Indian oral traditions. In stories recorded from American Indian oral traditions, Coyote is probably the trickster best represented and given most attention in critical analysis. For these reasons readers will find an unavoidable dominance of Coyote even in this book. Nevertheless, even in some of the cultures that Bright mentions, Coyote was not the prominent figure his assertion suggests. Barry Lopez ignores the diversity of American Indian trickster characters even more seriously in *Giving Birth to Thunder, Sleeping with His Daughter: Coyote Builds North America* when he changes tricksters of diverse character and name from varied traditions into Coyote, one archetypal figure.

North American tribal tricksters are often of different breeds with different traits emphasized. For example, there are a number of tricksters in parts of the Northwest; among Puget Sound and Pacific Coast tribes, Raven, Mink, Eagle, Fox, and Blue Jay are more important than Coyote, perhaps the most famous Indian trickster.[5] Finally, we must be careful not only to distinguish among tricksters but also to recognize that not all coyotes are tricksters. While tricksters may share a number of characteristics, many are distinguished by traits as well as name. Thus, Northwest Coast Raven tales tend to emphasize Raven's cleverness and, even more, his hunger over the sexual promiscuity and the gullible stupidity that the prairie and southwestern Coyote generally shows.[6] Hunger is an important trait in the Plains tricksters also, but it is often secondary to their pride and lechery. The Yurok trickster Wohpekumeu seems largely represented through his sexuality—sexuality so dangerously potent that his look alone impregnates women.[7] Similarly, most stories about the northwestern trickster Mink are about his sexuality and his marriages.[8]

In addition to cultural differences in characterization, there also seem to be occasional differences in the tricksters' status in their societies and in their cultures' attitudes toward them. Among the Pawnees the trickster was less important than other culture heroes and his transformer character less prominent than his trickster traits.[9] The Winnebago Wakdjunkaga and the Clackamas Coyote are headmen, while the Coyote of the New Mexico Pueblos has no apparent social status. Luckert sees the Navajo Ma'i (Coyote) as a manifestation of the trickiness needed by the "archaic" hunter—thereby giving him a status of sorts—while among the Hopis, an orderly, agricultural people, Coyote is a comical but dangerous weak link in society.[10] Ricketts asserts that among agricultural tribes tricksters are likely to be seen as tricksters only rather than as trickster-transformers, the latter types being more characteristic of hunter-gatherers.[11] In yet another indication of cultural perspective, Alan Velie argues that how often a trickster is the tricker rather than victim seems to depend in part on how a tribe views itself.[12]

While there are some character differences among tricksters, it is common for different tribes' oral traditions to have similar story episodes, trickster or otherwise. Such sharing does not mean, however, that similar episodes are really the same story. Certainly, different tribal audiences understand the stories differently. Wiget has compared Plains Cree and Winnebago versions of the same trickster episode, noting that the Cree version reinforces the Cree practice of arranged marriages, while the Winnebago version is a satire on the misuse of authority and social position.[13] This example makes clear that a story's meaning resides as much or more in the audience than in the tale itself, thereby guaranteeing diversity in trickster traditions.

It is clear that tricksters come in a variety of packages, a fact appropriate enough for a type often characterized as a shape shifter. One particular area of diversity and ambiguity is the theriomorphic as opposed to more obviously human tricksters. Some tricksters are quite definitely human: Wakdjunkaga, Napi, Wisaka, Old Man, Widower-from-across-the-ocean, Kamukamts.[14] While we do not often receive detailed descriptions of tricksters, we have some details for a few of those who are human. For example, we do not know what Nanabush looks like in other respects, but we do know that his penis is so long that he must carry it in a box on his back. Alice Marriott and Carol K. Rachlin tell us that the Kiowa Sendeh has a handlebar moustache and bulging arm and calf muscles.[15] Iktomi, commonly referred to as Spider, is—at least in the minds of some—a human with a big, round body like a bug, slim arms and legs (like a spider's?), and large hands and feet. He wears clothes of buckskin and a robe of coonskin.[16] Finally, most tricksters are said to talk in funny ways—for example, in a falsetto voice.

"Spilyay/Coyote and the Stars," by Roxanne Chinook (Wasco). Reproduced by permission of the artist.

Some tricksters are known by animal names—most prominently Coyote—and sometimes behave like animals, yet they seem at the same time human. Rabbit is the southern trickster. Nanabush is sometimes depicted as a rabbit, and the Menominee name for this trickster, Ma'na-bush, means Great Rabbit, but the character is generally presented as human.[17] In a version of Wenebojo's birth told by Ojibwe Delia Oshogay, a woman finds a moose that someone has killed. Hoping to get meat from the body, she finds only blood clots. She fills her mittens with the clots, one of which becomes Wenebojo, who briefly turns himself into a rabbit.[18] Nih'a^n'ca^n, the name of the Arapaho trickster, means both *spider* (or *slender* or *narrow-bodied* like a spider or an insect) and *wise* or *skillful*.[19]

Many readers probably think of tricksters in general as animals for the obvious reason that so many carry animal names. Inevitably, then, the question arises: Why have a number of tricksters in American Indian oral traditions been animals or associated with animals? Coyote is no doubt the best known of the animal tricksters, but there are many others: Raven, Mink, Fox, Blue Jay, Skunk, Coon, Spider, Dragonfly, Turtle, Mud Hen, Wolf, Rabbit, Canada Jay, and Wolverine. Why did these animals become the tricksters of some tribes? Did they possess traits that made them appropriately tricksters? At least two writers pursued this question for two of the best-known animal tricksters, Raven and Coyote.

Levi-Strauss asked, "Why is it that throughout North America [the trickster] role is assigned practically everywhere to either coyote or raven?"[20] He bases his answer on the assumption that both of these creatures are primarily carrion eaters, which places them between herbivorous animals (plant eaters associated with agriculture) and carnivores (predators associated with warfare and killing). This ambiguous position of betwixt and between makes tricksters mediators and is, he says, the source of their power. Unfortunately for Levi-Strauss's structuralist theory, his fundamental assumptions are problematic. First, it simply is not true that "throughout North America [the trickster] role is assigned practically everywhere to either coyote or raven." While coyotes are now at home in many places on the North American continent, Coyote's mythic habitat is restricted to the continent's western reaches (and he is not universally the trickster there). He appears nowhere in the East and Southeast as a trickster; nor do trickster coyotes reside in the woodlands. Trickster Raven is confined to an even more limited range in the Northwest. Second, while coyotes do eat carrion, it is not their sole—and perhaps not even their primary—food source. Nor is meat the only food coyotes eat; they eat fruit and seeds as well.[21] When it comes to food, coyotes seem to be quite opportunistic, eating what is "in season," with carrion probably most often their winter diet.[22] So coyotes are only part-time scavengers. With Raven, Levi-Strauss is safer, for carrion does seem to be a significant portion of ravens' diet, although they too prey on small creatures such as nestlings and eat fruits and seeds. Resting on his assumptions about these two creatures, Levi-Strauss's theories are on very tentative ground. Consequently, his conclusions are questionable for tricksters in general. Even if they were valid for Coyote and Raven, they still would not be applicable to most tricksters.

William Bright went well beyond Levi-Strauss's superficial notions of Coyote by comparing the natural animal with the mythic trickster animal in *A Coyote Reader* and "The Natural History of Old Man Coyote." Bright's question was, Is there something about the behavior of the biological coyote that makes him especially fit for the mythic role of trickster?[23] His answers attempt to create parallels between the trickster Coyote and zoological observations of the animal coyote. He asserts that "in the areas where coyotes were best known to American Indians in pre-Columbian times, *Canis latrans* was an especially appropriate actor—biologicallly, ecologically, ethnologically—to play the trickster role. From this . . . has followed the widespread significance of Old Man Coyote in American Indian mythic traditions."[24] However, there are so many Coyote traits that are not found in biological coyotes (including some that Bright comments on) that the correlations he attempts fail. For example, natural coyotes are not as impulsive as Coyote. Hope Ryden describes coyotes demonstrating extraordinary patience as they stand "at point" for as long as eleven minutes while hunting.[25] Nor are they as scurrilously licentious and promiscuous as Coyote.[26] Their relatively brief breeding period checks promiscuity and, further, many coyote mates bond for life.[27] The solipsistic self-centeredness of Coyote also appears to be fictional only. Among other "altruistic" behaviors, male coyotes bring food to mates while they are nursing pups, and coyotes have also been observed feeding wounded or entrapped coyotes.[28] Nor are coyotes always as solitary and individualistic as the American Indian Coyote, for they commonly hunt in pairs and families.[29] Even Coyote's propensity for wandering requires some qualification among biological coyotes, for while male coyotes seem to wander over large areas, females are more territorial.[30]

It appears that supposed correspondences between the behavior and traits of Coyote and those of coyotes are at best dubious, as Bright himself finally acknowledges: "it appears that human beings, perceiving such traits of coyotes as their wandering habits and their appetites, have projected other characteristics onto them—reflecting, above all, the rebellion of humans against their self-imposed domesticity."[31]

There are a few aspects of coyotes' nature that are consistent with Coyote. Like the mythic character, biological coyotes are difficult to characterize. They also demonstrate a remarkable capacity for survival, thanks largely to their adaptibility:

> the adaptable coyote not only is capable of bivouacking where he pleases, but seems able to adopt any number of life-styles. He can hunt either by day or night, dine on fresh meat or survive off carrion, raid town garbage pits or feast on wild fruits and berries, den in burrows or whelp in conduit pipes, run in packs or operate as a loner. Bold coyotes can be observed in the alleyways of Los Angeles. . . . Even the coyote's physical being reflects his protean quality. In *The Mammals of North America*, E. Raymond Hall and Keith R. Kelson identify nineteen subspecies of *Canis latrans*.[32]

Perhaps we can see in this protean adaptability, the natural prototype for Coyote's transformative capabilities.

Bright's investigation is interesting for suggesting the degree to which mythic details about Coyote may or may not be grounded in experience, but because the focus is so narrow, his efforts, like Levi-Strauss's, tell us little if anything about tricksters as a whole, to say nothing of the animal tricksters. The fact that coyotes and ravens might scavenge for even a significant portion of their diets at some times of year or that they are clever does not tell us anything about Rabbit and Spider as tricksters. And what about other animal tricksters? Are there correspondences between the biological animals and their trickster counterparts? As always in questions about tricksters, there is no one, simple answer.

Sometimes a trickster's animal characteristics may be of no more than secondary importance in a tribe's trickster traditions.[33] In these instances, the situation is probably much as in the Navajo tradition. Navajo descriptions of Ma'i are not always explicitly descriptions of an animal; rather, they sometimes imply that he is very human. What is important is his character, not natural history.[34] The Yurok Coyote, for example, is "wholly humanized."[35] In other instances, the fact that a trickster is an animal may be significant, although the type of animal may be less so. A case in point is the Comanche Coyote, who, Buller tells us, "assists the Comanche in that he fictionalizes all aspects of the question, 'What part of me is animal (natural) and what part of me is human and, for that matter, what constitutes those parts of our lives we classify as being supernatural?'"[36] Even when a point is made of a trickster's animal appearance, the actual animal's behavior might have no bearing on the character's behavior, as in the case of the Cree Wesucechak, who most often takes the form of a wolf or moose but sometimes also appears in human form, or the Haida Nanki'lslas (Raven), who would put on his raven skin only when he wanted to act like a buffoon.[37] Similarly, Nanibozhu can take the form of a rabbit when he does not want to be seen.[38] The most that we can say about such a transformation into a rabbit is that rabbits are quiet and elusive—appropriate qualities for one not wanting to attract attention. Perhaps Ojibwe belief suggests an answer. Because the power of transformation inheres in many beings, the trickster among them, the Ojibwes do not draw hard-and-fast lines between human form and animal form. What appears to be a bear may sometimes be the animal itself but may also sometimes be a transformed human.[39]

Another perspective on why tricksters are so often associated with animals can be gained from considering the narrative and mythic roles of animals in American Indian traditions. Animal characters talking and in general behaving and living like human beings—even while they are also their essential animal selves—are commonplace in American Indian stories, whether in mythic or "modern" history or fiction. Animal characters in American Indian oral traditions are sometimes a stumbling block for non-Natives, because we see such characters as appropriate for children's stories only. Part of the problem here is that many consider "folk" literature to be primitive and unsophisticated, the stories of childlike minds in undeveloped cultures. Reinforcing this point of view are the popular animated Disney movies (and their imitators) directed toward children. But there is nothing childish about American Indian and other tribal beliefs and experiences with animals. For American Indians, at least before the onset of the European fur trade, animals were not an inferior part of the Creation to be exploited without remorse. Animals are our relatives (at least metaphorically) in the universal community of humans, holy people, and animals, and we are bound to them by certain obligations just as we are to our human relatives. Their way of life is much like humans' as well. The Ojibwes, for example, say that the animals have villages of wigwams headed by chiefs just as the People (the Ojibwes) do, but the animal villages are under the hills or in deep lakes.[40] More than one American Indian story recounts how, at night in the privacy of their homes, the animals take off their animal skins, revealing their humanlike forms. Such portrayals are not childish anthropomorphism but are rather manifestation of animals' personhood; they are nonhuman persons, to be sure, but persons nevertheless—that is, beings with consciousness, intelligence, and spirits. Looking at animals from an American Indian mythic perspective reveals their significance even more, as Bright indicates: "in the Native American context, Frog, Bluejay, Bear, and Coyote are not animals: They are First People, members of a race of mythic prototypes who lived before humans existed. . . . When humans came into existence, the First People were transformed into the species of animals that still bear their names. All this is to say that the First People were not animals. They more resembled gods, although they were not much like any gods ever worshipped in Europe."[41]

As the stories make clear, tricksters are commonly among these First People. Tricksters' animal identities are, then, evidence that they are mythic presences, and as such they are tied to the world of beginnings. Some writers, emphasizing tricksters' mythic significance and role, see them as "mediators" between animals and humans.[42] It is in such a role, for example, that Nanabozho "brings words over" from animals to the people.[43] Consequently, that many tricksters are animals or have animal names is not a disparaging sign—as in our culture—that a trickster story is a children's story.[44]

Animal or not, because they are so often among the First People, tricksters commonly contribute to—or even orchestrate—the creation or transformation of the earth upon which humans will live, along with displaying their more comic, less admirable traits. Their creative character has led many to refer to a number of tricksters as culture heroes, that is, personages who, through heroic endeavors, transform the phenomena of the mythic world into—or create outright—the natural and cultural world of the People. In some uses, the epithet refers to one who embodies a culture's values to heroic degrees. Not everyone agrees that American Indian tricksters should be regarded as culture heroes. Ramsey dismisses this perspective on the trickster: "most sophisticated Indians I know emphatically reject the notion that their traditional trickster represents a 'culture hero,' and there is literary as well as ethnographic evidence to support their objections. Many western tribes have, in fact, one or more well-developed, authentic all-purpose literary heroes."[45] Boas described what seems a similar attitude when he reported that in the minds of more sophisticated Thompson Indians a distinct line existed between trickster and culture hero. He also claimed that missionaries, who recorded many of the stories, introduced an altruism as characteristic of culture heroes that was inconsistent with actual Native belief.[46]

It is true enough that many western—and some non-western—tribes have specific nontrickster culture heroes. For the Atsugewis of California, Silver Fox is the creator, whereas Coyote—"born smart but not wise, conniving but not thinking, quick to suspect but unable to solve a situation that requires fidelity"—can only change things.[47] The Winnebago trickster Wakdjunkaga is clearly a different sort of character from Hare, an obvious Winnebago culture hero. Among the subarctic Athapaskans, Raven is the trickster/transformer, as contrasted with a specific culture hero, Yamode'ya (at Bearlake), Tsuguyain (in Kaska), while the northeastern Wabanaki oral tradition separates the culture hero/transformer Gluscap from a variety of animal tricksters, the most common being Wolverine, Hare, and Raccoon.[48] Among the southeastern Yuchis, the culture hero was separate from the trickster/transformer Rabbit, the former carrying religious associations not made with Rabbit.[49] Finally, in some stories of creative benefactors, the trickster figure is not particularly important. Among the Pawnees, for instance, the trickster Wolf, while having some transforming powers, seems to have been less significant in the origin of things than obvious culture heroes.[50] In the Western Mono tradition, Coyote plays a relatively minor role in origin stories as an example of an insatiable glutton and braggart.[51]

At the same time, it appears that some American Indians themselves were not always clear about whether culture heroes and transformers were the same. One case in point is the Crows, some of whom vacillated about whether Old Man Coyote and the culture hero were the same. While Old Man Coyote is often clearly a trickster figure, at other times there does not seem to be much of the trickster about him and he seems benevolently concerned about what shape the world must take, his solicitude being directed particularly toward humans.[52] On the other hand, many commentators, including some American Indians, have identified various tricksters as, in effect, culture heroes (even if they have not used that exact term).[53]

Perhaps we should not totally dismiss the possibility of tricksters as culture heroes. If we do, indeed, mean by "culture hero" one who embodies a culture's values, then certainly few tricksters could claim this status. But some tricksters' adventures and accomplishments make the earlier definition of culture hero a good fit. One might consider familiar trickster traits and episodes in the light of Gill and Sullivan's more detailed characterization of the personage called culture hero.[54] According to their treatment, a culture hero is one who through his transforming powers creates, establishes, or somehow brings about the cultural (and sometimes natural) environment or context of a people. Like a number of tricksters, the culture hero begins his career in a world that has already been created, but, again like many tricksters, he plays a critical role in fashioning a new world or transforming the old world into a new one. Examples of tricksters from First Peoples' traditions who fill the bill are numerous. In an act that introduces one of the fundamentals for culture of any sort, Nanabozho "brings words over" from animals to the Ojibwes.[55] Moreover, he is credited with producing such staples of human survival and culture as fire and corn. He was also the source of the *Mide'wi'win,* the rituals of which dramatize his teachings.[56] Most tricksters also share well-known character and other traits with culture heroes. Perhaps most importantly, they are often wanderers whose appetites for sex, food, and gambling are prodigious. Finally, like culture heroes, tricksters may take diverse forms and almost always have proper names: Wakdjunkaga, the Winnebago word for "the tricky one," and the Kiowa Sendeh, both human types; Iktomi, the Lakota spiderman trickster; Coyote (not a coyote but Coyote); Kiowus, the Comanche Coyote; and so forth.

There is one characteristic that only a few tricksters share with culture heroes. The culture hero's birth is often unusual, even unnatural in some fashion. He may be born from a blood clot, for example. Sometimes he has a nonhuman parent, grows quickly, and is raised by an isolated grandmother figure, as in the Kiowa tradition, in which the son of a human woman and the Sun is raised by Grandmother Spider and later becomes the twin war heroes. While a trickster's birth, parentage, and upbringing are generally unknown or not at issue, there are nevertheless some tricksters who fill these criteria as well. Some said the Ojibwe trickster was born to a woman impregnated by the sun, while others said he was born to a virgin impregnated by the wind, and yet others said Wenebojo and his brother(s) are children of a human and a turtle (hence Wenebojo's mediation between the human and animal worlds?).[57] Velie tells us that Wenebojo is the offspring of a spirit, Epingishmook, and a human, Winonah.[58] The Omaha trickster is always spoken of as living with his grandmother, Earth Woman, mother of Indians.[59] Finally, in birth relationships, like many culture heroes, a trickster may have an animal sibling such as a wolf or moose. Among the Achomewis of California, Silver Fox and Coyote are sibling cocreators of earth for humans and disappear just before humans arrive, while Wolf is sometimes the older brother of Coyote.[60] Other examples from the Plateau and Northern California areas are: Panther and Coyote, Eagle and Coyote, Fox and Coyote, Fisher and Weasel.[61]

Admittedly, this characterization rests on a Euro-American understanding of the culture hero, much of which, like the Boas example above, hinges on the characters' altruism, especially when it is directed toward humans. Nevertheless, considering that some American Indian tricksters fashion a world appropriate for humanity's needs, such results seem a fair measure of distinction between those tricksters whom one might also call culture heroes and those who are only tricksters. Some North American tribal tricksters manifest a beneficent awareness of humanity's needs. In one version of the Crow creation story, Old Man Coyote makes people so that he can be guided by them in further creations. Unfortunately, they are not much help, because they do not know what to do.[62] A common observation about the trickster Wenebojo is that he is a sort of mixed-blood hero mediator between man and god sent by the Manito to help humanity.[63] Contemporary Cree playwright

Tomson Highway says that his people's trickster "stands at the very center of [the] universe [and] essentially straddles the consciousness of Man and God, translat[ing] reality from the Supreme Being, the Great Spirit, to the people and back and forth."[64] A Hopi story tells how Coyote brings the Korowista Kachina and his seeds to the starving people of Walpi.[65] The Yuchi Rabbit steals fire for the people at the behest of the people's council.[66]

At the same time, we must acknowledge that such conscious benevolence is anything but a common trickster mind-set. More often than not, tricksters are motivated by something other than altruism or benevolence. The transformations he effects (most having to do with the physical world, such as naming animals and places or bringing about landscape features) are often the result of his self-indulgence or irresponsibility.[67] Thus myths of the Northwest Coast Raven record this transformer/ trickster's continuing efforts to satiate his hunger by whatever means necessary, commonly force and trickery.[68] In one version of the Hopi emergence/migration story, Coyote has the wearisome task of carrying a heavy jar. Fed up with his burden, he opens the jar, whereupon fragments of light fly out and become the stars.[69] Radin claims that "Where [Wakdjunkaga] is a full trickster he does not, except secondarily and unconsciously, bestow benefaction upon mankind."[70] Whether he is purposefully benevolent or not, a trickster's transformation of the world into one fit for humans stands as a valid criterion for identifying which tricksters might be called culture heroes.

In any event there is no doubt that tricksters frequently have a hand in the creation of our world or in the transformation of the raw and malleable mythic world into the world we presently inhabit. Sometimes a trickster's handiwork results in natural phenomena, ranging from the earth's creation from a little ball of mud to the crest on a kingfisher's head, from a depression in rocks marking where a trickster slid down a hill on his rump to the red eyes of a waterfowl. At other times his creativity is cultural: teaching people how to use bow and arrow, instituting joking relationships between relatives, introducing a rite. Whether in a genesis of epic proportions or an incidental ramification of a gesture, tricksters are undoubtedly capable of changing the world, and we see

Nanabush on Turtle Island as depicted in *The Walam Olum*, the oral epic of the Lenape (the Delaware tribe), from *The Lenape and Their Legends* by Daniel Brinton.

this effect even in stories that are not primarily origin myths. Whatever their roles, tricksters are certainly positioned to have an impact on the shape of the world, for, as discussed earlier, they are commonly among the first beings. In such circumstances a trickster might even be preeminent. Some Nez Perce, for example, said that a long time ago, before humans, there was a kingdom of birds, animals, and fish ruled over by Coyote.[71]

Tricksters are generally not creators in the sense of being originators; that is, they do not necessarily create something out of nothing, out of the Great Void, as does the Judeo-Christian Jehovah.[72] Rather, it is usually more accurate to think of them as transformers; Levi-Strauss's term *bricoleur* (handyman or jack-of-all-trades) may be applicable in that some tricksters contribute to the shaping of our world merely by manipulating what already exists. Often, what is called an American Indian "creation" story is, in fact, a story about a trickster's altering phenomena to their present condition.[73] Looked at in a broader context, transformation in trickster stories can mean either/both metamorphosing reality by manipulating existing forms, as when Raven raises some people lying on the ground and "acting as if ashamed" into mountains, or simply "changing things around" or "setting things straight," as when the Nehalem South

Wind shortens winter or the Arapaho Nih'a^n'ca^n directs a murderer in founding societies.[74] The idea of a trickster as one who sets things straight is also implied in George A. Dorsey's calling the Caddoan trickster a "regulator."[75]

In a paradox that is essential and inherent to their stories, tricksters— inveterate rule breakers and threats to order—are themselves often a source of order. Raven's Haida name, Nankilsl.as-kina'-i, identifies him as "the one who is going to order things."[76] Discussing George Sword's version of "When the People Laughed at Hanwi," Elaine Jahner shows how Iktomi's "disruption of order among the gods brings about new order in new places requiring new temporal divisions. . . . [T]hrough marriage, male and female, mortal and immortal are brought into ordered relationships that in turn create spatial and temporal order."[77] Similarly, among the Indians of the Columbia River basin, Coyote destroys the power of monsters and other evil beings. After changing the good ancients into Indians, he groups and settles them in different places, giving each a name and a language.[78]

Sister Bernard Coleman, Ellen Fragner, and Estelle Eich's point about the Ojibwe Nanabozho is valid for most transforming tricksters: tricksters are a "force in the development of a pattern in the universe."[79] Among the patterns that tricksters bring about are the rules of hospitality, in-law hostility, ritual rules for fishing for salmon, the introduction of incest among humans, and the seasons.[80] Wiget suggests another approach to tricksters' founding patterns by observing that in trickster-transformation tales, "More than science or religion, a perception of homologies of form is at work . . . , as when the felling of a tree produces a river system: the ponds replace leaves, rivulets the stems, rivers the branches, and so on."[81] Such homologies may even extend to tricksters themselves, as when we see the correspondence between Nanabozho's body and nature: vines on trees are his intestines, fungus is the mark of his knees, a house creaking and thumping in winter is Nanabozho bumping his head against the outside walls.[82]

Sometimes tricksters' roles in the creation are less clearly proactive than a transformers' role but significant nevertheless. In some stories tricksters are "announcers" of changes in the world; that is, having observed, participated in, caused some phenomenon, event, or experience, the trickster announces (in a convincing display of the power of the word) that it will be the pattern or rule for all time. In one version of the coast central Pomo creation myth, Coyote does not create in the sense that he is a fabricator; rather, he only says what will be. Phenomena, objects, cultural features, and so forth, come into being as a result of his announcements.[83] In a Clatsop Chinook story, Coyote learns fishing taboos after considerable trial and error. He then says:

> So the people will do.
> They will not catch salmon
> if they are murderers,
> corpse-handlers,
> menstruating girls,
> widowed people.
> Those are all the taboos
> for generations to come.[84]

Often a trickster's announcement following an action (his own or that of others) can be understood as a confirmation or assertion of the inevitability that follows choice in this world. Sometimes a trickster makes such announcements in a marplot's role, as in the Maidu origin story, when Coyote opposes Earth Namer's intention to make humanity's life in this world easy and deathless.[85] Earth Namer states how things will be in the world, but Coyote contradicts him and in doing so guarantees that women will have a hard time in childbirth; that there will be sexual intercourse; that unmarried girls will sometimes have babies; and that there will be death, burial, and mourning.[86]

Given the creative role that tricksters often play in the Beginning, another question that naturally arises is whether they are gods. Clearly, in the minds of some American Indians, tricksters are significantly more than merely entertaining literary characters. Whether animal, human, or indifferently both, their presence among the First People and their frequent role as creators or transformers place them among sacred, divine beings. But here as elsewhere in the trickster universe, there is diversity. In a discussion of monotheism, Radin argues that the trickster, the transformer, and a supreme being were commonly combined.[87] In his later book-length treatment of the Winnebago trickster, he discusses in more detail the apparent contradictions between the divine and roguish sides of tricksters, which led to the perplexities some of whose "solutions" I have already summarized:

> In all these tribes we find the same break between Trickster conceived of as a divine being and as a buffoon. Nor is it only the outsider who feels this. Many Indians themselves felt it, and tried to explain it in various ways. An educated Tlingit told Boas that the buffoon-like incidents were added [to trickster stories] to offset the serious parts of the myth. . . . That, originally at least, Trickster was not a deity in the ordinary sense of the term seems evident. That attempts were constantly being made to elevate him to such a rank is, however, equally clear. . . . Broadly speaking, it can be said that only when Trickster has been definitely separated from the cycle connected with him, as among the Fox, the Ojibwa and the Winnebago, does he definitely become a deity or the son of one.[88]

After considering his evidence, Radin determines that "On the basis of all these facts only one conclusion is possible, namely, that Trickster's divinity is always secondary and that it is largely a construction of the priest-thinker, of a remodeller."[89]

On the other hand, while the Ojibwe Wenebojo assumes many forms and his power status seems to vacillate, he possesses, finally, both human and divine qualities. He created the world, to be sure, which makes him a higher being than humans, but he is still less than the *manitou* (the spirits that inhabit all living things). And so, it would appear, he is a mediator between humanity and the gods, just as he is a mediator between humans and animals.[90] W. W. and Dorothy Hill claim that the two aspects of Coyote were definitely separated in Navajo myths: While they are one and the same character, they wrote, the Coyote of the Navajo origin myth is one of the Holy People but the "trotting" Coyote is a trickster. This difference in roles rather than character or personage is clear in the Navajo mind, they say.[91] Among the Navajos' neighbors, the Hopis, Coyote has a "savior's" role in a few stories, but all in all, the Hopi Coyote carries much less religious aura than the Navajo Coyote.[92] Some Shoshonis—perhaps under the influence of Christianity—said that God created Coyote (*tei apo* or "little father"); hence, he is a kind of god who helped God create life (along with Bear, Wolf, and other "ancient animals").[93] Christianity seems definitely to have influenced Klamath thinking about their trickster, so that for some the trickster Kemukampsh became identified with the Christian god and his son Aisis with Jesus.[94] For some Sahaptins, the transformer/namer Coyote was an emissary of Jesus.[95]

If we insist upon thinking of the divine and the sacred in the literal, simplistic terms of a child's Sunday school lessons, then assuredly no trickster is a god. But if we can conceive of divinity as a being or force of multifarious creative energy, perhaps many creative-transforming tricksters are as sacred as other more obvious gods of American Indians. Unfortunately, many in the dominant culture have not advanced beyond their misconceptions about American Indian "idolatry" and "pantheistic nature worship." Our mistaken beliefs notwithstanding, tribal religions are anything but simple and primitive. The tribal peoples of this continent experience divinity, the holy beings, much more complexly than many have thought. The Navajos, for instance, see the Holy People as powers that can be both beneficent and hostile, and they recognize that these beings are not contained within the finite objects that symbolize them and that the sacred is not confined to one mode of revelation. Nevertheless, it is true, as Bright says about the First People, that American Indian tricksters on the whole are not divinities who would pass Euro-American muster as gods: they are not worshipped at all, to say nothing of being worshipped as supremely powerful self-aware creators who create a world ex nihilo.[96]

Whether one regards tricksters as divine or sacred depends, of course, on one's definition of the godhead or the nature of the sacred. It is clear that tricksters do not satisfy traditional Judeo-Christian conceptions of divinity. But how have American Indians defined the sacred, and do tricksters conform to that definition? Ricketts claims that Trickster is a religious, sacred figure because he is a myth figure. Furthermore, trickster "myths are sacred because they establish and explain the reality of things. . . . Not the trickster as a living being, but the deeds he does and what they reveal about man and the world are the sacred reality."[97] There is truth in Ricketts's description, but the conclusion, not drawn but implicit in his description, is the significance of creative or transforming power. The power to transform the objective world as well as themselves seems to be an essential quality of the Holy People, or *manitou*, or the sacred ones by whatever name a tribe knows them. Among the Ojibwes, for instance, the ability to metamorphose is a sure sign of the power possessed by "other-than-human" persons such as the *manitou*.[98] The power to transform themselves is also possessed to a lesser degree by humans such as shamans and by other characters in the oral traditions. For example, it is through his abilities to transform himself into different shapes—a tree stump, a bird, a feather—that the Arapaho Blood Clot Boy is able to defeat his enemies.[99] But these mythic personages generally receive their power from sacred nonhuman beings, and their power to transform does not usually extend to the objective world, while the power to transform the world is inherent in many tricksters. Not everyone who is funny and clever, lascivious and gluttonous is a trickster, but the possession of transforming power seems to be a prerequisite for tricksterhood of many sorts. Such power certainly appears to be the means by which the Klamath trickster is distinguished from otherwise similar figures.[100]

Not every trickster has the power he needs or thinks he has. Before we become too hyperbolical, let us remember that it is still trickster we are looking at, and we must be appropriately watchful and cautious, just as characters in the stories are; for they know that even though Coyote has the power to transform his appearance, nothing alters his personality. Just as we begin to relax in the aura of mythic power, he will turn us topsy-turvy. Sometimes this transformational power has a dark side, as in many Pueblo stories when witch transformations are into Coyote, and Coyote is associated with witching powers.[101]

While the above efforts to characterize tricksters are full of variations and exceptions, one trait seems consistent for all tricksters, no matter who they are or what tribes they are associated with: tricksters are inveterate travelers. It is in tricksters' wanderings that we see most dramatically the difficulty of saying exactly who or what an American Indian trickster is. We can go beyond Levi-Strauss and Ramsey and say that an American Indian trickster is not contained within simply polar opposites and is more than either/and or either/and/and, and so forth. Or we can observe with Bright that "Whatever we say Coyote *is*, he answers, with the ancient Sanskritic sages, *Neti neti:* 'That's not it, that's not it.'"[102]

Actually, to talk about tricksters as travelers suggests too much of the purposeful, for most often tricksters' journeys have no destinations. Tricksters simply wander, as the beginnings of so many trickster stories suggest: "Coyote was going there," "Trickster started wandering around the world again," "as he was walking along . . . ," "And then he travelled on." To what can this habitual wandering be attributed? We could examine the roving habits of some of the trickster animals—coyotes are an obvious choice, for they do a great deal of trekking—but that, of course, would suggest an answer for only one or two animal tricksters and none for human trickster characters. In a few cases explanations for tricksters' rambling are to be found in their characters. The Keresan tradition says that Coyote's wandering is punishment for his gluttony.[103] An Ojibwe version of a trickster-marries-his-daughter story ends with everybody knowing of his shame wherever he goes, so "he kept on going. No one knows what became of him."[104] This story suggests that the cause of his wandering is to be found in his alienation from society. We will see that it is not always true that tricksters are removed from society, either physically or relationally, but we cannot deny that their wandering from their homes and from the rules—like their behavior in general—often smacks of hostility to ordered society and to its controls.[105] Looking at tricksters from a social standpoint, we might also notice that the frequent lack of information regarding their birth or parentage contributes to their image as footloose and fancy-free.

It should be considered, too, that narratives of journeys are common in the North American Indian oral traditions as a whole, not just in trickster traditions. Frequently, as a result of a protagonist's adventures on a journey, some change comes to human life; often rituals are learned and passed on.[106] Hence, while the hero leaves human society (often because he has violated some taboo or social rule), he is ultimately the means by which the human community increases its relations with the nonhuman persons composing the larger community of life. Myth commemorates and reiterates the journey to community, and rituals are the communal enactment of certain kinds of social relations attending the experience. Rituals are as well "an attempt to create and maintain a particular culture, a particular set of assumptions by which experience is controlled. . . . The rituals enact the form of social relations [in this case, those created in the journey] and in giving these relations visible expression they enable people to know their own society."[107]

Trickster's wanderings are both an embodiment of this pattern of mythic journeys (except that his journeys seldom have ritualistic ramifications) and a comic inversion of the process. For a number of tribes, it is on his journeys that he sets the world straight, taking a hand in shaping both nonhuman and human communities (those which some other mythic hero will later link as one). In this context the accuracy and helpfulness of saying that a transformer trickster is a "vagabond who lives beyond bounded communities"[108] becomes questionable, for his seemingly aimless wandering is in a world whose boundaries, physical or social, are still being defined at least in part by his actions. In fact, since traveling expands the limits of our known world, mythic tricksters' wanderings are necessary to define both the physical and social worlds as we experience them. But at the same time, another element of Trickster's wanderings serves as a comic inversion of the mythic journey. Rather than defining social limits, he deconstructs them; and instead of affirming the greater social order, his journeys continually threaten social disorder. Rather than wandering to define the larger sacred social geography, he journeys within the circumference of his own constricted self. In this role Trickster represents not the creation of social reality but the comic cautionary social image of potentially dangerous human behavior.

Raven Steals the Moon

Raven . . . traveled northward. After he had traveled for a while he came to where a village lay. He then put himself in the form of a conifer needle into a water hole behind the chief's house and floated about there awaiting the chief's daughter.

The chief's child then went thither for water, and he floated in the water that she dipped up. She threw this out and dipped a second time, but he was still there. And when close to her he said: "Drink it."

Not a long time after that she became pregnant. Then she gave birth [to a child], and its grandfather washed the child all over and put his feet to its feet. It began to creep about. After it had crept about for a while it cried so violently that no one could stop it. "Boo hoo moon," it kept saying.

After it had tired them out with its crying they stopped up the smoke hole, and, having pulled one box out of another four times, they gave it a round thing. There came light throughout the house. After it had played with this for a while it let it go and again started to cry. "Boo hoo, smoke hole," it cried. They then opened the smoke hole, and it cried again and said: "Boo hoo, more." And they made the space larger. Then he flew away with it [the round thing]. Marten pursued him below. *TaLAtg.a'dAla,* too, chased him above. They gave it up and returned.

He then put the moon into his armpit. And, after he had traveled about for a while, he came to where Sea-gull and Cormorant sat. He made them quarrel with each other. And he said to Cormorant: "People tell me to brace myself on the ground with my tongue this way [when fighting]." He then did it, and [Raven] went quickly to him. He bit off his tongue.

Then he made it into an eulachon. And he put on his cape and rubbed this all over it, and then he rubbed it on the inside of the canoe as well. Then he also put rocks in and went in front of *Qadadjâ'n*. And he entered his house. "Hi, I, too, have become cold." *Qadadjâ'n* was lying with his back to the fire and, looking toward him, saw his canoe, covered with slime, lying on the water as if full. He then became angry and pulled the screen down toward the fire. Eulachon immediately poured forth. He [Raven] then threw the stones out of the canoe and put them into it. When it was full, he went off with them.

After he had distributed the eulachon along the mainland in the places where they now are and had put some in Nass inlet, he left a few in the canoe.

He then placed ten paddles under these, of which the bottom one had a knot hole running through it. And he shouted landward to where a certain person lived. She then brought out a basket on her back, and he said to her: "help, yourself, chieftainess." After she had put them into [the basket] a while, and her basket was nearly full, he stepped upon a stalk of *lqea'mawhich* he had provided and said: "A-a-a, I feel my canoe cracking." He then pushed it from the land, and when she stretched out her arm for more [eulachon] he pulled out the hairs under her armpit.

Fern-woman (*SnAndja'n̄-djat*) at once called for her sons. Both her sons knew how to throw objects by means of a stick, they say. He [Raven] immediately fled. And one of them shot at him and broke his paddle. And after they had broken [it] he paddled with the one that had a knot hole. When they shot after him again he said "Through the knot hole," and through the knot hole went the stone. Thus he was saved. He had dexterously got her armpit hair.

He then left the canoe. He came to a shore opposite some people who were fishing with fish rakes in Nass. And he said: "Hallo, throw one over to me. I will give you light." But they said: "HA ha-a-a he, who is speaking is the one who is always playing tricks." He then let a small part shine and put it away again. They forthwith emptied their canoe in front of him several times.

He then called a dog and said to it: "Shall I make (or ordain) four moons?" The dog said that would not do. The dog wanted six. He (Raven) then said to him: "What will you do when it is spring?" "When I am hungry I will move my feet in front of my face." And he made it as he (the dog) told him to do, they say.

He then bit off a part of the moon. After he had chewed it for a while he threw it up [into the sky]. "Future people are going to see you there in fragments forever." He then broke the moon into halves by throwing it down hard and threw [half of] it up hard into the air, the sun as well.

Thence he traveled northward.

John Swanton, *Haida Texts and Myths*, 116–18

CHAPTER THREE

Living Sideways

Social Relations in Trickster Stories

It is clear that many trickster stories from American Indian oral traditions are like the Clackamas Chinook trickster stories that Mrs. Howard told to Melville Jacobs in that they stress social relationships.[1] Whatever else might be said about trickster stories, we must recognize that they serve social purposes—most obviously entertainment, but even while they entertain, they instruct and act as societal control by dramatizing community values and behavioral limits. Navajo Coyote stories teach children (and adults) some of the same lessons typically found in other tribes' trickster stories: "that an inordinate ambition to equal others in accomplishment invariably leads to failure [and] the necessity of staying within proper bounds."[2] At first glance, some trickster stories suggest that ours is an absurd world with no physical anchor, social stability, or moral center. After all, what are we to make of a world in which a trickster can dismantle himself or habitually escape his acts of incest, often with little more than a few bumps, if that? But there is nothing "amoral or nihilist" about these stories; rather, they are grounded solidly in tribal norms.[3] Some are, no doubt, the outlet for protest against repression they have been claimed to be; some reinforce community values in positive, some in negative ways; some may contribute to reassessment of culture and belief (whether in religion or other facets of human experience), perhaps leading to change.[4] Regardless, all are rooted in community.

It should be no surprise that these tales serve social ends, for all literature—oral and written—is a social discourse, a dialogue between an individual and his or her community, and trickster stories are just such a dialogue par excellence.[5] Babcock-Abrahams rightly argues that American Indian trickster stories dramatize the ever-present conflict and interplay "between the individual and society, between freedom and constraint."[6] The ambivalence with which we respond to tricksters is due to the contradictions the conflict or interplay raises in us. Such interplay is the source of the social functions of trickster stories. It is in the context of the conflict between individual and society that we can best understand the role of humor in American Indian trickster stories. Humor, which helps us endure what often seems the absurdity of the universe, also buttresses social stability.

American Indians do not have a corner on the market for humor, of course. All peoples have their own traditions of humor—stories, jokes, tricks—but acknowledging and understanding the role of humor in the lives of the American Indians is important if for no other reason than to counteract stereotypes. After his journey west in the nineteenth century, Washington Irving observed about American Indians:

> [They] occasionally indulge in a vein of comic humor and dry satire, to which the Indians appear to me much more prone than is generally imagined. In fact, the Indians that I have had an opportunity of seeing in real life are quite different from those described in poetry. They are by no means the stoics that they are represented: taciturn, unbending, without a tear or a smile. Taciturn, they are, it is true, when in the company of white men, whose good-will they distrust, and whose language they do not understand; but the white man is equally taciturn under like circumstances. When the Indians are among themselves, however, there cannot be greater gossips. Half of their time is taken up in talking over their adventures in war and hunting, and in telling whimsical stories. They are great mimics and buffoons, also, and entertain themselves excessively at the expense of the whites with whom they have associated, and who have supposed them impressed with profound respect for their grandeur and dignity. They are curious observers, noting everything in silence with a

keen and watchful eye; occasionally exchanging a glance or a
grunt with each other, when anything particularly strikes them;
but reserving all comments until they are alone. Then it is that
they give full scope to criticism, satire, mimicry, and mirth.[7]

Irving's observations may not do full justice to the depth of humor's
role in traditional American Indian life. Deloria explains that "Indians
have found a humorous side of nearly every problem."[8] As in ceremonies
with clowns, even mythic materials might contain amusing material.
Melville Jacobs observes that of the Clackamas stories he examined, 60
percent of myths contained "fun" as contrasted with 20 percent of the
nonmythic tales.[9] The Nez Perce ethnographer Archie Phinney said that
humor is the "deepest and most vivid element" in Nez Perce mythology.
It is "[t]he element that animates all the pathos, all the commonplace
and the tragic. . . . There is nothing hilarious or comical but there is the
droll, the ludicrous and the clever exaggeration."[10]

Keith Basso tells us that among the Western Apaches, "a striking
feature of . . . life [is] that serious things are always getting said in what
appear to be unserious ways."[11] Mimicking certain kinds of "serious"
behavior—innuendo, faultfinding, insults—in jokes emphasizes that
those behaviors can have disruptive social outcomes, particularly if taken
seriously. Jokes, therefore, are "simultaneously 'funny' and 'dangerous.'"[12]
Tricksters' behavior, too, implies for their audiences both "funny and
dangerous" behavior. Telling a trickster story can become an occasion
for parodying behavior threatening to tribal values. Toelken reports that
among the Navajos, telling a trickster tale can lead to a "hearty discussion
about Navajo values, language, and cultural history."[13] Trickster stories
are so important as educative tools that one matures as a "true Navajo"
only after being well grounded in the traditions of Ma'i.[14] Laughter is an
important instrument in such tribal enculturation. Deloria reminds us
that "For centuries before the white invasion, teasing was a method of
control of social situations by Indian people."[15] Navajo adults—and no
doubt those in other tribes as well—often use laughter to rebuke children.[16]

The laughter that accompanies many trickster stories is, indeed, an
element of social control, and a trickster's failure to fit into that social

world is at the center of many trickster stories. As stand-ins for humans, tricksters prove absurd when their bungling immoral or amoral behavior contrasts with the normal and tolerable.[17] Failing to fit normal social constructs—often even while he manipulates them to his own ends— makes trickster laughable, or perhaps not trickster the character but rather the character's behavior. The Navajo storyteller Yellowman claimed that listeners do not laugh during Ma'i stories because the stories are funny; they are not. Rather, they laugh at "the way Ma'i does things."[18] Hearing the laughter, those with ears to hear understand that Coyote's escapades are not acceptable.

Trickster stories, then, are satirical, but they are not always satirical in ways they are claimed to be. Radin says that some of the humor in the Winnebago trickster stories is satirically directed at ritual. While there is certainly nothing static about American Indian societies, it is unlikely that many American Indian storytellers told their stories to transform ritual that experience had proved must be for the community's spiritual and physical well-being. Speaking of humor in Nez Perce mytho- logy, Dell Skeels makes a point that may bear on many trickster stories as well, at least those of mythic import. Conscious satire, he says, is unusual, no doubt because the "timeless quality" of mythology obviates its use for satirizing a present person, group, or situation.[19] Radin may be on safer ground when he describes the stories as an "outlet for voicing protest against the many, often onerous obligations connected with the Winnebago social order and their religion and ritual."[20]

It is true that some trickster tales satirize group customs and the restrictiveness of Native societies. The dominant culture's romanticizing of American Indian ways notwithstanding, there were many restrictive elements in tribal life. At one time or another, no matter how conven- tional one might be, no matter how accepting of social demands, we all chafe against one or another of society's fetters. Tribal taboos, ritual requirements, and the expectations assumed for ideal values must at times have seemed to hem a person in. These circumstances may well have led to ridicule of even the social conventions that contributed to one's physical survival, as in a Salish story when an apparently lazy and inept Blue Jay proves to be a better and more tireless hunter than his much praised and socially prized brother-in-law, Wolf.[21] The Winnebago trickster Wakdjunkaga drives home the difference between the ideal and the real when he, a tribal chief, not only goes on the warpath but also has sex with a woman in the middle of the war-bundle feast in violation of all tribal rules and taboos.[22] In another example, awakening from a nap, Wakdjunkaga finds himself lying on his back without a blanket: "He looked up above him and saw to his astonishment something floating there. 'Aha, aha! The chiefs have unfurled their banner! The people must be having a feast for this is always the case when the chief's banner is unfurled.' With this he sat up and then first realized that his blanket was gone. It was his blanket he saw floating above. His penis had become stiff and the blanket had been forced up."[23] Here the satire is directed toward an important yearly feast at which the tribe's chief raised a long feathered crook, the symbol of his authority, and delivered lengthy speeches exhorting the people to observe tribal ideals.[24]

Sometimes the satire of trickster stories is directed at others than the trickster himself. Wiget examines another episode from the Winnebago tradition in which the trickster marries a chief's son in order to have easy access to food. Disguised as a woman—with a vulva made of an elk's liver and breasts made of the elk's kidneys—Wakdjunkaga not only marries the son but has a child by him as well! Wiget explains clearly and in some detail the chief's failings in this matter.

> He has given his son's hand and his tribe's future to a woman he does not know, who is in fact without "place," without kin of any kind in the village. He has done so on the recognizance of "an old woman living on the outskirts of the village," a conventional Winnebago character type the audience would understand as untrustworthy. Rashly encouraging his daughters to acknowledge the relationship and hastily gathering a wedding party, he puts the satisfaction of having his son marry a beautiful woman ahead of the prudence and judgment required by his position. . . . If, in the exercise of authority, passion and self-interest can override the demands of tradition and responsibility for the common good, then no one is safe. Such a story reminds us of the danger of confusing the person and the role.[25]

Certainly, trickster stories sometimes protest the constraints of social rule, but in the service of society's rules and expectations they much more frequently ridicule tricksters. All in all, most satire in trickster stories is directed at human failings and quirks as parodied in the tricksters themselves. To complicate matters more, as tricksters violate the limits of social law and propriety, they also commonly establish such boundaries in a positive way.

The key to understanding American Indian trickster stories as social exempla is American Indian attitudes about the individual's relation to society. The romanticism that has shaped the dominant culture's privileging individualism does not operate in the American Indian world. Among American Indians, it is not taken for granted that the individual's well-being may be distinct from society's or that the community may have to sacrifice its needs in the name of individual or minority rights. It is difficult for many of us in individualistic American culture to accept traditional peoples' social relationships in which the group's (family's, clan's, community's) welfare is the center of concern. We fear that such commitment leads to suppression of the individual's desires and well-being. However, the truth may be that in American Indian cultures individual needs and desires are accepted more tolerantly than they are in our individualistic society. The individual's personality is honored and respected perhaps to degrees that we might find indulgent. By and large, persons are allowed to follow with impunity what they perceive as their own course. Of course, if one's passions or appetites bring one into conflict with the "real" world (the world that stands apart from the individual, including both the realms of natural phenomena and of social phenomena), there are inevitable consequences. Trickster stories commonly dramatize these consequences.

What makes traditional American Indian attitudes different from American individualism is the belief that the individual is not an island, not a freestanding integer whose identity grows from some inner seed with no external referent, not an identity possessing a destiny separate from others; rather, one's identity develops from his or her presence in and interaction with community. To cite just one example, among the Navajos all human individuals in a community—like all nonhuman experiences and phenomena—are seen as integrated and interreliant, and the ostensible self-sufficiency that the dominant culture associates with individualism is not encouraged, particularly in the religious life of the community: "[I]ndividuality [when permitted] is . . . always tailored to the larger ritual expectations of the group."[26] Traditionally, not only is the American Indian individual's identity united with that of the group (family, clan, village, and so forth); so too is his or her fate, and, in turn, the group's welfare may depend on the individual's choices. Egoistical behavior can bring danger or suffering to family or community. For American Indians, "social reality . . . is coexistent with the individual, both constraining and in its turn being constrained by him."[27]

The matrix of individual and social reality is relationships, "the cornerstone of Tribal community."[28] Through relationships—family, clan, and tribal—American Indians discover who they are and how their identities give them presence in the social web.[29] In fact, this knowledge is probably essential to American Indians' sense of well-being. Discussing how Navajo family relationships extend beyond immediate family to include clan, Toelken explains that extended and reciprocal relationships are a source of personal stability.[30] Reciprocity characterizes and controls many aspects of American Indian social life, as, for example, in giveaways. Among the Algonquins, one honored by a gift will honor another by gifting the object after wearing or using it for a time, a passing on which eschews possession and consumption at the expense of others in the community and which sees reciprocity in community terms.[31]

Living in such a society requires a continual awareness of oneself in relationship with and heightened sensitivity to the needs of family and community. Not all, of course, sustain this awareness successfully or even possess it. Some act as though they are, indeed, islands unto themselves. Perhaps the impact of such self-absorption is most noticeable and most immediately destructive on a family level, a truth dramatized in some trickster stories. Toelken observes that one of the severest Navajo criticisms that can be made of one is, "[H]e acts like he doesn't have any family," a charge that denotes the "epitome of personal degradation and lack of responsibility."[32] Unlike African tricksters, who are commonly seen interacting with their wives and offspring, most American Indian tricksters are only infrequently seen in the context of their own families, and even when they are in that context, the interactions are seldom of the complexity that we see in African stories.[33] North American tricksters generally act as though they do not have family, even when they do have it.[34] Toelken also points out that among the Navajos such self-absorption is thought to be evidence that one is a witch. He goes on to identify the main traits of witches: "selfishness, acquisitiveness, lack of concern for other family members and for clan relationships."[35] Readers will recognize tricksters here. Appropriately, in Navajo myths, Coyote is often associated with witchcraft, as is the Coyote trickster in many Pueblo stories.

In a social system where the individual's significance is social as well as personal and the ideal is to refrain from self-interest in favor of others' interests, public opinion plays a consequential role in community life. The community may well appraise individuals "on the basis of their contributions to the collective well-being," as Julian Rice says of the Lakotas.[36] Public gossip—the "news" of someone's failure to meet social expectations—can be merciless, which for many is certainly a significant context for self-awareness concerning their behavior. Radin recognized this self-awareness when he said of American Indian social controls "that every mistake, every deviation from accepted opinion, every individual and purely personal interpretation, every peculiarity and eccentricity may call forth ridicule. . . . As a conserving force . . . the fear of ridicule is every individual's personal balancing wheel."[37] We have already seen that Ramsey refers to American Indian cultures as "shame" cultures. A. C. "Chuck" Ross makes clear that such forces still operate in American Indian communities: "we're group oriented. And because we are tribal people, the minute you become an 'I,' then you're an outsider. As a result, the group will ridicule and/or ostracize you to try to get you back into the group."[38]

Although ridicule is a plentiful commodity in trickster stories (even while fear of ridicule is rare in tricksters), not all stories are simply about trickster follies. Generally speaking, we can identify the following foci in trickster stories.[39]

Enlargement of social boundaries in expanding the limits to what is possible and allowable as well as defining (as in limiting) the

boundaries of the acceptable, perhaps what Yellowman meant
when he said of Ma'i, the Navajo Coyote trickster, "if he did
not do those [terrible] things then those things would not be
possible in the world."[40]

Defying and confusing social rules and expectations such as the
rules of hospitality or socially determined expectations about
such activities as rituals.

Dramatization of the contradictions inherent in social life as well
as the internal clashes attending confrontation between instinct
and reason, emotion and thought.

We have seen that tricksters are often transformers who alter a preexisting or recently created world so that it becomes the familiar world
we live in. Generally, these transformations are for humanity's benefit,
even if humans do not necessarily see it that way. For example, in myths
dealing with the origin of human mortality, a trickster's common
explanation for death's necessity is that the world would become too
crowded with people or that humans would not feel affection or pity
for one another if there were no death. More obviously beneficial are
tricksters' creative acts introducing social customs and boundaries. Hence,
in a scenario played out in more than one location on the North American continent, especially in the West, Wolf (or some other elder brother
of Coyote) creates a utopian world, but Coyote transforms it into a
human world; that is, he "transforms the natural order into a cultural
one."[41] Because of our stereotypical outlook on trickster as a boundary
buster, his instituting social boundaries of one sort or another or punishing
others for transgressing them may seem out of character, but such acts
are not at all unusual among American Indian tricksters. Hence, when
the Second Mesa Hopi Coyote positioned boundary stones for the people,
he also left restricted strips between clans or town lands that were not to
be cultivated. As "enforcers" of the boundaries, he buried prayer feathers,
a blind beetle, and a poisonous spider, saying that if anyone cultivated a
restricted strip, he would go blind or die of poison.[42] The Sanpoil Coyote
makes Beaver the Salmon Chief, with the charge that he must share the
salmon with all who come to fish and must not let anyone become

greedy.[43] The Sahaptin Coyote establishes hospitality.[44] The Clackamas Coyote helps his grandson get revenge on the latter's unfaithful wives by causing the moon to shine on their infidelities.[45]

In addition to specific social/cultural traits, tricksters' creations or transformations are often immediate and concrete—a landform, for instance, or perhaps an animal trait. It may well be that even these transformations carried social implications for traditional audiences. We know that often American Indians have regarded familiar aspects of their landscape to be "persons" in one sense or another, as when a Tsimshian myth shows ancestors transformed into rocks and islands.[46] At other times geographical features may be thought of as manifestations of nonhuman beings or regarded as peopled by nonhuman beings that merit the same ethical-social responses as humans. Discussing the prominence of the theme of relationships among American Indians, John Epes Brown has written how "relationships do not stop [with family, clan, and tribe] but extend out to embrace and relate to the environment; to the land, to the animals, to the plants, and to the clouds, the elements, the heavens, the stars; and ultimately those relationships that people express and live, extend to embrace the universe."[47] Therefore, by transforming the landscape or the animals within that landscape, tricksters are also shaping the social geography of the American Indian world, the cosmic social order of which humans are a part as surely as they are a part of the human social order. Granted, there is nothing explicit to indicate that storytellers or audiences would have made such associations. Still, given traditional American Indian attitudes toward the natural world and the highly allusive nature of American Indian oral art, there might well have existed an unspoken understanding that Trickster's transformation of the physical world had social implications as well.

In any event there are many instances in which a trickster's actions or choices as he wanders have direct and clear social consequences. When the Caddo Coyote frees the buffalo for the people to hunt, he provides the material basis for culture and the institutions of social control of hunting.[48] This example shows a trickster establishing the material foundation for society and formalized social institutions. What may be more significant about many tricksters' behavior is that they are also responsible for human social behavior on various levels. For better or for worse, tricksters occasion the realities of human social behavior as a kind of primal prototype. Tricksters having been a part of the prehuman flux, their choices and actions become existential reality. The Crow Old Man Coyote rationalizes his sexual fickleness as the basis for the custom of the Lumpwood and Fox warrior societies' kidnapping each others' wives: "One thing I'll tell you. Newly married women are wont to satisfy us; when we have been married for a long time, we get dissatisfied. When we marry others, in the beginning it is the same way, once more we have a lively interest [in our partner]."[49] In another Crow story, Old Man Coyote decrees joking relationships:

> It was Old-Man Coyote. He was going about, looking for food. He went where there were a great many buffalo tracks. He got there trotting. A yellow calf was lying in the buffalo track. Its feet were swollen. "E-e-k a!" he exclaimed, "this younger brother of mine is miserable. I'll put you on my back and shall soon catch up with your mother." He carried it on his back, he took him along the tracks, he got tired. "Elder brother," said the calf, "you are tired now, kill me and eat me." "My dear younger brother, don't say that again. My dear younger brother, do not say that. If I killed you, my bad joking-relatives would laugh at me." We do not know who Old-Man-Coyote's father was. This is why we practice the joking relationship. Whatever Old-Man-Coyote said, that we also say.[50]

In an Upper Cowlitz story, Coyote destroys Soft Basket Woman's vaginal teeth and kills her cannibalistic children, whom he visits. He announces that in the future sexual union between men and women will be more congenial and guests will not have to fear their hosts.[51] Considering the lasciviousness of tricksters in general, here too there is a notable irony in Coyote's role in vaginal dentata stories.[52] In most stories the trickster's sexuality is always extravagantly unbridled and hence repeatedly the cause of many social transgressions. In any event, we see in these examples how a trickster sometimes contributes to defining social limits in positive action rather than being a negative example.

Nevertheless, tricksters commonly delineate limits by violating them. Repeatedly, a trickster confronts and crosses social boundaries with little thought of consequences. In spite of the above instances of trickster stories satirizing society or its conventions, most of the social satire is directed against tricksters—or rather, the trickster in each of us. Our laughter at their undisciplined egocentricity and weak-willed flesh defines the psycho-moral limits and the nature of our humanity. Time and again, we see the usually amusing misfortune that befalls tricksters (and us, as well) when they are driven by individual desires and appetites, act alone or as though they do not "have any family," or project their appetite-driven energies onto others as aggression of one sort or another.[53]

American Indian tricksters are inherently at odds in their societies; they are what all are at one time or another and what some are all the time: unsocialized or asocial humankind. We see in a multitude of stories the tension between the individual and the community to which Babcock-Abrahams refers. Much of this tension comes from a trickster's choosing self over community. Thus in one story he destroys his canoe as a way of discouraging others from accompanying him on the warpath—a foolish exclusion, but one that frees him from the demands of being in a community of warriors.[54] We also see tricksters repeatedly following their own counsel rather than heeding the acquired wisdom of the community. Repeatedly, we see them asserting their independence by ignoring advice and directions.[55] Victor Barnouw also points out that when Wenebojo accepts advice from others, things turn out satisfactorily for him: conversely, when others accept advice from him, the misfortune is usually theirs, probably because his advice has its origin in himself, not community wisdom.[56] Similarly, Melville Jacobs says that the Clackamas Coyote is a bonehead whose efforts fail when he responds to internal stimuli only, but when he responds to something external, his responses are powerful, adult, even deitylike.[57]

There are occasions when we see tricksters alone, and even then we see what happens when someone tries to live as a society of one. When the Winnebago trickster wanders off and is briefly isolated from the greater society, he is especially likely to be the victim of his own nature, for it is in these episodes that—apparently free of social context—he acts foolishly in ways that are hilarious to his audience but painful for him. Alone and free of anything like social direction or restraints, his own fatuous instinctual energies turn upon him; he becomes a society at war with itself. In one Winnebago episode he begins to skin a buffalo he has killed.

> In the midst of these operations, suddenly his left arm grabbed the buffalo. "Give that back to me, it is mine! Stop that or I will use my knife on you!" So spoke the right arm. "I will cut you to pieces, that is what I will do to you," continued the right arm. Thereupon the left arm released its hold. But, shortly after, the left arm again grabbed hold of the right arm. This time it grabbed hold of the wrist just at the moment that the right arm had commenced to skin the buffalo. Again and again this was repeated. In this manner did Trickster make both arms quarrel. That quarrel soon turned into a vicious fight and the left arm was badly cut up. "Oh, oh! Why did I do this? Why have I done this? I have made myself suffer!"

In another episode he punishes his anus for failing to guard his game while he slept.[58]

Perhaps fortunately for these wandering buffoons and certainly unfortunately for their victims, such moments of isolation are frequently relieved by tricksters' social forays. As we have already noted, some see tricksters' wandering as a mark of their marginality, but it is a mistake to consider their meandering without also considering the frequently implied social contexts in which it occurs, for these circumstances are a significant part of tricksters' didactic function. Rather than merely arguing that tricksters' travels represent their living "physically or psychically" beyond bounded communities, we should notice that most of their shenanigans do indeed occur in one way or another within social boundaries, although they certainly strain or violate the values that produce cohesive societies. As they wander, tricksters are seldom removed from one social situation or another for long, seldom free for any length of time from some sort of bounded community, whether the human social world or nonhuman relationships. This is also true whether or

not they are in a village or encampment, for as we have seen American
Indians do not necessarily believe themselves removed from community merely because they are away from the collection of dwellings that
are the center of human society. In fact the impossibility of escaping the
social eye or social relationships and responsibilities may be the theme
in some stories in which at first glance a trickster appears to be removed
from society and alone. This can be seen in the story in which Coyote
commits self-fellatio and is discovered by the clouds or others even
though he believes he is alone and hidden from anyone's sight.[59]

Moreover, we must not overlook the fact that often a trickster is shown
to be, even as he wanders, a thread in the social fabric. Commonly,
others are not particularly enthusiastic about a trickster's appearance
on the scene. When a trickster arrives, the other characters become suspicious and are on their guard. Sometimes, however, his relationship to
them is emphasized and he is greeted accordingly. In one Winnebago
episode, as Wakdjunkaga arrives at Muskrat's village, "All its inhabitants
were happy at his arrival. The children exclaimed, 'Our uncle has come!'
This they repeated again and again. Then the old muskrat spoke to him,
'Ah, my older brother has come! It is good.'"[60] Sometimes tricksters are
acknowledged as being connected to the natural world in kinship terms:
Nanibozho is "brother to animals, plants, trees, and many different
aspects of nature," Wakdjunkaga "ambled along calling all the objects in
the world younger brothers when speaking to them. He and all objects
in the world understood one another, understood, indeed, one another's
language."[61] At times a trickster is a headman of some sort, as in Winnebago trickster stories when Wakdjunkaga is a chief or among the
Chinooks when Coyote is a headman. At other times he has a sidekick,
for example, Skunk among the Chinooks. Sometimes he is husband or
father (on occasion, mother or wife). At other times a trickster may be
addressed as "elder brother," a kinship phrase which, even if not meant
literally, still operates as a reminder that he is in others' view part of the
whole cloth of society.[62]

Tricksters' self-delusions notwithstanding, many American Indian
stories make clear that no one living alienated or detached from human
society can be whole. In a Lakota story a man wandering alone finds

himself in a disordered, fearful world. When a wolf asks him where he is going, the man admits that he has "no clear goal." "In that case," the wolf responds, "follow me, and I will lead you to a camp." Arriving at a village, the wolf tells the man "Here is where you should live."[63] Sometimes, even a trickster acknowledges the necessity of society. The Crow Old Man Coyote creates the world because "that I am alone is bad. If I looked at someone now and then, if I talked with him, it would be well."[64] After Crow makes the world, in a Tagish Tlingit story told by Angela Sidney, he similarly realizes that he is lonely and needs people. He makes them from the bark of a poplar tree.[65] Deloria's assessment of the relationship between individuals, society, and religion is relevant here: "The possibility of conceiving of an individual alone in a tribal religious sense is ridiculous. The very complexity of tribal life and the interdependence of people on one another make this conception improbable at best, a terrifying loss of identity at worst." Even ethics, Deloria asserts, "flow from the ongoing life of the community and are virtually indistinguishable from tribal or communal custom."[66] Applied to tricksters, these observations suggest that while their behavior and motives are often indisputably contrary to the well-being of the community and they prove to be asocial in their community-ethical failures, American Indians might not have viewed tricksters in terms of the marginality that Euro-American scholarly metaphors suggest.

Wander as they will, tricksters cannot escape the bounded community. However, having a place in the social universe does not mean that a trickster is socially congruent; quite the contrary. But rather than seeing him as a marauding outsider, as unraveling fringe on the social fabric, or as caught in some undefined marginality, it may be that American Indian storytellers and audiences have traditionally perceived the trickster as an insider gone awry. A more apt image for his relationship to society might be to say that he lives sideways: he moves on a diagonal to the rest of society's parallels. As such, he is a warning. What Melville Jacobs says about Chinook humor, actors, themes, and plots is applicable to tales about the trickster figure, the dangerous insider, the one who lives sideways: tricksters were "indicators of those parts of the social structure which creaked or failed to grant security. Laughter covered over or resolved disapproving or anxious feelings which the Chinooks had about those many characteristics of their way of life which did not measure up to wishes and ideals."[67]

As a trickster wends his way through human and nonhuman societies, we see, comically, how vulnerable community ideals, values, and institutions are to the twistings and inversions of the ego-centered individual ensconced in that society. In fact, social apparatus may be necessary for his schemes; it is the trickster's devious grasping of the social that underlies much of his asocial behavior. He usually knows the limits; otherwise, why would he find deception necessary or even possible? Moreover, much of his rule-breaking behavior is socially derived or at least social in origin. Compelled by self rather than by community as the American Indian ideal would have it, the trickster often pursues no uncommon desires but rather socially acceptable goals or values (only the degree of the trickster's desire is extraordinary) and manipulates the social contract in some fashion, violating it in the process. Errant and aberrant, he lives sideways in society, many times bending normal wishes and values, whether personal or social, to his own ends and knocking awry—sometimes temporarily, sometimes permanently—the social will they customarily satisfy.

In all societies there are mechanisms by which individuals achieve socially approved status and reputation, title, and role beyond what they receive through happenstance such as birth. Such mechanisms mediate social and individual needs, in that the social approval attending status provides a good deal of ego satisfaction for the individual while also reaffirming the social order. The individual is made, thereby, a cohesive part of the social structure. Ideally, these mechanisms instill social appetites that satisfy community needs by satisfying individual needs. Tricksters show us, however, that such links between the individual and society fail, that the mechanisms go awry, when the balance between community and individual is tipped by self-indulgence, self-delusion, or any other failure in self-restraint. In the individual's pursuit of community-sanctioned goals, he subverts the very values he pursues or even possesses, as when the Clackamas Coyote is a headman whose delusions and deceptions corrupt the status he has achieved in his society.[68]

Perhaps the best examples of social appetites gone astray in trickster stories are to be found in Bungling Host and Foolish Imitation episodes.[69] In both story types a trickster is ridiculed for his presumptions to social status through magic power. The typical Bungling Host story has a trickster visiting an animal of one sort or another who magically provides food for his guest, for example, by cutting meat from himself without suffering pain or loss, poking sticks up his nostrils, holding fingers over the fire so that edible fat drips from them, even killing his children but reviving them later from carefully preserved bones. When the erstwhile host later visits the trickster at the latter's insistent invitation, the foolish one tries to be an equally impressive host even though he lacks his guest's powers. The results are dire: the trickster suffers pain or kills his children or otherwise fails miserably to provide food for his guest. In fact the guest usually ends up having to exercise his powers to provide his own hospitality. All the while the trickster insists that he does not understand what went wrong, for he has always worked the trick successfully before. Even unmasked, this fraud continues his pretense to status through magic power.

Foolish Imitation stories similarly ridicule the trickster for his presumptuous efforts to gain magic powers or social status. An obvious example is the common Eye Juggler episode, in which a trickster is taught—after insistent pestering—to make his eyes fly into a tree and return into his eye socket on command. He is warned to do the trick only a few times, but, of course, the trickster ignores the rules and loses his eyes. Two Zuni stories make explicit the absurdity of Coyote's pretenses. In one, Coyote tries to imitate Badger's sword-swallowing trick, a trick practiced by the Badger clan, which was associated with the Lewekwe medicine society. When Coyote fails, cutting himself and bleeding, Badger says, "You don't belong to Lewekwe and you can't do that."[70] The other, a Bungling Host story of Coyote and a bumblebee, is equally explicit.[71] In other Foolish Imitation stories, a trickster's insatiable ego seeks the gratification of status not appropriately his, which leads to mindless brutality against his relatives. In yet another Zuni story, he is tricked into beheading his grandmother as he attempts imitating the Burrowing Owl's dance.[72] Given such cruelty, it is no wonder that for some Coyote is associated with witchcraft.

We know that in most American Indian societies spirit power was a source of both individual and communal well-being, physical and spiritual, and hence was socially valued. The possession of such power was evidenced variously, ranging from skill at hunting or fishing to healing or magic ritual abilities. It is important to remember that among American Indians individual power commonly extended beyond the individual. Douglas points out that "beliefs which attribute spiritual power to individuals are never neutral or free of the dominant patterns of social structure."[73] In an American Indian context, Karl Kroeber shows how personal vision power among the Ojibwes is transmitted from the individual to the tribe through feasts, dances, or the creation of ceremony.[74] It follows, then, that a failure of individual power could have community consequences.[75] It is in such contexts that we might say the Bungling Host and Foolish Imitation stories draw amusing contrasts between those who legitimately possess communally efficacious spiritual power and those who do not (usually the trickster) and stimulate other social observations as well.

Ricketts and Ramsey argue that trickster tales parody shamans, but as noted earlier, a satirically antinomian Trickster is essential to Ricketts's portrait of the figure as a kind of Native secular humanist.[76] While it is no doubt true that some stories satirize shamans in particular, the evidence of most stories suggests other and perhaps more plausible interpretations. Among other social observations, these stories dramatize the difference between those possessing power, and hence status, and those lacking it. The personages a trickster mimics in Bungling Host and Foolish Imitation stories possess power; interestingly, these are sometimes animals that outside of the stories are regarded as powerful or essential to the people's well-being: a seal, an owl, a bear, an elk. Of course it is not unusual for such animals to have ceremonial significance also. In trickster stories they may well be associated in the American Indian mind with shamans or simply with any persons who have demonstrated noteworthy spiritual power for themselves or their communities. It is these individuals who have crossed conventional boundaries. By stepping beyond the limits of individual self, they establish relationships with the nonhuman world, thus extending the social connections of the human world. The possession of power is not most important because it originates in private revelation but because in crossing the frontiers of human community one has also passed the limits of self, thereby binding self and human community to the larger community. In Bungling Host and Foolish Imitation stories, tricksters, on the other hand, are sterile individuals warring within the precincts of self. It is usually not clear in the stories whether the tricksters actually believe that they can successfully imitate others or they are simply trying to pull a con job, but ultimately it does not matter; in either case they are caught in the internecine warfare of self and social deception. Grasping at social status, tricksters attempt to draw upon resources they do not have and call the attempt "power," when in fact it is nothing but warped and self-defeating self-aggrandizement. The magic acts of self-immolation by those the trickster imitates are signs that they have lived beyond the self in ways that serve others' well-being, not merely their own. In the trickster's hands ostensible power becomes derangement or self-mutilation. Driven by an appetite for the social status that magic power would give him, a trickster is doomed to defeat and frustration, even danger, because he fails to see two things: first, that true power does not come from self alone (and certainly does not derive from boastful claims); and second that true power leads one beyond self (evidenced in Bungling Host stories by the power holder's ability to provide for others). All in all, in spite of the trickster's violations of moral and social restraints—the crossing of boundaries that some mistakenly call "marginality"—he fails to cross the most important boundary of all if there is to be community: the boundary of self.

On a less metaphorical level, trickster Bungling Host stories demonstrate how social relationships can be turned topsy-turvy by illegitimate claims to status. In a number of stories the host is well aware of the trickster's proclivity for imitation and tries to avoid his reciprocal invitations. When good manners make further avoidance impossible, he accepts the trickster's invitation to visit but, as we have seen, invariably ends up having to provide the food, for the would-be host has failed to act like a host. Thus the putative guest becomes the actual host, and the imposter becomes a guest in his own lodge. Matters become more confused when the visitor refuses either to eat the food he has provided or to take leftovers home (as guests have often been encouraged to do in a number of cultures). In the trickster's lodge, the guest refuses to act like a guest because he has become the host.[77]

Pursuing socially approved and significant values in these stories, tricksters are also pursuing individual confirmation in the community, but they do so in self-deceptive and self-destructive ways as they pursue what they perceive as their communities' values and expectations. What their communities in fact expect are qualities not in plentiful supply among tricksters: self-control, self-discipline, the "resolute endeavor to observe a proper measure or proportion in all things,"[78] and, finally, that people be themselves. Buller's discussion of the Comanche concept of *puha* makes clear the importance of the American Indian value of being oneself.

> Because Coyote doesn't always live within his limits, physically or psychologically, his misfortunes tend often to be short lessons in the morality of being one's self. . . . [In Comanche culture,] medicine (*puha*) plays an important role in the way a person reacts to his own environment. It is important for the Comanche to obtain and understand his *puha* early in his adult life and then to conform to the criterion that particular *puha* determines. To live outside the limitations established by the power of a particular medicine would be to invite danger and tragedy. Coyote fails time and again to live within the limits of his own *puha*.[79]

In other stories the relationship between individual and community values shifts: through a reckless manipulation of social form, tricksters seek gratification of physical appetites, both gustatory and sexual. Thus, in order to cheat Mink out of food, the Winnebago trickster Wakdjunkaga parodies the means by which a member of the Thunderbird clan originally became chief of the tribe.[80] The machinery of social relationships becomes weaponry in his self-oriented campaigns. When considering such stories, we must remember that even personal physical needs have social components. Sexuality gives rise to interpersonal relationships as well as physical passion, and it is, of course, the biological basis of perpetuating the community's life even while it can also threaten community cohesiveness. Our need for food has been ritualized as social communion in various ways: the ethics governing family eating, feasts, and host-guest relationships as well as rules governing securing and preparing food. In the case of both sexual and gustatory needs, individual appetites have been transformed into affirmations of communal life. But tricksters manipulate, turn askew, and violate these social forms and expectations, turning them into instruments of their own desire. Time and time again, to gain their self-indulgent ends, tricksters take advantage of or contrive social situations—dances and ceremonies, feasts, innocent gatherings of girls, contests—to mask their intentions. Or they take advantage of their status as headman, father, husband, and provider or of kinship, offering these as a kind of illusory social collateral for their seemingly good intentions.[81] Even in those few stories that begin with a trickster's searching for food for his family, his ego, ravenousness, or self-delusions turn his respectable domestic venture into an occasion of self-indulgence.[82] There are numerous stories in which we see a trickster manipulating some social form to satisfy his voraciousness. For example, in Pawnee and Wichita stories, a trickster as head of the household takes advantage of the conventions of entertaining male guests so that he can prohibit his family from entering the lodge. While pretending to feast with guests who are not really there, he devours the food himself, leaving nothing but offal and bones for his family.[83] Another favorite trickster social manipulation is the contest. Having been found with game or having come upon someone who has found game, he proposes a contest, often a race, for possession. Sometimes he wins the contest, sometimes he loses, but invariably he cheats. Thus, as Luckert points out, the trickster recasts "basic hunter ethics in terms of sportive [and deceptive] game."[84]

In a variation on the theme of tricksters manipulating social convention, a Micmac and Passamaquoddy story tells how starved Wildcat decides to catch and devour Mahtigwess, the trickster Rabbit. Mahtigwess senses that something is up and brings his great powers to bear against Wildcat. As he follows Rabbit's tracks, Wildcat comes upon a "fine, big wigwam" in which sits an "old, gray-haired chief, solemn and mighty. The only strange thing about him was that he had two long ears standing up at each side of his head." This distinguished chief feeds (quite well) and shelters the hunter, but the next morning, when Wildcat awakens and finds himself lying in the middle of a great snowfield, he realizes that the wigwam and even the food were an illusion created by Rabbit. And so it goes through various personages offering Wildcat conventional hospitality, all illusory: a preacher (with "two long ears sticking up at each side of the priest's cap"), a Sagamore ("with long white locks sticking up on each side of his head"), another chief ("who wore two long feathers at each side of his head" and who has two beautiful daughters to feed strangers), an elderly, gray-haired, gentle-looking man (with "two scalp locks sticking up at the sides of his head"), and finally, a French ship captain (a "gray-haired man with large, gold-trimmed, cocked hat that had fluffy plumes right and left"). With the last charade Wildcat finally catches on, only to be threatened in a hilarious conclusion with scalping by the captain-Rabbit.[85]

Stories in which tricksters' sexuality plays a prominent role are also frequently stories in which they test or manipulate the social order.[86] In an Arapaho story the trickster Nih'a^n'ca^n tries to maneuver around kinship rules about who is available for sexual relations. He challenges Coyote to a contest to determine which of them is the more cunning, but Coyote wants nothing to do with such a contest. Nevertheless, Nih'a^{n}ca^n transforms himself into various creatures, none of which fools Coyote. Coyote then decides to enter the game.

> So Coyote went around Nih'a^n ca^n and became a woman sitting on the ground with a robe on. "Where are you going, woman, what is the matter with you," said Nih'a^n ca^n. 'My mother scolded me and I didn't like it, so I wandered off' said the woman. "She told me to go to my brother, Nih'a^n ca^n." "Oh, you are mistaken, I am your brother-in-law; you are not related to me," said Nih'a^n ca^n. "My mother told me plainly that I must come to you, as a sister," said the woman. Nih'a^n ca^n then grabbed her and laid her on the ground. He was about to have intercourse with her when she turned into a coyote and jumped away from him and ran through the bush. "I was just fooling you," said Nih'a^n ca^n. "Yes, but I fooled you all right," said Coyote, howling at him.[87]

Even the grand social occasion of a feast becomes a sexually dangerous time for women when the Maidu Coyote transforms himself into a woman and his penis into a baby, invites women to a feast, then transforms himself into a man again to have sex with them while they doze in their after-feast stupor.[88]

Tricksters' sexual adventures defy and threaten all sorts of social relationships. The Hopi Coyote's lust for a spider woman creates tension in the friendship between his and Spider's families and results in Coyote's death. In another Hopi story Coyote's lusting after a woman that he and Badger have resurrected and intend to use as a housekeeper in their bachelor quarters results in her dying again, this time irrevocably.[89] Perhaps there is no more unsettling threat from a trickster's sexuality than when it threatens his own family. In these cases, along with his other physical appetites, a trickster's sexuality is a constant reminder of the unspeakable urges, passions, and intrafamily hostilities that must be kept in check if domestic discord, even disintegration, and pain are to be avoided. In these stories latent sexual tensions explode into public view when through one ruse or another a trickster marries his daughter, has sex with his mother-in-law, or deceives his son or causes him to be killed so that he can marry his daughter-in-law. In Clackamas stories Coyote dupes a succession of females including his grandson's young wife, whom Coyote steals after a sexual reawakening.[90] When a trickster marries his daughter, he invariably manages his heinous crime through a series of deceptions laid on social grounds.[91] After giving his legitimate wife specific directions about his obsequies and the exact kind of man his daughter should marry, thus appearing the concerned father to the end, the trickster feigns death. When the survivors have completed their public, and sometimes communal, observation of his death, thus unwittingly giving communal reality to an illusion, the trickster returns to his village in the guise of the very man described as husband for his daughter. Sometimes this "stranger" is distinguished by his ability to provide, sometimes by his fine clothing or some other socially distinguishing trait (not familiar traits for tricksters in their usual identities). Apparently he intends to keep his daughter as a sexual partner for some time; this is not one of those brief seductions or casual rapes so common for tricksters. He marries her, thus using a fundamental social institution to legitimize his crime and to give him continued access to his daughter. Important elements in the protagonist's success are the underlying social assumptions that make his deception possible: the apparent reality that public rituals, such as burial and mourning, provide our beliefs; status automatically conferred—without further questioning—upon one who appears to meet our social criteria; unthinking acceptance of an interpersonal relationship as viable because it has the trappings of a social institution.[92] Society frequently does creak, and never more than when the dangerous insider trickster tests and exploits its forms and institutions. Fortunately, as Melville Jacobs points out, our laughter at Trickster's doings assuage some of that frightening reality as both a release and a kind of social control.

We have been examining tricksters as dangerous social insiders, a description appropriate for most tricksters. There is one, however, who can accurately be called an outsider, perhaps the only trickster who is truly and consistently outside of human society: Iktomi the spider of Lakota oral tradition. Iktomi is son of Wakinyan (Thunder, "terrifying and destructive" in this aspect but the "laughter-loving clown" Heyoka in his other aspect) and is therefore one of the Sacred Beings. He begins existence as Ksa, wisdom, but because of the tricks of Gnaski, a demon, and because Ksa follows Gnaski's bad advice, he finds himself named Iktomi by Skan (the spirit that gives life to all) and forbidden to sit in the circle of Sacred Beings. Tired of being the butt of the other Sacred Beings' laughter, Iktomi swears that he "shall laugh and cause others to be laughed at. . . . Let all who have laughed at me beware, for I will cause them to be laughed at."[93] As punishment for another scheme that causes embarrassment to Hanwi (the moon) and Tate (the wind), Iktomi is forbidden to associate with the Sacred Beings; rather, he is banished to the world, where he lives in eternal isolation without friends.[94] In this world the one who was once wisdom becomes the opposite, the embodiment of foolishness and illusion. He continues his deceptive, ridiculing ways, sometimes with his tricks backfiring, as happens with tricksters. Among his pranks is his causing discord among animals and birds, all of whom—with the exception of wolves and coyotes—have refused to participate in his deceits.[95] It is Iktomi who, having promised the wolves prey in the form of Pte Oyate (Buffalo People), engineers the seduction by which the Buffalo People leave their region under the world and enter this world, where they become the Ikce Oyate (Real People), the first people in this world and ancestors of the Lakotas.[96] That the world that the Ikce Oyate live in is clearly one in which a trickster has a hand is best summarized by Iktomi's advice to Gnaski: "always tell the truth, but never tell the whole truth."[97] In this world Iktome continues his deceptive ways, "a powerful enemy of human welfare"[98] who appears in Lakota stories as various enemies and monsters. He also acts out in stories that are reminiscent of or cognates to trickster episodes in other American Indian oral traditions: hence, he too manipulates and violates kinship rules. In fact, the only way he can relate to his family is by taking advantage of them.[99] And he also frequently tries to pass himself off as a source of spiritual power for the people. As an enemy of people, his stories become lessons to youngsters about recognizing one's enemies as well as learning about the ugliness and absurdity that can exist behind a friendly facade.[100] Iktomi is such a serious problem for humans that finally the Wise One calls them together so that he can direct the shamans in effective ways of protecting the people from the spider. One of the social controls he advises is that their camps be formed in a circle with each lodge door toward every other door, thereby allowing all to see if Iktomi enters a lodge.[101]

Much that has been discussed in this chapter demonstrates that American Indian tricksters exercise their outrages within the context of American Indian social life. This is not to deny the creative, self-liberating nature of trickster's violations, either in the literal, physical sense of his transformations or in the psychological sense of his freeing our perceptions from the conventional. In acknowledging this creative, liberating aspect of the trickster, we recognize the necessity of those times when we look at social forms through an individual, self-interested eye; when, following our own bent, free from excessive social consciousness, even at the risk of social displeasure, new realities materialize for us. At the same time, however, we must remember that one boundary tricksters do not cross, cannot cross, is the boundary of self—a "transgression" indispensable to finding community. A trickster-related Pawnee custom demonstrates this familiar paradox. Children were encouraged to dance during the songs that were part of trickster stories, the intention being to set them free from shyness.[102] On the one hand, we can infer a desire to free children from a debilitating and enslaving self-consciousness (in this case, shyness) that the social eye creates in them as they mature. On the other hand, in circumstances truly worthy of the trickster's inversions, perhaps they were being encouraged to turn from isolation of the self (another way of looking at shyness) to a forgetting of the self even while hearing of one thus isolated. In amusing dance and song, perhaps these children were beginning to experience what was socially requisite for American Indians and what Allen identifies as the goal of all ceremony: shedding the isolated individual consciousness to "fuse the individual with his or her fellows, the community of people with that of other kingdoms, and this larger communal group with the worlds beyond this one."[103] In spite of himself, the trickster encourages us to see through the collective social eye and thus to look beyond the individual self. Public performances of trickster tales "[m]ediated between . . . children and their unverbalized fears and uncertainties about themselves, especially about their growing bodies in relation to their developing selves and render[ed] such anxieties harmless or at lest subject to normative laughter . . . shared openly with the adults of the tribe."[104] Of course in their corrective function, trickster tales also expose adult behavior to shared normative laughter. At least in part, what we see in many trickster stories is a socialization process.

Looking at trickster tales through the lens provided us by social relationships among American Indians, we see cultures that may have been more successful than the modern dominant culture at nurturing the individual. Such success was perhaps a consequence of a fundamental faith and belief in community as the soil of individual growth, not of a romantic disdain for the group or deference to nearly illimitable rights of one person.

Iktomi Takes Back a Gift

Iktomi, the tricky Spider-Man, was starving. There had been no game for a long time. Iktomi was just skin and bones. His empty stomach growled. He was desperate. Then it occurred to him to go for help to Inyan, the Rock, who has great powers, and who might answer his prayers.

Iktomi wrapped himself in his blanket, because it was late in the year and cold. Then he went to a place where a large upright rock was standing. This rock was *lila wakan*, very sacred. Sometimes people came to pray to it.

When Iktomi arrived at that place he lifted up his hands to Inyan: "*Tunkashila, onshimalaye*, grandfather, have pity on me. I am hungry. If you do not help me, I will starve to death. I need meat, grandfather."

Iktomi took his blanket from his shoulder and draped it around Inyan. "Here, grandfather, *Tunkashila*, accept this gift. It is the only thing I have to give. It will keep you warm. Please let me find something good to eat."

After praying to Inyan for a long time, Iktomi went off to search for food. He had a feeling Inyan would answer his prayers, and he was right. Iktomi had not gone very far when he came upon a freshly killed deer. It had an arrow piercing its neck, the feathered nock sticking out on one side of the neck and the arrowhead on the other.

"*Ohan*," said Iktomi, "the deer has been able to run for a distance after being hit and the hunter has lost it. Inyan has arranged it that way. Well, that is only fair. Did I not give him my blanket? Well, anyhow, *pilamaya, tunkashila*—thank you, grandfather!"

Iktomi took his sharp knife out of its beaded knife sheath and began to skin and dress the deer. Then he gathered wood and, with his strike-a-light and tinder, made a fire. There was not much wood and it was wet. It was'nt much of a fire. And it had grown very cold. Iktomi was shivering. His teeth were chattering. He was saying to himself: "What good is my blanket to Inyan? He is just a rock. He does not feel either cold or heat. He does not need it. And, anyway, I don't think Inyan had anything to do with my finding this deer. I am smart. I saw certain tracks. I smelled the deer. So there, I did it all by myself. I did not have to give Inyan anything. I shall take my blanket back!"

Iktomi went back to the sacred rock. He took the blanket off him. "*Tunkashila*," he said, "this blanket is mine. I am freezing. You don't need this blanket; I do."

Iktomi wrapped the blanket tightly around his body. "Ah, that feels good," he said. "Imagine, giving a blanket to a rock!"

When Iktomi came back to the place where he had left the deer, he discovered that it had disappeared—vanished, gone! Only a heap of dry bones was left. There were no tracks or any signs that somebody had dragged the deer away. It had been transformed into dry bones by a powerful magic.

"How mean of Inyan," said Iktomi, "and how stupid of me. I should have eaten first and then taken the blanket back."

CHAPTER FOUR

Coyote, He/She Was Going There
Sex and Gender in Trickster Stories

We have seen that tricksters commonly exploit social forms and expectations in order to achieve their individualistic, self-serving ends, and a trickster is seldom more self-serving than when his libido is the impetus behind his efforts. Tricksters' amusing—and sometimes frightening—licentiousness is a significant danger to the social fabric. One aspect of tricksters' sexuality that writers have given little attention to is its gender implications. Furthermore, few have considered the implications of the fact that tricksters are commonly, but not exclusively, male. Of the great many trickster tales I have read, in no more than a few dozen are the trickster protagonists female, and some of these stories can be found in other American Indian oral traditions in versions with male protagonists. Moreover, even in those tribes whose trickster stories have female protagonists, such stories are apparently in the minority. These facts suggest that exploring trickster stories for an understanding of sexuality and gender expectations may provide some unique—if not revolutionary—insights into American Indian trickster stories while underscoring the richness of the trickster tradition as a socially formative kind of entertainment (as opposed to the Euro-American scholarly cliché of Trickster as a sort of romantic overreacher).

Along with Siobahn Senier, who also considered questions of gendering, I "ask why [a trickster story] is gendered and relayed as it is . . . and [I] speculate as to what kind of impulses [a] narration might be reinforcing or subverting."[1] Even if American Indian storytellers and audiences have not commented on or otherwise explicitly acknowledged the role of gender in trickster stories, there are clues that gender roles are sometimes part of their underlying didacticism and satire. The thesis of this chapter is, then, that in a number of American Indian trickster stories, gender matters. The use of either male or female tricksters as well as a storyteller's gendering narrative details may point to a storyteller's critical cultural judgments or personal observations on a tribe's gender assumptions—for example, attitudes toward male headmen, or the nature of men's and women's behavior, or ideals of male or female social roles— or may offer corrective commentary directed at an individual. Certainly, this is so in male trickster stories, and it is likely true in at least some stories with female tricksters. Further, there are a few trickster stories that are interesting to consider in the context of the Two Spirit people (once known as *berdaches*).

Readers might question the value of focusing on the topic of tricksters' gender, considering that it seems of little or no significance in the discussion of so many trickster stories. However, the effort in recent studies of American Indian oral traditions has often been to approach stories as works of individual creativity, not as the products of a homogeneous, traditional voice. The fact that trickster gender was a matter of indifference to many trickster storytellers may make all the more significant those instances in which gender does seem to be an issue. Some storytellers certainly would have been more responsive than others to opportunities for social commentary and teaching afforded by trickster stories, just as some were more sensitive to and skillful at practicing the aesthetics of the community's storytelling tradition. In this context, we must proceed carefully in any interpretations. Readers should not assume that a particular story is an authorized reflection of a culture's values.[2] Rather, a storytelling represents a single storyteller's understanding of how the story's narrative details open a window on his or her culture's values. Clearly, the cultural value dramatized in one telling of a trickster story may not be at all present in another telling. Nevertheless, some cultural generalizations may be possible as an entry point for this topic.

Melville Jacobs first stimulated my curiosity about gender issues in the Trickster tradition. One of the few writers to consider why female tricksters are relatively rare, Jacobs argues that male tricksters are exclusive in the Chinook oral tradition because Coyote's main personality traits—particularly inordinate, vulgar sexuality and traveling for the sake of adventure—were considered male traits. He further conjectures that a male storyteller would have recounted "more and better" Coyote stories than his storyteller/consultant, Mrs. Howard, because the "Coyote personality would surely have been identified with more often by men than women."[4] In some other cultures as well narrating trickster stories was apparently associated with men only. One example is that Ojibwe Wenebojo stories related to the *Mide'wi'win* were told mainly by men.[5] Also, associations between the trickster and male characteristics were made in other tribes; the Cayuga trickster, to cite a specific instance, "represents unrestrained male sexuality."[6]

To call such assumptions and understandings stereotyping would be ethnocentric. However, in matters of social expectations for men and women, North American indigenous peoples assumed specific and different social and family roles for men and women. While such assumptions do not, in general, seem to have been justification for oppressing or otherwise belittling women (men's and women's roles and responsibilities commonly being accorded equal significance), there do seem to have been clear-cut assumptions and expectations about gender character and responsibility. Consequently, given the licentiousness associated with men, it is no accident that most tricksters are male.

In any event the hyperbole that abounds in dramatizations of male trickster sexuality carries that sexuality to levels traditionally unacceptable to many Euro-Americans, but many American Indian societies traditionally have been less priggish than the dominant Euro-American culture. In early times among the Klamaths, anal and erotic details were essential features of some myths (both trickster and nontrickster) and were recounted even in the presence of children.[7] American Indian playwright Hanay Geiogamah acknowledges that "among the boys" trickster stories were commonly pornographic.[8] Nevertheless, while these stories may have provided juicy entertainment, the social dangers and disorder attending or threatened by men's unbridled sexuality is at the heart of a number of trickster tales.[9]

Tricksters' prodigious sexual appetites and energy are hilariously and powerfully dramatized by the gamut of their lusts and the size of their penises. The Yurok trickster, Wohpekumeu, to cite one instance, is so sexually robust and so promiscuous that he impregnates women with a mere glance. Because of his sexual threat, the people once literally leave him in the world alone, making him temporarily one of the few truly outcast tricksters.[10] No doubt the best-known depiction of a trickster's sexuality is the Winnebago Wakdjunkaga's extraordinarily long penis (long enough that it can snake across a stream and insert itself into a woman's vagina), which he carries in a box on his back, giving the illusion of control—a control essential to good social order but clearly beyond a trickster's capabilities, as the evidence of the stories shows.[11] Even though such a phallus is not explicitly characteristic of all male tricksters, the image has become synecdochic for all tricksters' licentiousness.

Males in many cultures tell themselves that size is everything, the bigger the better. However, in one Crow trickster story it is the little things that count—at least temporarily, and we get a wonderfully comic image of the lengths to which Old Man Coyote will go to have sex with a pretty girl. During a dance, a young woman tells the men to expose their penises because she wants to marry the man with the smallest. Old Man Coyote exchanges penises with Mouse. The girl chooses him, of course, but his triumph lasts only until the onlookers see Mouse trying to walk through the encampment dragging Old Man Coyote's huge penis.[12]

No woman is safe for long from a trickster's penis; not virgins or other men's wives, not his daughters, not his mother-in-law, not even his grandmother. Nor, as we have seen, is any social relationship or institution safe. Community well-being and harmony, friendship, marriage, family: all fall before a trickster's incorrigible penis. Sometimes a trickster's sexual rapaciousness drives him to violate very specific tribal moral customs. Crow married women were vulnerable to being kidnapped by former lovers in the rivalry existing between the Lumpwood and Fox societies. It was shameful for a man to take back a wife who had been abducted. However, Old Man Coyote brags that he has done so three times. In fact his mere glance reminds a woman of the sexual favors he has shown her, so that regardless of any disgrace she will return to him.

Human females are not a trickster's only victims; a buffalo cow mired in a wallow is on occasion as acceptable as a human woman.[13] In a sense Trickster even sexually abuses men when in some stories he marries a chief's son. Thanks to his prodigious penis, Trickster even "abuses" himself when he performs self-fellatio.[14] The issue in many of these stories is not sexual victimization as such but rather the cruelty, self-deception, and absurdity of a man whose unrestrained sexuality poses a threat to the community. Such stories dramatize the power of human sexuality to whirl us beyond the boundaries of human social constraints.[15]

These facts notwithstanding, there are occasions when a trickster's sexual assertiveness *is* stimulated by hostility and aggression toward a woman, and women become his victims because of their gender. In a Nez Perce story an old woman ridicules his eyes because they appear wide open in the dark. "Coyote then thinks to himself, 'Your saying such a thing, woman, makes me want to make you my wife and get even with you' [that is, have sex with her]."[16] Sometimes, he acts out his anger or hostility toward a woman for other reasons and perhaps in nonsexual ways. Coyote becomes so angry when Eagle's daughter refuses to marry him that he turns women into rock.[17] More often sex seems a weapon, as when, in some Nez Perce stories, Coyote rapes and impregnates the young women of enemy tribes.[18] In the common story type called "vaginal dentata," female sexuality is the cause of trickster's hostility. In these stories female sexuality—not male, as is usually the case in trickster stories—poses a threat, at least to the availability of women to men.[19]

Male tricksters' dealings with women are often directed by their response to or manipulations of gender expectations for women. Sometimes a trickster shapes women's lives, in some instances introducing a few benefits but more often, limitations—even controls—on women's lives. Hence Coyote institutes pregnancy in a Wishram story.[20] In a Havasupai story Coyote gives origin to women's menstrual cycles by flipping fresh fawn blood between his sister's legs, apparently in order to prevent her sharing in his freshly killed deer meat.[21] Similarly, Manabush originates menstruation by throwing a clot of bear's blood between the legs of Nokomis, his grandmother.[22] Finally, Crow legend tells us that it was Old Man Coyote who made women's very existence possible, for he created women to keep men company and to assure that the people would increase in number.[23]

In another common trickster episode, one not overtly sexual but with sexual and gender ramifications, women—or at least, a certain kind of woman—are clearly a trickster's victims and the object of the story's satire. The so-called "well-behaved" (a euphemism for chaste but maybe also prudish?) girl stories tell of a young woman who arrogantly rejects all suitors and all thought of marrying. She pays a high price for her pride: Trickster hoodwinks her into marrying him or at least having sex with him, a grave humiliation given women's usual disdain for Trickster. The Yurok trickster Wohpekumeu impregnates two young women who refuse to marry.[24] Similarly, the Arapaho Nih'a^n'ca^n sleeps with two pretty sisters who will not marry.[25] In a Tewa version, Blue Corn Girl and Yellow Corn Girl refuse one by one to marry the Cloud Boys of the four directions, who offer them marvelous gifts as marriage tokens. Coyote says that these women are "lazy about [marriage]." When he dances and sings for them, they want to marry him. The next morning before the girls awaken, others in the village see that the girls have married Coyote and chase him away.[26] From a contemporary Euro-American point of view, particularly if the point of view is informed by feminism, this latter story type may seem an assertion of male sexual-social authority over women. However, imposing such views here would be a mistake. It is likely that this trickster's audience—male and female alike—would have approved of his victim's chagrin in these cases, for they have violated their roles as women.

Clara Sue Kidwell has pointed out how different from middle-class white women's values are those of Indian women. "The tribally oriented societies of Indian cultures and the extended family situation in which several generations may live very closely together give a different definition to the roles of women than do the nuclear family orientation and the technological aspect of the dominant society. . . . Marriage was a necessity for the survival of the community."[27] While a woman might have chosen not to marry and perhaps would have been allowed to live out her choice, she was nevertheless subject to community disapproval, for such a woman was considered prideful and her "rejection of her

[social] role was in a sense a rejection of the whole society."[28] Looked at
from this point of view, we see a trickster in an uncommon and ironic
light: as enforcer of social stability teaching a woman a lesson. When a
woman is the satirical butt of a male trickster story, it is usually because
she (for once not the trickster) has—her culture agrees—resisted the
community's values and needs.

But it is not only women who suffer Trickster's chastening for not
fulfilling society's gender expectations with respect to marriage. Male
versions of the "well-behaved girl" stories involve what might be called
Trickster's transgendering, yet another way that tricksters cross the boundaries of the conventional. In these stories a trickster poses as a woman
and marries a man. An Ojibwe story of this sort satirizes a chief's son's
arrogant refusal to marry. When the beautiful woman he has married is
unveiled as Wenebojo, the young man is appropriately humiliated.[29] In
a Swampy Cree version of this tale, the trickster Wichikapache hears of
a conceited young man who wants a wife but who cannot find a "good
one," finding fault with every women he sees.[30] The trickster transforms
himself into a beautiful woman, whom the young man "quickly likes."[31]
Wichikapache proves to be a good wife, even giving birth to children.
However, the children are wolf cubs, a fact that makes the young man
the laughing stock of the community. It is immediately obvious to all
that the beautiful woman must, in fact, be the trickster.

In any event, well-behaved girl stories notwithstanding, it is safe to
say that the laughter stimulated by most sexually oriented male trickster
stories is not a result of what the trickster does to women but of what
he reveals about himself (and males?) as he victimizes others.

Tricksters' relationships with women are not always based on sexuality
alone; sometimes their attitudes and behavior toward women grow from
their own failures to fulfill their gender roles. Deward E. Walker points
out that Coyote possesses none of the skills a woman might want in
a husband: "fathering, hunting, or fighting"; hence women reject him
repeatedly. His aggression toward women, then, is—at least in part—a
consequence of his own limitations. In episodes involving adult males,
we also see tricksters failing to fill gender expectations. Walker points out
that hunting is the usual ground of the Nez Perce Coyote's interactions

with males.³² The same is true for other tricksters. Commonly in these circumstances, their incompetence, lack of self-discipline, and unseemly competitiveness lead inevitably to their failure as hunters. Episodes in which a trickster demonstrates his incompetence as father and provider abound. Those that come to mind most readily in this context are the Bungling Host stories discussed in chapter 3. Walker also recounts a Nez Perce story in which Coyote cheats Porcupine in a rivalry for a buffalo carcass. He fetches his wife and children to help him carry home all of the meat rather than just taking home what he can carry. However, Porcupine kills them all. This fatal—but predictable—ending comes about because Coyote has foolishly brought his family "to a place where enemies are present, thus placing them in danger."³³

On the basis of such evidence, it seems clear that the satire of many trickster stories focuses on gender values. But what about those relatively few stories in which a female trickster is protagonist? The first, obvious question is why are there so few? Given the vagaries of recording and translating stories from oral traditions, it may be that female tricksters were more common than current publications indicate. Perhaps many recorders—largely dominant-culture males—simply showed no interest in female tricksters, or perhaps, as Wiget has suggested, women storytellers—more likely to tell female trickster stories—were not sought out by male investigators in the mistaken belief that only the men of the community carried the tribe's traditional cultural knowledge.³⁴ Perhaps they suppressed such stories for propriety's sake. Or maybe the storytellers themselves—noting Euro-American moral predilections and cultural assumptions about women—suppressed the stories. We could conjecture further, but the fact remains that there are far fewer female than male tricksters, in the academic record at least and possibly in American Indians' oral traditions as well.

Even when female tricksters have appeared in American Indian stories, there has been little or no printed commentary on the protagonist's gender by either storyteller or ethnographer. The inevitable question is, given the socially formative or didactic nature of so many trickster tales, might it not make a difference whether a trickster is male or female? Are female tricksters assigned certain kinds of motif or episode? Another question is whether American Indians had/have different attitudes about male and female tricksters. As far as the published record is concerned, it appears to some—again, from the points of view of storyteller and ethnographer—that the presence of a trickster personality is more important than the trickster's gender. Writing about a Hopi story with a female protagonist, Wiget asserts: "the female sex of the trickster seems only a contrivance to initiate the action, an element of setting, and is not integral to the central action."[35] Further support for this general point of view may be an Acoma trickster tale in which the protagonist's gender seems of so little consequence to either the storyteller or the recorder that pronoun gender references change a couple of times in the course of the story.[36]

Perhaps a trickster's gender is a matter of narrative and thematic indifference to many storytellers, but it is not always so. At least on occasion, and maybe more frequently than we know, gender plays a role in plot and narrative details and reflects something about either a culture's or a storyteller's gender attitudes. Or perhaps the plot and narrative details of an episode type (for example, the borrowed-feathers episode below) encourage a storyteller to use a gender-appropriate protagonist. On the few occasions that tricksters have status or authority in a community, their positions are generally of a sort associated with males in patrilineal societies. If it is reasonable to assume that such satirical narrative details of some trickster stories are male directed, it seems equally reasonable to assume that some storytellers used female tricksters because they saw certain episodes as gender appropriate.[37] Although there may be no particular kinds of episode assigned exclusively to female tricksters, when a story has a female protagonist it sometimes seems to frame a gender-related theme or to be gender appropriate. In the relative absence of analysis and commentary by American Indians, we can only conjecture about these matters. It must be understood, then, that much of the following is hypothesis, not unflinching assertion; it is inference based on available cultural and narrative evidence. The many variables and the insufficiency of evidence in this area would make anything more than hypothesizing foolish. Still, it is interesting to speculate.

Partial evidence for intentional gendering in a trickster story may be the fact that in one tribe a particular trickster episode may have a male protagonist, while in another it may have a female protagonist. For example, the common Bungling Host story among Plains and Central Woodlands tribes has a male trickster imitating his erstwhile host by killing his own children for food, while versions among the Tewas and the Hopis use female tricksters.[38] The presence of male and female tricksters for the same or similar episodes in respectively patrilineal and matrilineal societies is not likely casual happenstance.[39] However these changes in gender came to be, it seems reasonable to assume that, for some storytellers at least, cultural values and assumptions led to considering certain stories as particularly appropriate for female coyotes.

In the few female trickster stories available to us, she is commonly the object of the satire. The questions arise: Is she satirized because she is a woman or because she is a trickster who incidentally is female? What, if any, relationship exists between the trickster's gender and the narrative elements in the stories? It appears that in most female trickster stories the protagonist's trickster personality causes her to fall short of her community's gender-role expectations. She is, therefore, fair game for satire, as is the male trickster personality when he fails his society's expectations, some of them gender related (for example, when he fails both as a warrior and a chief in the Winnebago tales or when he perverts his father's role by marrying his daughter). Furthermore, it seems that cultural context implies particular, if not essential, appropriateness for the narrative events and/or details of some female trickster tales.

As we begin considering female tricksters, we should note that there are two specific trickster attributes not represented among published female trickster tales. This is not to say that stories of either type do not or did not exist; collections simply do not seem to contain them. First, there seem to be no female trickster/transformers of the mythical proportions of many male tricksters. The closest we get to a female trickster/transformer is a Crow story in which Old Man Coyote's wife proves as creative as her husband through "sacred reversals" (to use Gerald Vizenor's term) when she causes various transformations of the world by contradicting the transformer Red Woman's edicts. Like her husband and other transformer tricksters (particularly those who act as marplots in the creation of the world), she contributes to making the newly shaped world into the human world by establishing the possibility of early human death through giving origin to *batés* (the so-called *berdaches*), as well as to roots for medicine, and so forth.[40] The relative absence of female trickster/transformers is not likely due to denigration of feminine creativity, for many American Indian tribal mythologies contain female personages who transform the physical, social, and ceremonial worlds. This includes mythologies of matrilineal societies with female trickster stories.

A second trickster attribute absent among published female trickster stories is the trickster's prodigious sexual appetite. A possible exception is a Hopi episode in which a widowed female coyote grinds her dead husband's penis into powder, which she applies to her vulva whenever she desires the same rollicking, rapturous sex the living husband provided her.[41] However, this mother Coyote lacks other identifying trickster traits, and her motivation seems not so much reckless bawdiness—what we would expect from a male trickster—as simply a widow's longing for the continuing benefit of her husband's sexual prowess.[42] Whatever the explanation for the paucity of sexual content, it is generally speaking not prudishness about women and sex, for there are other kinds of stories—including male trickster stories—in which women prove equally lusty as men.

The most obvious fact we should note about stories with female tricksters is that they are all from matrilineal and/or matrilocal tribes, most from southwestern peoples but a few from Caddoan peoples. In most and maybe all of these tribes, women have generally had significant either de facto or socially endorsed authority or power. For example, among the western Tewas and the Hopis women have traditionally controlled the economic system and the home that is at the core of that system. Women own the houses, the fields, and the fruits of cultivation through their clans, with the clan mothers having final say in matters of distribution. Furthermore, strong ties among mothers-daughters-sisters create solidarity of opinion, which in turn carries much authority. Among the Tewas it is the women who have traditionally cared for family ritual possessions—no mean office, to be sure. John J. Honigman reports that a Hopi wife, as household head, sprinkled corn over ceremonial paraphernalia, and on these grounds women claimed to be more important than men.[43] Among the Navajos, in addition to an authority attending matrilineality and matrilocality, women have traditionally benefited from the liberation and influence of having independent incomes and owning property, often more than men.[44] It should come as no surprise, then, that at least some trickster stories are about women in societies where women are notable social and economic forces.

Because some male trickster stories satirize men who are in positions of authority or power—for example, headmen or shamans—we might be tempted to approach female trickster stories in matrilineal societies as satires of women's authority. But when Mother Coyote is satirized, the reasons seem to be other than her authority or power. In fact, she is so incompatible with her society's expectations of her that she seems to have neither. And this may be the point of the stories: Perhaps she is the object of satire because she is incapable of being the strong woman her society expects her to be. These possibilities are underscored by a second fact: In these stories trickster is always a coyote. To be sure, among the tribes whose female trickster tales I have examined, male as well as female tricksters are coyotes. As wandering hunters and as social transgressors, all coyote tricksters—male and female—live wayward lives of risk and transience. Nevertheless, the female coyote trickster's incongruity with her community is even more pronounced, for to have a hunting mother in a culture where mothers traditionally control the agricultural means of production (as they did in most of these tribes) seems in itself a comment on her fecklessness.[45]

Interestingly, it is not only general plot details but also specific narrative details that might reflect gender awareness. In some female trickster stories, particularly Hopi stories, we find narrative details befitting women's roles. For example, in New Mexico and Arizona Tewa versions of the borrowed feathers story, both using male tricksters, the birds at the beginning of the story are either picking up wheat that lies about or dancing in gratitude for a grasslike wheat available to them.[46] Among the eastern Pueblos, women were the gatherers of seeds and nuts. Perhaps we see another example in the eastern Pueblo version of Coyote's once more placing himself out of his element, in this case gender-fitting sustenance activities. In a Hopi version of the story, a female Coyote chances upon the Bird Girls as they grind corn, typically women's work at which, the storyteller informs us, they are always busy. While they grind, they sing songs whose images suggest the integral relationship between grinding, their identity, and even their physical traits.

> Bird Girl, Bird Girl
> Brush the cornmeal off the grinding stone.
> Bird Girl, Bird Girl
> Brush the cornmeal off the grinding stone.
> Callous, callous are the nails,
> Callous, callous are the horns
> [Presumably, calluses from using the grinding stone]
> Meehe'e'e'e hew, hew, hew.[47]

When the song ends, they briefly fly into the air; then they return to their grinding, repeating the work-ritual sequence again and again. Into this scene vagrant Coyote intrudes. She sees, perhaps, not the stability of women's work ritual but rather a game and, one assumes, an easy meal of Bird Girls. At her request the Bird Girls allow her to join in the grinding, which she does awkwardly. This is not, after all, her usual work. Next, she wants to learn the song and then the dance flight, both of which are as alien to her earthbound life as the customary women's work of grinding corn. The Bird Girls give Coyote some of their feathers so that she too can fly. The consequences of her whim are predictably disastrous when the Bird Girls pluck the feathers from Coyote while she is in the air. There are at least two other Hopi versions of the Borrowed Feather. In the first of these, Mother Coyote and Father Coyote are hunting for their children. Mother Coyote sees Blue Jays dancing in the trees and asks to borrow feathers so that she can join their dance. In the second a male Coyote is apparently out hunting on his own.[48] It is certainly not far-fetched to suggest that the storyteller knew some of these other versions and intentionally chose the corn-grinding activity. The point is that the storyteller's use of a gender-related activity such as corn grinding gives to the story a more pointed and focused satirical thrust than the Tewa male version. Once again, Mother Coyote demonstrates how miserably she fails to meet the demands of her role in addition to proving that her blundering imitations take her into unfamiliar territory where she does not belong. While such gender-specific details are by no means a consistent difference between male and female trickster stories, even their occasional occurrence suggests that some storytellers were aware of the difference gender makes in the import of a story.

It should also be noted that in almost all stories with female tricksters, some reference is made to her children. In all tribes' male trickster stories, references to trickster's family are relatively infrequent. When his family is referred to or family members are even made characters in a story, their roles are, with a few exceptions, quite perfunctory, with no essential plot or thematic function (except, of course, for the Bungling Host and trickster-marries-his-daughter stories). To be sure, in some female trickster stories references to or uses of trickster's family may be equally perfunctory. Still, there are other instances in which the family as a whole or Coyote's children or husband in particular seems to fill a significant plot or thematic role. Sometimes a story merely opens with a reference to the fact that she has a family; sometimes the beginning shows or implies that Coyote is trying to meet her maternal duties—for example, by hunting or fetching water for her children. She starts, then, with the best of intentions—something we can seldom say about the male tricksters. But in each instance her good intentions dissolve under more immediate enticements. Greed, envy, curiosity, her inability to postpone gratification, her ambition to possess what is not rightfully hers, some vanity or some characteristic bungling leads her to grief. On those occasions when she decides that she wants something not rightfully hers (for example, pretty spots for her children, a certain song, an improved scheme for hunting), her children's presence in the story underscores their trickster mother's foolishness, lack of self-control, or unnatural desires. Considering the frequency with which the children appear in or are referred to in female trickster stories, we are, no doubt, to understand a female Coyote's failings as specifically a mother's failings.

A Coyote trickster's character may be particularly threatening to the values attached to women/mothers in American Indian stories. In most American Indian traditions, a woman was expected to play a stabilizing role in a community through her steadfastness and creative powers. While men's traditions were, according to Laguna writer Paula Gunn Allen, largely about risk and change, women's and mothers' traditions and rituals were devoted to food, household, medicine; that is, to the maintenance and continuity of life.[49] Another source of stability and continuity, particularly for the extended family but also for the community as a whole, can be seen in the expectation that women would defer willingly (though not irrevocably) any immediate personal goals they might have.[50] Even without reading the stories, we can guess that Mother Coyote will fail to meet such ideals and expectations. If nothing else, her wandering undercuts the domestic stability she ought to provide.

A Hopi story illustrates Mother Coyote's failings dramatically and also reveals that not all trickster stories are comical, for this stunning trickster story ends tragically, if ironically. While it may evoke laughter, as do most trickster stories, the laughter is an uneasy, even grim laughter. In this story Mother Coyote learns—or thinks she learns—sorcery.

From the story's beginning, we can see that this mother is in a difficult position. Her husband is dead, and as she—being Coyote, after all—is alone without the support of an extended family, she must do all the hunting to feed her children. Once, while hunting, she comes upon a kiva where witches ("Two Hearts" as the Hopis call them) are engaging in their ceremonies. The most important of these is jumping through a hoop to transform themselves into animals, a common ritual for witches, as is their killing others—even relatives—for their hearts so that the witches can survive.[51] Curious Coyote spies on the witches, who discover her and drag her into their kiva much against her wishes. Told that she must now become a Two Heart, Coyote decides that she wants the power to turn herself into a cottontail, for in this form she can chase down rabbits, changing back to a coyote for the kill at the last instant. The hoop rolls; Coyote jumps through and becomes a cottontail, but unknown to her the head witch spits, which means that Coyote will not be able to transform herself back. When the ceremonies end, Mother Coyote heads for home, delighted at her new power, which is sure to increase her ability to care for her little ones. As she approaches home, she says, "I'd like to turn back to a coyote," but because it is dark she cannot see that she does not transform. In addition we might assume that because Coyote possesses so little self-awareness, she is unable to sense any difference in herself. Eager to rejoin her children, she rushes into the lair. One can imagine the reception this cottontail gets from the starving coyote pups.[52]

A characteristic failing of Coyote's—nosiness, being where she has no business—places her in a circumstance that must inevitably lead to evil, destructive ends. Of course anyone's joining witches would be horrendous, but a mother's doing so seems especially appalling. Moreover, rather than a ceremonial tradition that maintains life, as women's traditions do, she joins a ritual whose participants survive only through others' deaths, a ritual which is a menace to the community and to the family— the very people a mother's steadfastness and selflessness should sustain. Part of the grim irony of this story is that Coyote joins the Two Hearts who survive by killing even family, but her children kill her as they struggle to survive. While her desire to find a better way to provide for her pups is understandable, the fact remains that her desire for an unnatural advantage leads her to violent change and death, not to life's perpetuation.

In brief, Mother Coyote unwittingly teaches us exactly what Old Man Coyote teaches us: more often than not, we will pay a price for yielding to the moment's whim and trying to be someone we are not. But it does so in narrative terms that seem particularly appropriate for the gender and cultural context of its protagonist.

There is little doubt that gender expectations play a significant role in trickster stories with male protagonists and at least some of the time in female-protagonist trickster stories. Such an observation about males and females is a relatively straightforward matter. One particular trickster story, however, complicates the issue of gender and tricksters and elicits more questions than answers. An Omaha trickster story published in Richard Erdoes and Alfonso Ortiz's *American Indian Trickster Tales* raises other sorts of gender questions about tricksters, concerning the persons in the past called *berdaches* and now called by many writers "Two-Spirit people."[53] This person is male bodied but chooses to live as a woman does and may, therefore, dress and behave like a woman, including taking part in a woman's occupations and having sex with a man. At times in the past, such a person might be a man's second or third wife in a society that permitted multiple wives. Unlike Euro-American cultures, whose gender distinctions are binary and focus on heterosexuality only, a number of American Indians generally defined gender in terms of occupational propensity and behavior rather than sexual choices or biology.[54] Some contemporary students of American Indian gendering assert that American Indian traditions often recognized not only male and female but also Two Spirit womanly males and Two Spirit manly women as genders.[55] This rejection of a dualistic either/or gendering is consistent with the American Indian ability to accept what in our culture would be regarded as ambiguous or as an unacceptable boundary transgression, such as that in which the tricksters themselves engage.

A young man might become a Two Spirit because he demonstrated interest in women's work and kept company with women.[56] Therefore, choosing life as a Two Spirit was not first and foremost a matter of sexual preference. A Two Spirit's sexual practices were a consequence of choosing this gender role, not a cause of it.[57] As with other genders, some kinds of sexual behavior for a Two Spirit were considered more appropriate than others. Thus, a male-bodied Two Spirit's having sex with a masculine man was not considered homosexuality, for the Two Spirit was of a different gender.[58] On the other hand, sex between two male-bodied Two Spirits would have been considered homosexuality, for they were of the same gender. Many nations accepted what amounted to marriages between a Two Spirit and a man, the Lakotas and Winnebagos among them.[59]

The presence of Two Spirit people in some indigenous cultures is also consistent with the tendency of American Indian societies to find a contributory role for many kinds of people with diverse characteristics, knowledge, and skills. Often, these Two Spirit people were respected for their artistic natures, hard work, and generosity.[60] In addition, they were frequently honored for their spirituality. In some tribes—for example, the Shoshonis, Miamis, Hidatsas, and Lakotas—Two Spirit people were assumed to have accepted their gender in response to a vision.[61] Two Spirits figure prominently in the religious traditions of some tribes. Among the Navajos, Hidatsas, and Assiniboins, Two Spirits were considered holy. A *nádleehé* plays a significant role in the Navajo creation story. It was the supernatural gift of birds and animals that lead to the first Arapaho *haxuxana^n*. Kroeber identifies the Trickster Nih'a^{n}ca^n as the first *haxuxana^n*, for he "pretended to be a woman, married the Mountain-Lion, and deceived him by giving birth to a false child."[62] The Lakota *winkte* was traditionally regarded as fulfilling a spiritual destiny and as being a possessor of special powers, especially magical and ritualistic powers.[63] Northern Plains nations believed that a Two Spirit might receive special powers for performing women's activities—for example, quilling or tanning. Or their powers might have to do with healing or heterosexual matchmaking.[64] Often, Two Spirits performed specific ritual functions such as handling corpses (Yurok), cutting ritual lodge poles (Crow), or performing prominently in scalp dances (Cheyenne).[65]

Even before Euro-American perspectives influenced many indigenous people's views of gender crossing, choosing life as a Two Spirit was not without its ambivalence. While claiming that among the Cheyennes, the Two Spirit enjoyed high status, James Steele Thayer also points out that such a person among most northern Plains peoples was "both feared and prized because, and even in spite of, the supernatural vocation and power" of the person's life, to say nothing of the fact that the Two Spirit lived in a manner some in Plains society would consider "abnormal," even if accepted.[66] Among the Dakotas, *winktes* lived on the fringes of camp, the same location where orphans and widows lived, thus manifesting a marginal presence in the community.[67] Moreover, the Two Spirit people themselves may sometimes have adopted this gender role with some ambivalence. As occurred in other instances of living a vision-led life, a Two Spirit was faced with a challenge through obligations imposed by the vision, in this instance, taking on a new gender role and perhaps new ceremonial responsibilities. Thayer claims that some were so reluctant to take up this challenge that there were occasional suicides. Similarly, some Omaha men who had Two Spirit dreams chose suicide over the life in a new gender identity. Others sometimes attempted to keep their vision secret.[68] Following James Owen Dorsey, Thayer claims that *miati*—the Hidatsa word for a Two Spirit)—is derived from *mia* (woman) and the suffix *ti* (to feel an involuntary inclination).[69] Finally, an Omaha became a *winkte* as a result of a vision in which the Moon offered him a choice between a bow and a burden strap. If the person chose the bow (thereby indicating the choice of a traditional male role), sometimes the Moon would force the bow strap on him.

Appropriately enough in a study of tricksters, the issue of the Two Spirit's life is not a cut-and-dried matter. The Omaha story referred to above—entitled by Erdoes and Ortiz "The Winkte Way"—carries its own ambiguities. The editors' introductory note says, "Iktinike [the Omaha trickster] and Rabbit are always chasing women, but sometimes, just for a change, they turn themselves into *winktes,* doing it the *winkte* way."[70] Meeting up with Rabbit, Iktinike suggests exactly that. Rabbit objects when the trickster wants him to be the passive partner and bend over, allowing Iktinike to get on top of him. After they argue about positioning for a time, it is Iktinike who gives in and bends over so that Rabbit is in the superior sexual position. After he finishes Rabbit jumps off and runs away, with Iktinike calling after him, "Hey, come back! It's my turn now!" to no avail. As Iktinike approaches home, one group of boys after another tells him that Rabbit is spreading the word that he mounted the trickster. Soon Iktinike feels that he must relieve himself. When he squats, little baby rabbits rather than feces come out![71] Arriving home, he is greeted by his amorous wife, who wants to have sex. Iktinike begs off: "I've got a headache."[72]

It is impossible to say how "traditional" this story is, although the conclusion's use of a clichéd Euro-American joke is perhaps a fairly recent twist. In any event, what or who is being ridiculed here? One possibility is that—under the influence of Christian missionaries—the story ridicules *winktes.* In this perspective *winktes* would be identified with trickster—master of the perverse violation of all standards and limits—in that they, like him, try to be what they are not, that is (according to this view) women.[73] The story also seems to equate homosexuals and *winktes,* thus emphasizing sexual practice over other aspects of a *winkte*'s cultural role. Yet a quite different perspective is possible, also based on gender expectations. In *winkte*-male sex, the *winkte* either performed oral sex on the man or took the passive role in anal sex. Sometimes, however, perhaps "just for a change," like Iktinike and Rabbit, the partners might reverse sex roles. In such circumstances the man would not want his part to become known, for taking the passive role would reflect badly on his masculinity.[74] Does this story satirize swaggering machismo by making public the humiliation of the trickster's usual aggressive masculine sexuality? (After all, it is he who initiates the sexual contact.) Even the boys—who presumably would have looked up to a masculine role model—know Iktinike's secret. And his mortification is so complete that for once the sexually extravagant trickster is curbed. From this point of view then, the story may be a satire on the pretense and posturing involved in men's notions of masculine gender images. Finally, we have seen how trickster stories often show a trickster posing as one with sacred power and usually suffering a penalty for this hubris. Is the Omaha story, then, yet another example of a trickster's fooling around in sacred territory where he has no business being?

Arapaho tradition says that Nih'a^n'ca^n, the Arapaho trickster, was the first haxuxana^n.[75] What more obvious original could we ask for in this matter: Trickster the shape changer and violator of boundaries. What is even more revealing is the fact that an Arapaho myth explains that this came about when Nih'a^n'ca^n "pretended to be a woman, married the Mountain-Lion, and deceived him by giving birth to a false child."[76] Such stories occurred throughout Native America. The Arapaho story and the Omaha story of Iktinike's brief experience as a winkte encourage another look at the male versions of well-behaved girl stories. Could some of these stories be satires of Two Spirits, or might they use Two Spirits for satirical purposes?

In a Winnebago version of such episodes, Wakdjunkaga—in a scheme with his companions Fox, Jay, and Nit to survive the winter—"marries" a man.[77] He makes a vulva from an elk liver and breasts from an elk's kidneys and dons a woman's dress. As the final step in his transformation into a pretty woman, he lets Fox (followed by Jay and Nit) have intercourse with him and impregnate him. His arrival announced by an old woman who lives at the edge of the village, the trickster enters the village and marries the chief's son, a good hunter, and provides him with three sons. Wakdjunkaga's secret is revealed when he playfully jumps over the fire and "drop[s] something very rotten" (one assumes, the liver-vulva) and runs off from the village.[78] This story is full of the sorts of violations we expect in a trickster story, although they are not all of his doing: a "woman" goes visiting alone (unheard of among the Winnebagos); an old woman of little social status appoints herself town crier to announce the arrival of a handsome woman; and the trickster bride devours the bridal meal most unceremoniously.[79] A major point in the story seems to be the implied criticism of the chief, who "puts the satisfaction of having his son marry a beautiful woman ahead of the prudence and judgment required by his position."[80] Ironically, trickster—the one usually driven by passion and instinct—becomes the chastening agent of the chief, whose self-interest has made him ignore "the demands of tradition and responsibility for the common good."[81]

Wiget goes on to say that the story "reminds us of the danger of confusing the person and the role."[82] Of course in this instance, the confusion is intentional. Still, Wakdjunkaga does fulfill part of his assumed role: curiously, he/she does give birth. Nevertheless, the humiliating joke rests on the same ground as in the female versions of this episode: The haughty one who defies the culture's gender expectations is duped by Trickster, in this case because the victim assumes that the one he takes as wife is who the person is. However, given the ambivalence sometimes accompanying the tradition of Two Spirits, the gender-crossing Trickster's shenanigans could be a burlesque warning to both Two Spirit and husband not to take their "marriage" too seriously—that, in fact, there is no real spousal relationship but only a relationship of convenience. Finally, ever mindful of the polyvalence of Trickster stories, let us not forget how commonly they prove the imperfections of human categories. Trickster's occasional transgendering adventures comically demonstrate the inadequacy of what seem to be "natural" gender expectations but which are, in fact, artificial—that is to say, only human— boundaries. Trickster prepares us for the necessity of Two Spirits.

Earlier in this chapter, I acknowledged the role that conjecture would play in my discussion. My treatment of female tricksters and of Two Spirits is the focal point of most of this conjecture. As we have seen, there is often a satirical, didactic thrust in Trickster stories. That the stories serve[d] such ends has long been recognized. Only occasionally, however, have scholars and other writers examined the stories for their specific lessons, Ramsey and Wiget being two notable exceptions. In any society satire is usually directed toward culturally specific issues rather than general human foibles (the much-acclaimed "universality" of Western world literary "classics" notwithstanding). We should not be surprised, then, that American Indian trickster stories target particular behaviors and kinds of people within their cultures. And just as female-male relations and gender expectations have been at the heart of much Euro-American satire, so, too, in American Indian oral traditions gender expectations come in for their share of hilarity. While American Indian cultures traditionally have been more tolerant than Euro-American ones of the ambiguities that sexual behavior and gender roles can comprise, most were nevertheless clear about what the roles were and about expectations surrounding them. It is clear that Trickster stories were significant instruments for enforcing tribal sexual/gender mores. A part of this effort—for some storytellers, at least—involved gendering the plots and details of some trickster episodes.

Bluejay and the Well-Behaved Maiden

Bluejay went to the menstrual lodge. There at the menstrual lodge was the well-behaved maiden. She sensed his approach from within. Bluejay let his feet hang inside. She saw his legs from within. "Oh, such good legs." They had large calves. "Such good legs. Who can he be?" she thought. Thereupon he stood up and went. The well-behaved maiden now thought, "Who could it have been? Let me peep at him." Now she climbed up and watched him go. Hooded he went on. "Just who was it coming here to me?" she said to herself. At this point she turned around to discover that the men at the men's lodge were looking at her. "Now they have seen me peeping at a man." She was abashed. "Now it is that I will follow him became all of them have seen me." She packed her things, climbed up, and followed him. The people there said to one another, "What now, the well-behaved maiden follows Bluejay." Here she followed and caught up to him and found that it was Bluejay. Then he took her with him. They came to a stream, a stream of large flow. Bluejay said to her, "We are wading." They took off their shoes but he, Bluejay, left his legs still wrapped. His calves were so large. The woman said to him, "your legs are still wrapped. You will wet them."—"Yes, but let them remain like that." Now they waded. Bluejay took the upstream side. Shortly the woman said to him, "just what is tangling about my legs? Like pine tree moss; whence floats this pine tree moss?" All the way across it entangled her legs in this manner. They were about to wade ashore when Bluejay dashed ashore alone. There he suddenly gave the call of the bluejay, and oh, those which had been his good large calves were suddenly only bones; not at all like calves. "Is that why pine tree moss was entangling me; his calves were made up of pine tree moss." Bluejay then took her to his lodge and they lived there. He would go out every day and in the evening would bring back only pitch gum. He would give his wife pitch gum thinking that she, too, liked only that. Thus far Bluejay.

Archie Phinney, *Nez Percé Texts*, 17–18. Copyright © 1934, reprinted by permission of Columbia University Press.

CHAPTER FIVE

Blood Kin

Trickster, Hero, Clown

While the European folk tradition includes tricksters, none in the modern era seems to have achieved the popularity and cultural importance of the American Indian trickster. Certainly, none has the mythic significance of the North American character. None even exists with culturally specific identities, as do American Indian tricksters (and many other world tribal tricksters). To be sure, the picaro may be a literary descendent of the European folk tradition's tricksters, but he is no chip off the old block; the bloodline has thinned considerably. He is a victim of the selective moral-ontological breeding attending the Western Judeo-Christian search, under the influence of the absolutist technocratic-rationalistic mind-set, for moral certitude. On the other hand the American Indian trickster's blood is still thick and vigorous, not only in his traditional and modern manifestations but also, it would seem, in other characters in the American Indian oral heritage. Radin has noted trickster characteristics in the other oral-tradition figures.[1] I believe that in such American Indian protagonists as the various brother (often twin) heroes (the Zuni Ahayutte, the Kiowa Half Boys, Lodge Boy, and Thrown Away), the Navajo Chantway heroes, assorted theriomorphic characters, and others we can see a strong family resemblance to tricksters.

With a tolerance of the paradoxical and the equivocal in reality as deeply implanted in the American Indian worldview as it seems to be, it is no surprise that the dramatization of paradox that tricksters manifest is found in other American Indian stories as well. In Dennis Tedlock's

translation of the Zuni Beginning, paradox and equivocality as well as
indeterminacy characterize events, conditions, and processes by which
the primeval Zuni world was transformed into the present reality. For
example, after the People have emerged from the underworlds in which
they began and have wandered about their new, sunlit world for a time,
a witch emerges from the underworld. "Having you in this won't be
good," say the Ahayutte (twin heroes). "Indeed/ that's the way it IS," the
witch responds. Apparently, the continuing threat of evil and disorder
that the witch represents is necessary to the scheme of things; that is the
way of the world, like it or not. Still, the sorcerer's presence is not
unmitigated evil, for he brings with him corn, which will sustain the
People's lives. Rather than kill the witch and lose the corn, the people
choose for their own lives. To make matters even thornier, the House
Chief must sacrifice his own child at the witch's command; but even
that sacrifice brings blessings, for the child promises, "when the time
COMES? Then I will enter upon their roads," presumably as a rain
cloud or as one of the creative kachina powers. So out of the presence of
evil comes fertility and hence life, but the price of these is death, which
further contributes to life.[2]

While the Zuni sorcerer is not a trickster, the equivocal and paradoxical
to which his presence gives rise is the same sort of reality that tricksters
repeatedly create. As a model of reality, tricksters—to whose lives such
traits are fundamental—would seem to be quintessential American
Indian oral-tradition characters. Perhaps it was something along these
lines that Ramsey intended when he wrote, "The Trickster figure is
ubiquitous in the native literature, and . . . is conceptually central to it."
Trickster is the "one native type whose protean nature seems capable of
subsuming all other possible types sooner or later . . . a type who is all
men's epitome."[3] The qualities that make tricksters what they are and
the world they create what it is do, indeed, appear frequently in American
Indian oral traditions. In fact, it may be that the dramatization of the
equivocal and paradoxical is a distinguishing trait of American Indian
mythologies, even when there is no trickster present in a story. In the
myths, in both human and supernatural aspects of the world, we find a
swirling configuration of trickster realities: good and evil intermingling

with order and disorder, and all giving rise to creation and destruction, change and stability. American Indian oral-tradition protagonists are often the expression of these realities. There is a specific circumstance that these characters and tricksters share: violation of physical, social, and taboo boundaries of all sorts.

Traveling inevitably leads one to cross frontiers, and trickster experience, as we know, is no exception. For tricksters, the crossings are most often sheer self-indulgence. They wander in order to escape the consequences of some recklessness, and thus they find themselves in circumstances ripe for new transgressions. But why is violation such a common element in American Indian trickster stories? Dundes would answer, perhaps, by pointing out that the theme of disobedience (leading to violation of some sort) is fundamental to the structure of American Indian stories in general.[4] However, while he would undoubtedly be correct, his observation would not help us understand the connection in trickster stories between tricksters' violations and their power.

Makarius argues that Trickster's mythic power derives from his transgressions: he is the "magician violator of taboos," the "transgressor for the good of all."[5] Drawing upon a limited range of trickster stories about the Menominee Manabozo (and a few other midwestern trickster incarnations), she sees in stories of the death of Manabozo's brother symbolic transformations of the hero-trickster's sacrificial murder of his brother in order to obtain the magic power available in the *Mide'wi'win* ceremony.[6] He does so not out of self-interest but for the good of humanity, his altruism therefore making him no longer asocial but rather fundamental to the people's social/ceremonial life. Manabozo's sacredness "is to be understood [as] the quality accruing from the dangerous, efficacious, and ambivalent power of the hero, due to the violation of taboo, and consequently to the acts of profanation and sacrilege expressing such violation in myth."[7] Following Makarius's argument requires great inductive leaps—as well as leaps of faith—that even her own sources do not seem to justify. At one point she concludes that the brother's death by the Monster Snakes (or some other evil *manidog*) is actually a symbolic concealment of the fact that the trickster-hero has murdered his brother in order to gain magical power.[8] She rationalizes her position by saying "It is quite understandable that in addressing a popular audience, the narrator of the myth, anxious not to blacken the figure of the hero by depicting him as a fratricide, should want to cover up the crime."[9] Unfortunately for her hypothesis, this explanation does nothing to help us understand why a narrator would be so protective of a trickster's reputation, considering the many unspeakable crimes tricksters commit. Citing Clyde Kluckhohn's "Navajo Witchcraft," among other sources, as evidence that American Indians regarded "the murder of a near-kin . . . as a means to acquire magical powers, and that this is the traditional way to obtain initiation into magic," she ignores the fact that Kluckhohn writes about witchcraft, not at all the same thing as a ceremony like the *Mide'wi'win*.[10]

It is true that violating a taboo or some other form of disobedience sometimes leads to creative, even sacred ends for American Indian tricksters (as well as Navajo Chantway heroes and others). Their rule-breaking and common-sense-defying actions on their journeys keep them in conflict with the conventional social and even natural order. As in the picaresque novels, a trickster's transgressions involve defiance or inversion of accepted codes and categories and opposition to community values or actions, but in a trickster tale such behavior is often crucial to his shaping the natural and social worlds. Repeatedly, a trickster's whims and caprices, his ungoverned appetites, his psychic disorder carry him willy-nilly beyond social or other limits, where he creates or orders a new reality. His higgledy-piggledy way of going about things or being driven by an improvisatory whim leads him to violation, and in consequence the world often ends up with a new scheme of things. The scatological becomes the creative in one version of Nanibozhu's creation of the earth, for he makes the earth to escape his own feces, which are floating in a deluge he caused. In a Wasco tale the trickster betrays his hunting partners, the wolves, by stranding them in the sky, where they become part of the constellation we call the Big Dipper. Treachery, always a threat to order, ends in natural order. In a Navajo story the First People throw a hide scraper into the water, saying that if it floats people will not die. Capriciously opposing community choice, Coyote throws a stone, which, sinking, negates the first act and guarantees that

there will be death. In response to the First People's anger, he rationalizes that the world would get too crowded without death, and hence a
rationalized caprice becomes part of the natural order. The shaping of
new order is not the only consequence of trickster's peregrinations into
forbidden territory, for his abuses also reaffirm the story audience's
existing values and limits.

It is one of the many ironies of tricksters that their digressions across
borders should result in confirmation of those boundaries as well as in
defining new order, but in trickster stories—as in the myths of Navajo
Chantway heroes and the twin heroes of many tribes—"the character of
well-defined rules and boundaries is established not by dogmatism but
by permitting infringement upon proper place."[11] As in other trickster
affairs, here too there is another way to look at things. American Indian
stories and ceremonies represent creative acts not as cause of anything
but as evidence that one possesses power, medicine.[12] For twin heroes
such as the Zuni Ahayutte or the Kiowa Half Boys, it seems that possession
of sacred power makes defiance of taboo and other boundaries possible.
Like the twin heroes, tricksters contravene order and limits *because* they
possess magic power, not in order to acquire it. Thus, tricksters are able
to shape-shift across the boundaries separating humans from sticks or
adult men from infants.

Regardless of the source or nature of their magic and transformative
powers, what the figures we will examine—Navajo myth heroes, twin
heroes, clowns—have in common with tricksters is that they all violate
the rules in some way, and their violations are fundamental to their
careers. The nature of the violation is not constant among them, however.
The twin heroes break the rules most often by ignoring their grandmother's (or someone else's) warning not to go to a particular location
because of the dangers that reside in that place, usually in the form of
some monstrous animal or humanlike being. The Navajo hero, on the
other hand, violates the rules of his group in some way so that he is
ostracized. His journey outside the society of humans puts him in positions of taboo violation, which brings him into conflict with the Holy
People. Clowns most often defy the limits of what is considered "decent"
and holy, and as they do so, only they—among all of the preceding

figures—are consistently funny. Tricksters combine all of these traits and rule-breaking behavior—and more.

Consider first the protagonists of Navajo Chantway myths. In *Mythology and Values: An Analysis of Navajo Chantway Myths,* Spencer's analysis of myth protagonists suggests that the human heroes (sometimes heroines) of Chantway myths behave in ways more than a little reminiscent of tricksters, but admittedly without their comedy.[13] Sometimes, Spencer says, these protagonists intentionally ignore prescribed rules and aggressively search for peril out of recklessness or curiosity or through sexual exploits or some other willfully self-assertive or irresponsible behavior.[14] Further, analysis of the tales reveals "what seems to be a covert preoccupation with the hero's own active share in provoking the mishaps which befall him."[15] Because of his "misadventures," he must leave his family and community. Having done so, he finds himself, in one way or another, in dangerous circumstances in the natural/supernatural world because of some further violation, for instance improper contact with an animal or spirit. Initially he may even be the object of divine hostility. In any event the life forces among which he moves are out of balance, and he is in need of healing. Finally he is reconciled to and saved by the gods. After being healed by them and learning from them the ceremony associated with his story, he returns briefly to human society with new-found power. Commonly returning to the company of the gods, he leaves this power with his people in the form of a new ceremony—if not a new reality, at least a new way of perceiving and controlling reality. The protagonist has obtained "relief for his immediate misfortune [and] the power for his own and his people's future use."[16]

The trickster reality in human experience asserts itself in a few very specific ways in Chantway myths. There is, first of all, the hero's self-indulgent and, commonly, unsocial behavior. Like tricksters and the twins, whom we will consider presently, he is difficult to control and wanders away from home in search of adventure.[17] Part of the myth's "value theme" (Spencer's term) is the recognition that self-assertion is necessary for breaking away from the restraints of family and achieving maturity. In addition, when we consider the consequences of the hero's self-assertion, we can see that perhaps the social rules are rightfully challenged, because order and security are society's greatest vulnerability in that they can be enemies to creativity and change. Although he is no magician, the Navajo Chantway protagonist seems to share much with Makarius's "violator of taboo" for the good of all. Moreover, like the Navajo trickster Ma'i, the protagonist roams about the various levels of experience.[18] At the same time the hero's story may remind us that he is denied human society because of his self-assertion or self-indulgence, that rebellious behavior can also be extremely dangerous, and that self-discipline is an essential quality. The point is not that the protagonist of a Chantway myth is a trickster. He is not. His career is markedly different from a trickster's. He is probably a young man, and his adventures—unlike those of tricksters—are part of a maturation process that will lead to his acquiring discipline and responsibility.[19] Nevertheless, the hero's career and personality do parallel those of the trickster, not least in the union of "hostile elements in aggression . . . with the positive."[20]

The twin heroes of many tribal oral traditions also share more broadly in tricksters' reality. As noted above, Ramsey says that tricksters subsume all other American Indian characters. Radin, on the other hand, says that the twin myth in North America is "the basic myth" of the Indians.[21] Looking at the many twin heroes in American Indian myth traditions, one cannot help but conjecture that they are related in some fashion to tricksters. Together, the brother heroes share many of the trickster's traits of character and behavior, including: mixed altruistic and egoistical motivation; pushing—often overstepping—acceptable boundaries in their mischievous disregard of or challenging of the rules and prohibitions; a transforming creativity that establishes both natural and social realities; and sometimes, at least partially divine parentage. There are two types of twin stories to consider in this context: those in which there is a pronounced opposition of values between the twins and those in which there seems to be a more indiscriminate mingling of trickster traits.

In the first kind of oral-tradition twins, we often see differences between the brothers that are reminiscent of the split between tricksters and culture heroes, at least in the sense that there is a division of positive and negative or admirable and contemptible qualities. Thus, in a number of western tribal stories we find a "culture hero" and a trickster at odds in the creation. For example, the Maidu Earth Namer states how things will be in world, but Coyote contradicts him and in doing so guarantees that there will be sexual connection, that unmarried girls will sometimes have babies, and that women will have a hard time in childbirth. Coyote also says there will be death, burial, and mourning. When his son is bitten by a rattlesnake, he tries to retreat from this proclamation of death, but Earth Namer prevents it.[22] In northwest California, Silver Fox creates the world by the power of his thought, but Old Man Coyote wants to make it a more disagreeable place. He is restrained, but only with difficulty. After much discussion they reach a compromise. Coyote is responsible for the evil of the world.[23] Sometimes the opposition is between a mischievous trickster marplot and an exemplary, powerful elder brother. In a Ute story, for example, Sunawavi (Wolf) argues with his brother Coyote over the nature of death.[24]

The antithetical, quarreling and transforming twins of Eastern and Central Woodlands mythologies dramatize the nontrickster twin brothers who embody conflicting creative energies. In the Seneca origin story Djuskaha (Sprout) and Othagwenda (Flint) manifest their antagonism even in the womb, for they debate how they will leave their mother's body at the time of birth, Othagwenda saying that he will emerge from her armpit while Djuskaha intends to be born through the normal birth canal. After they are born (in some versions killing their mother in the process), their grandmother throws Othagwenda into a hollow tree away from the lodge. Eventually reunited, the brothers travel about separately in order to transform the world. Othagwenda creates landscape features and natural phenomena that will make life hard for humans, while Djuskaha's creations will make life easy for them. Each then sets about revising the other's transformations. For instance, Othagwenda creates a mosquito so big that it can pierce a sapling and make it fall; Djuskaha shrinks it to its present size, making it less dangerous to humans. Djuskaha, on the other hand, has made rivers in which half the water flows upstream and half flows downstream, thereby making canoe travel much easier; Othagwenda changes this so that rivers flow in only one direction.[25]

While the Seneca story dramatizes a balancing of opposing forces, the frequently told story of Lodge Boy and Thrown Away, an element of which is present in the above story dramatizes the necessary coexistence of contraries. The names of the twins may vary in different versions, but in most we see that willful violations, creative destruction, humanity, and "naturalness" are accompanied by contrasts between the twins— contrasts which suggest that together they are truly mediators between the human and the natural (as tricksters have been claimed to be). Although differing in details, most versions of this tale follow much the same pattern.[26] A woman ignores her husband's warning against looking at or speaking to any stranger who visits their lodge while he is away. A stranger does arrive, kills the mother, and cuts her open, finding twin boys in her womb. He throws one of the boys someplace in the lodge— for example, behind the tipi curtain—and the other outside, in a spring most often but sometimes in another natural location such as a river or under a tree.[27] In some versions of the tale the discarded twin is named After-Birth Boy because he develops from the placenta of his brother's birth, which is cast in a spring or under an oak tree. In all versions a violent division occurs between the world of the lodge and the natural world. One boy stays willingly with his father, learning about society, the arts, hunting skills, and so forth. The castoff, on the other hand, is identified with the natural world, frequently taking on animal characteristics such as an otter's sharp teeth. While the father is away, the castoff often leaves his natural habitat to play with his socialized brother. When the father discovers the second boy's existence, he and his other son capture the castoff, usually through some sort of trickery and often with the bow and arrow as a key prop. After reviving their dead mother, the twins—acting as one—go on their adventures, usually undertaken in willful disobedience of their father's orders, during which they destroy various monsters or bring other good to the world, often through mischief. The rightful unity of values that the twins represent and their mediating function between the human and the natural are obvious. At the same time they must operate in—and sometimes even contribute to—a world of violence, deception, disobedience, and, occasionally, black humor. Only by submitting to and manifesting such a world can their unified power act creatively. Seeing the twins only dualistically would be misleading; it should be noted that their creative, transforming powers can be effective only when they act as one. We can see in these two kinds of twins the inevitable and necessary interplay of positive and negative, social and natural forces contributing to creative transformations of the sort we see in many trickster stories.

The second kind of twin-trickster story is one in which the twins represent a less obvious bifurcation of traits. Interestingly, in many of these stories the twins begin postnatally as one, but through some foolish or prohibition-defying act the one becomes two, as when Doldal splits himself with an arrow or the Sun Child splits himself with a hoop (as in the story below). Beginning as one, the hero becomes two, but the two share traits and powers and continue to function as one.

One version of the Kiowa Half Boys myth recorded by Marriott and Rachlin is a particularly good example of how these twin heroes can seem to be embodiments of tricksters' ambiguous yet powerful reality.[28] This story begins with the common American Indian motif of the woman who marries a star (except that in this case she marries the Sun), but it soon becomes the story of their son. Leaving the human world for the sky world of the Sun, the young woman marries the Sun and gives birth to a boy. After disobeying her husband's prohibition against digging any wild potato with the top chewed off, she discovers a hole in the sky that allows her to look down on her earthly homeland. Homesick, she makes a sinew rope to lower herself and her son to earth, but she miscalculates the length she needs and ends up dangling above the earth on a rope too short, where her husband discovers her. The Sun makes a rawhide-laced willow ring and rolls it down the rope so that it leaps over the boy but kills the mother, both of them then falling to the earth.[29] The boy is subsequently raised and named Talyi by Spider Woman, mother and comforter of all living things and beings. Raised by Grandmother Spider, an earth figure, Talyi combines the natural, human, and divine—the heritage of a few tricksters as well.[30] Warned by Grandmother Spider Woman not to throw his play willow hoop (which in this story is both an instrument of destruction and a game hoop), the boy, of course, does just that. But first he indulges in some tricksterlike rationalization: "'Nothing bad will happen to me', Talyi [says] to himself, for after all he is his mother's son. Everything will be all right. Grandmother is getting old, so she imagines things." He plays with the hoop properly a few more minutes, until impulse overwhelms him and he throws it into the air. When it falls it cuts him in two, so that there

> was no longer one boy standing here, but two. They were identical in appearance except that one was right-handed and one was left-handed.
>
> "Well," said the right-handed twin to his brother, "here we are. Who are you?"
>
> "I am I," the left-handed twin answered. "Who are you?"
>
> "I am I, but when we are together we are we," his brother answered.
>
> "Then *we* together must be stronger than either I," said the left-handed twin.
>
> "Together we make one strong person," the right-handed twin agreed.[31]

As in tricksters, here too opposing but complementary identities make for a powerful reality.

When she discovers what has happened, Grandmother laments that the boys must leave: "now that there are two of you, you have double strength . . . you must leave me and go out on your adventures, to save the Kiowas from the dangers that threaten them."[32] So, like some tricksters, off they go, making the world safe for humans. Their adventures result in the tribe's acquiring the Ten Grandmothers, a sacred bundle. In brief, as in many trickster episodes, disobedience, defiance of rules and limits, and unity of complementary powers create good.

The Ahayutte, twin heroes of the Zuni origin myth, also possess between themselves a tricksterlike polyvalence, and they too transform reality by killing various monsters, undertaking each of their search-and-destroy missions after being explicitly warned by their grandmother against going to particular locations where the monsters live (just as Lodge Boy and Thrown Away disobey their father's specific warnings and the Half Boys disobey Grandmother Spider). Their successes come largely through an assertive and confident application of their wiles. They are most like tricksters, however, in their exuberance and self-indulgence and in their often comic trickery. In one story they show humorous disregard for themselves, laughing and joking about their own deaths, as they gather firewood for a cannibalistic old woman who intends to cook them. They outwit her by separating their souls from their bodies (reminiscent perhaps—but with different ramifications—of the dissociation of thought and body frequently seen in tricksters, including their dismantling themselves). When she begins to eat their bodies, their souls tell her that they have defecated and urinated in the meat. Entering her nostrils, they cause her to cough and sneeze herself to death. When they return home, having regained their bodies, they trick their grandmother by stuffing the cannibal's skin with grass and tying it to the younger twin, who runs, screaming that he is being chased. The grandmother beats and smashes the stuffed corpse while the Ahayutte laugh, pleased at pulling off a successful stunt. In another episode they demonstrate a trickster's comic-tragic indifference to nature's powers when they steal thunder and lightning and play with these phenomena until they cause a flood that kills their grandmother.[33] Not all of the twins' deeds are so amusing. As is often true with tricksters (especially when sex is the issue), the twins can be profoundly indifferent to others' well-being. For instance, they habitually murder girls they sleep with. One of their victims meets them again the next night, but they do not recognize her. Blinded by lust, as tricksters often are, all they see is WOMAN. They are unable to make personal distinctions or to conceive of the hideousness of their acts. This woman, however, gets a measure of revenge on the twins. The next night they sleep with her again, but when they prepare to kill her the next morning, as is their wont, they discover that she is already dead, with dirt covering her. When they realize that they have had intercourse with a ghost, they take her heart, but she follows them anyway, chasing them until they arrive at the place of emergence and the origin place of the sacred societies. There the Flint Society helps them put her ghost to rest, and the twins are told that they failed to observe the ceremonial requirements for dealing with killing, just as tricksters often learn that their adventures and dangers occur because they have failed to meet certain ritualistic obligations.[34]

The above twin episodes seem to emphasize traits such as wiliness and deception (including self-deception), impulsiveness, dissociation of mind and body, the paradoxical integrity of opposing qualities, and other trickster traits. The exact generic relationship between tricksters, the twin heroes, and Navajo myth protagonists is problematic at best. There is nevertheless ample evidence in these stories and others to suggest that tricksters can stand as a prototype for many American Indian mythic protagonists, if not as a matter of genesis then certainly as a critical model for understanding characterization in the myths. This connection is made even more evident when we consider that sometimes the twins appear in episodes that are also often trickster episodes—for example, stories of women with vaginal dentata. There are instances in which tricksters appear in episodes with twins as protagonists. In a version of the Ojibwe origin myth, Wenebojo is the grandson of a woman who falls from the sky onto a turtle—as in the Iroquoian origin story. His mother dies giving birth to him and his brother Flint (who have argued in the womb about who would be born first). In yet another myth Wenbojo develops from a blood clot.[35] Pakwis, whom some believe to be the trickster's brother, argues with him about what the world should be like. For instance, the trickster wants January to be warm, while his brother wants it to be cold.[36] Makarius summarizes a number of birth episodes for Wenebojo\Manabozo\Nanabush that are also found in twin stories.[37]

The correspondences between tricksters and the other mythic personages discussed above also demonstrate a crucial element in the American Indian worldview that I have already touched upon in various ways. All dramatize the fundamental paradoxes of human experience: that defying the restraints to the point of disorder can create order; that the comic can also be tinged with the tragic; that wrong, even evil, might carry something of the comic; and that good and evil are inextricably fused, so that there are occasions when they seem to blend into one another. The Euro-American tradition presses for resolution of the ambivalent, the paradoxical, the equivocal; this resolution always seems informed by absolute and inflexible moral principles. Rather then accepting reality, much traditional Western world culture and literature have sought ways to resolve ambiguity through the dominance of moral certainty. Until fairly recently and still, perhaps, for many, it has been believed that ultimately the lion will lie down with the lamb and the picaro with the burgher, though only when the former become like their meek and conventional bedmates. But while the picaro—for all his adventuring—is snared by the constant pull to moral certitude, the tug to resolution, tricksters are brother to many American Indian heroes who embody the ambiguity of human nature and experience. Many stories in American Indian oral traditions seek no absolute resolutions but accept that both change and stability are consequences of life's ambiguities.

In ceremonialism—that human endeavor to manage change and stability—tricksters generally do not play a significant role. In fact the goal of much Navajo ceremony, the restoration of order, is exactly the opposite of what Coyote brought into the world when he haphazardly threw stars into the sky. Even when the Navajo Coyote makes an appearance in ceremony, his presence is disorderly. The plants associated with him are "unselected," while his songs—unlike the usual songs in Navajo ceremony—are not in orderly sets.[38] Occasionally, a tribal trickster provides some ritualistic element or the belief context in which a ceremony is performed. Hartly Burr Alexander recounts Manabozho's association with various aspects of the *Mide'wi'win,* while Coleman identifies him as the source of the ceremony.[39] Although generally absent from ceremony themselves, tricksters do have parallels in American Indian ceremonialism in the persons of ritual clowns. Non-Native observers of some American Indian ceremonies have often been startled and shocked by the appearance and behavior of ceremonial clowns, who seem profane or downright salacious and obscene and perhaps not at all amusing. American Indian ceremonial clowns handle burning embers or plunge their hands into boiling water; say the opposite of what they mean or do the opposite of what apparent common sense dictates (for example, taking a bath in a stream bank's sand rather than the water); eat and drink feces and urine;

simulate sexual intercourse with each other or with onlookers; parody ritual acts; satirize Native and white behavior (particularly white cultural quirks like being governed by the clock), threats from outside their communities (for example, the BIA and missionaries), and much more. Matilda Cox Stevenson claimed that she had seen Zuni clowns "bite off the heads of living mice and chew them, tear dogs limb from limb, eat the intestines and fight over the liver like hungry wolves."[40] Frank Cushing reported of Zuni clowns: "I have seen one of them gather about him his melons, green and ripe, raw peppers, bits of stick and refuse, unmentionable water, live puppies—or dead, no matter— peaches, stones and all, in fact everything soft enough or small enough to be forced down his gullet, including wood ashes and pebbles, and with the greatest apparent gusto, consume them all at a single sitting."[41] All in all, clowns' behavior seems to outsiders to be totally incongruous with the sacredness of the ceremonial setting in which they perform; they trample all the rules and are profoundly disorderly and libertine. In addition, they often dress eccentrically or are otherwise characterized by unusual appearance. The bodies of some Pueblo clowns, for example, are striped horizontally black and white. Other clowns are covered with mud and wear headpieces or masks that make them look like muddy Pillsbury doughboys.

Such antics may be at the least startling to us but perhaps only because Euro-American culture has forgotten its own tradition of sacred clowning. In medieval Europe the annual Feast of Fools sanctioned conduct that at any other time would have been punished as sacrilege. Subdeacons mocked the sacraments, sang pornographic songs in church, and doused a bishop or other officials in a river, all as release from restrictive religious demands.[42] Our modern American culture has generally banished humor from the cathedral as well as from other cultural arenas, but among American Indians humor continues to permeate every aspect of life, including the problematic and the sacred.[43] In fact, Kenneth Lincoln asserts that "having things both ways, sacred and profane— characterizes much ceremonial Indian humor."[44] W. W. Hill observed that humor among the Navajos was an important part of both social interaction and ceremony.[45] Finally, among some American Indians it has been said that everyone present—especially strangers—must laugh before religious ceremonies may begin.[46] The laughter elicited might be satirical and corrective, or it might be an acceptance of immutable reality or of the paradoxes of everyday life that suddenly and startlingly illuminate the enigma of the All, just like the laughter directed at trickster stories.[47]

The similarities between American Indian ritual clowns (Heyokas, Mudheads, Newekwes, Kosharis, Koyemshis, and so forth) and tricksters are immediately apparent to those who become familiar with both, and asking which came first may be a chicken-and-egg question. One might see ritual clowns as the "earthly" counterpart of tricksters or as "reification in the tribe itself of trickster figures who can ridicule custom, etc. with impunity."[48] Whatever the perspective, it is clear that clowns and tricksters are harnessed by many American Indian traditions. In one version of the Ojibwe origin myth, when the trickster's grandmother says "Your actions are like a Ne-naw-bo-zhoo, he replies, "I am the great Ne-naw-bo-zhoo on this earth." The storyteller Chief Mack-e-te-be-nessy, Andrew J. Blackbird, explains that the name means "clown."[49] A Dakota becomes a Heyoka by a vision of Iktomi (or at least by association with him), and among the Lakotas Iktomi is considered a Heyoka because he is always talking to the thunderers.[50] Makarius even claims that Heyoka is another name for Iktomi.[51] Among the Arapahos the founder of the "Fools' Lodge" is trickster, and in California clowns are identified with the trickster.[52] Both figures are dramatizations of the transgression of boundaries as well as of the paradoxes and contradictions of human experience.[53] And both are images of humanity's absurdity, of the disparity between what we are in our own minds and what we in fact are in the world's mundane reality. Clowns' backward talk and reverse behavior is coupled with their breaking of taboos and their violations of commonly accepted "decent" behavior, just as tricksters violate all of our assumptions and expectations about social rule and natural law.[54] In regard to their respective social roles, there are differences between clowns and tricksters in that clowns are also sometimes disciplinarians and peacemakers—rare roles among tricksters.[55] In addition clowns' violations of cultural constraints are, in a sense, sanctioned because of their sacred associations: Pueblo clowns have ceremonial authority, and

Lakota Heyokas gain their status from the Thunder Beings. Tricksters have no such authority; their license is self-proclaimed only.

Also like tricksters, clowns are often associated with the mythic beginnings of the world. In the earth-diver origin myth of the Maidus, Phe'ipe, a ceremonial clown, was among those on the raft floating on the Deluge before the present world was made, while among the Cheyennes, clowns—members of the Society of Contraries—are related to the "culture hero" Sweet Medicine.[56] In another example, Iktomi is the son of Wakinyan—Thunder. When Iktomi is banished from the company of the Sacred Beings, Skan tells him that "as the offspring of Wakinyan [a contrary] who is honored most by words or deeds which are the opposite of the intent of those doing or saying them, you should have accepted laughter and derision as proper homage to you."[57]

It is perhaps the clowns of the New Mexico and Arizona Pueblos that are best known. Certainly, they stand as fascinating representatives of American Indian ceremonial clowns in general. As is the case with other tribal clowns, their origins are commonly part of the story of the Beginning. For example, the Zia Koshare—mediator between earth people and the sun—was created by First Man.[58] Their performances in ceremonies are often allusive to the People's emergence. In "Way Back in the Distant Past," Albert Yava describes how before Tewa clowns perform in front of the village, they engage in their own ceremonies in their kiva.[59] Prior to their leaving the kiva, the leader climbs a ladder to the opening at the top of the kiva, sticks his head out, and shouts, "Yah hay" and then ducks back in four times. The clowns' eventual emergence from the kiva is a reenactment of the People's emergence from the third underworld into this world.[60] Emory Sekaquaptewa details the Hopi clowns' reenactment of the emergence:

> Before the Hopi left from the emergence place, one man chosen by them as their leader went up on a hill [and called out], "yaaha-hay!" four times. Thus gaining their attention he said "now you heard me cry out in this way. You will hear me cry in this way when we have reached the end of our life-way. It will be a sign that we have reached the end of the world. We will know then

whether we have fulfilled our destiny." . . . From this beginning when we have been resembled to clowns we know that this is to be a trying life and that we will try to fulfill our destiny by mimicry, by mockery, by copying, by whatever. . . . When the clowns come they represent man today who is trying to reach this place of paradise. That is why the clowns always arrive at the plaza from the rooftops of the houses facing the plaza where the katsinas are dancing. The rooftops signify that even though we have not reached the end, we are not necessarily ready to walk easily into the spiritual world. The difficulties by which clowns gain the place of katsina make for fun and laughter, but also show that we may not be able to make it from the rooftop because it is too difficult. We are going to clown our way through life making believe that we know every thing. . . . The clowns come to the edge of the housetops around noon and they announce themselves with the cry "yaahahay!" four times. This announces as foretold at emergence the arrival at the end of the life-way journey. And then they make their way into the plaza with all sorts of antics and buffoonery representing the Hopi life quest. . . . The clown skits and satiric performances done throughout the afternoon are reminiscent of the corruption that we experienced in the underworld, where we presumably had Conscience as a guide. We chose not to follow Conscience and it comes into play during the clown performances in the form of the katsinas that visit the plaza.[61]

Clearly, clowns have functions that transcend mere entertainment, important as that may be. For the Zunis—and quite likely others as well—their presence is salubrious.

Before each performance, [Newekwe] clowns are reminded by their leaders "to make your mind blank" and "to go out there with a happy heart, a heart free from worry, to help the people." Their whole goal is to startle and even shock the audience in order to get a response, perhaps a sudden laugh, or at least a gasp of disapproval. In so doing they "get to the people," they "open them," and release them from internal idle thoughts or worries. In the Zuni view, worry lodges in the stomach and is a primary source of general (and one might say visceral) worry at Zuni.[62]

Like tricksters, these clowns are very much a part of the contemporary world, not relics, for "clowns are always facing new dangers whether from Madrid, Washington, Rome or Houston Control." Unlike tricksters, the men who are chosen as clowns are known "as the wisest and most fearless people in the entire pueblo."[63]

Appearances suggest that American Indian clowns are the very embodiment of physical, spiritual, and social chaos and as such constitute a threat to the order and well-being of the community. How could it be possible, after all, that such moral anarchy in the most sacrosanct contexts would not take its toll on the character of a people? Certainly, many have inferred American Indian satanic barbarity from the behavior Stevenson and Cushing described. To counter appearances, however, we should first consider that these acts of moral turmoil occur within the well-defined and controlled limits of ceremony. Yava points out that Tewa clowns undergo disciplined preparation in anticipation of their ceremonial performance; for instance, they must abstain from sexual intercourse (in fact, they must stay away from women completely) and deny themselves meat, salt, and so forth.[64] Hence, their license is grounded in discipline. Their private ceremonies also create an ordered environment of protection against the terrible and destructive forces they will temporarily unleash in their performance. It is also critical that we recognize how clowns defy order in the name of order, for as in didactic trickster stories, clowns' antics teach us. Lincoln states that "Serious men make good koshares, or clowns, the Hopi say, for in their language the word for 'clowning' means 'to make a point.'"[65] Wendy Rose has written that "The sacred clowns are descended from the warrior societies and are as much police as clowns. They entertain, but they serve a serious function at the same time. They also demonstrate good and bad behavior through what they do and when they spoof someone in the crowd it's partly a police action."[66]

Given the clowns' behavior, this hardly seems creditable, but "that's the way it IS," to quote the witch in the Zuni origin myth. Just as order implies an understanding or definition of disorder, so disorder implies order. For a thing to be out of place, we must know its place. Just as their behavior tells the people how not to behave, so the clowns' intemperate antics define what order is; the breach clarifies the boundaries.[67] In some inexplicable manner, ceremonial clowns—whether Navajo, Zuni, Hopi, or Lakota—even as they defy the formal limits of ritual, add to the power of the ceremony and its consequent efficacy in the world: "their clowning is the disguise that makes mysterious influence effective in the world."[68]

The order-threatening capers of American Indian clowns take place, then, under the sheltering blanket of ritual. Only in ritual can the extraordinarily destructive powers set free by the clowns' performance be controlled; but at the same time, in a paradox worthy of these ceremonial tricksters, the sacramental setting redirects these powers toward the creative. Gill points out that the Heyokas pose a threat of destructiveness equal to that of the Thunder Beings, with whom they are associated, in storm and lightning but that the Sioux also recognize the possibility of creative results to such danger.[69] Following Douglas, he points out that dirt (tantamount to forbidden action), a "by-product" of creation, "has the ability to evoke . . . an experience of the powers that bring order into the world . . . , [hence] dirt is symbolic of the beginning stages of creation and growth as well as decay."[70]

Furthermore, the laughter that clowns evoke, Barbara Tedlock affirms, opens people to "immediate experience," that is, frees their minds from "whatever worries they brought with them."[71] As noted above, such release has significant ethical and health benefits.[72] But laughter also opens people up to seeing anew; it liberates onlookers "from conventional notions of what is sacred and dangerous in the religious ceremonies of men."[73] Just as at the beginning of things, when the world had not taken its final shape but lay inchoate and fertile with possibility before the First People, so clowns put onlookers in a similarly creative place and time—the place and time of the ceremonial world, which, tearing aside the illusions of the mundane world, reveal sometimes terrifying, sometimes transforming truths. Experiencing the sacred anew means also that clowns' creativity leads to an alternative way of experiencing humanity's everyday world and the particulars of the human condition. Like the

clown in the Night Chant, clowns in general are also the "living representative of that full world of good and evil" in our world.[74] They redefine
the limits and categories within which we live, enlarging the possibilities
of our lives. Like Yellowman's Ma'i, they are important because they are
not ordered, for like him they experience everything and are the expo-
nents of all possibilities.[75] The Newekwe clowns, whose "path is that of
the Milky Way, arching clear across the night sky . . . see boundaries, of
whatever sort, as easy hurdles rather than as walls. Which is why they
never laugh at their own jokes but, causing others to laugh at the leaping
of a boundary, share a moment of shamanic detachment with the
uninitiated."[76] Further, just as observers discover that the ugly, poor,
bedraggled appearance of the clowns belies the terrifying power they
possess and just as the contrary behavior of the Heyokas conceals the
fatal courage they possess, so observers begin to see new dimensions of
the sacred underlying the apparently mundane and profane. Just as the
clowns' presence and behavior blur the lines between the sacred and the
profane, so they also delegitimize the conventional categories that control
our thinking in everyday experience.[77]

Ultimately, in our deliberations, clowns bring us squarely alongside
tricksters, being among those who not only defy all frontiers and
boundaries but also simultaneously define the limits. Because the first
koshari of Acoma was afraid of nothing and accepted nothing as sacred,
he was allowed to be everywhere, just like the wandering trickster.[78] Like
these clowns, ubiquitous, traveling Trickster breaks the rules through
contrary behavior—his foolishness initially masking his power—and
discloses for us the limits of perceived categories and the possibility of
creative action even in a frequently threatening world.

Wenebojo in the Whale and the Fight with His Brother

Wenebojo and his twin were talking inside their mother and were
wondering who would be born first. The twin said, "I will." But Wenebojo said, "No; if you are, you will kill our mother." While they were
arguing, the twin jumped out and disappeared, and so did the mother.

The grandmother was surprised and wondered what had happened. She saw a speck of blood on the floor, picked it up, and wrapped it in some birchbark and said that that was Wenebojo. Each day she would look at the blood speck, and it seemed like it was growing. Finally she opened it one day, and there was a little rabbit inside the birchbark. She wrapped it up again, and the next day she looked again, and there was a human being in it. It was Wenebojo.

After a while Wenebojo found out where his brother was, so he told his grandmother that he was going to kill a whale and get some oil. She warned him that the whale was a bad fish and could swallow him and his canoe too. But Wenebojo went ahead and made a canoe and went out to sharpen his knife on a big stone. As he rubbed his knife on the rock, it seemed to say, "*Gigá, Gigá, Gigá*" (My mother, My mother, My mother).

He dropped his knife and went in to ask his grandmother where his mother was and why he had never seen her. She told him not to bother about it. She was afraid he would start to search for her too. Finally she told him that a big whale had swallowed her. Wenebojo got mad at this and went out to kill a whale to avenge his mother.

He went out fishing, and when he got out aways, he yelled, "Whale, come and swallow me!" The whale heard him, but they [sic] said it was Wenebojo calling, and he was a bad spirit. Finally, one big whale got tired of the yelling and opened her mouth and sucked Wenebojo in, his canoe and all.

Wenebojo looked around, and it was just like a wigwam inside. There was a squirrel and a bluejay there, and as Wenebojo could talk to anything, even a rock, he always addressed them as younger brother. He asked the bluejay where he was, and the bluejay told him that they were in the whale's stomach, and he told him where the whale's heart was. Wenebojo was still in his canoe, so he paddled over to the heart and poked it every once in a while with his paddle, until the whale got sick and tried to throw him up. But Wenebojo turned his canoe sideways. Finally he poked the whale's heart and killed it, and the whale turned over on its side.

Then Wenebojo told the wind to blow him over to his grandmother's landing. One morning the grandmother went to get some water, and there lay the big whale on the beach. She let it lie and soon ravens came and started to eat the flesh until there was a big hole in the middle. Wenebojo, the squirrel, and the bluejay crawled out. He had avenged his mother, so he took all the oil from the whale.

Then he asked, "How was it that the whale didn't get my brother?" She told him that his brother was on a solid rock island surrounded by pitch, and that he was a bad spirit anyway and that Wenebojo shouldn't try to get him. But Wenebojo set out anyway.

He took his canoe and some whale oil and paddled toward the island. All at once his canoe got stuck in the pitch. He put some whale oil on his canoe and paddle and got a little further, and then got stuck again, so he put on some more oil. Finally, after he had used up all the oil, he reached the island. He saw his brother chopping off bits of his leg with a stone axe, and *megis* shells would fly off at each stroke. He didn't know his brother's name; so he called him *Okakwáncagiga?ng* (hewing his shin). The brother greeted him and invited him into his wigwam and gave him something to eat. After supper Wenebojo said, "What if someone attacked us? What would you do?"

"I'd fight him first," said the brother.

But Wenebojo said, "No, I'd fight him first."

They argued for a long while, and then the brother lay down and went to sleep. Then Wenebojo went outside and stuck little feathers all around the edge of the island. He told each one to start to whoop and holler just as the sun rose. Then Wenebojo lay down but didn't go to sleep, for he was still afraid of his brother.

At sunrise the feathers started yelling, and the brother ran out to see what the noise was. Wenebojo started to follow him and was shooting arrows into his brother, but nothing happened. A chickadee then told Wenebojo that he would have to shoot his brother in the braid of his hair in order to kill him. Wenebojo shot at the braid, but the arrow glanced off. Wenebojo took his last arrow and waited until his brother turned around. Then he hit him in the center of the braid. The brother fell over dead.

Conclusion
The World As It Is

Conventional wisdom in contemporary scholarship asserts that a trickster's transgressions place him on the margins of society or even beyond the social pale. From a vantage point of "liminality," he liberates humans from traditional social-moral categories and dramatizes new ways of perceiving and the possibility of new orders. Wiget characterizes this capability of tricksters thus: "Outside the system of norms established by the myths of origin and transformation, he becomes a useful, institutionalized principle of disorder. As an 'outsider,' Trickster can suggest the dangerous possibility of novel relationships between form and function; sex and role; belief and practice; kin and clan; even appetite and will. He provides, to use Barbara Babcock's terms, the 'tolerated margin of mess' necessary to explore alternatives to the present system and to contemplate change."[1]

My skepticism regarding tricksters' putative outsider's status notwithstanding, Wiget's description is valid for tricksters in important ways. Tricksters do indeed free us from the imaginative and moral impoverishment attending enslavement to codified and solidified thinking. Along with American Indian oral-tradition heroes and ceremonial clowns, tricksters help us experience the visionary beyond the conventional and encourage us to reconsider the artificiality of our categories and perceptions and to imagine beyond the margins of the socially decorous and lawful. As they violate the rules, as they give free rein to the multifarious trickster personality, and as they shape the world, tricksters also shape human perception. The most significant creative power they bring to humanity is vision—of the world and of self. The common understanding of Yellowman's statements to Toelken—"Through [Coyote] stories everything is made possible" and "If [Ma'i] did not do all those things [the good, the foolish, the terrible], then those things would not be possible in the world"—is that tricksters' inversions realize the world and then establish the rich potential for human action in that world.[2] Tricksters become a model of human possibility. They derange the stability of order into disorder, and disorder, being illimitable and knowing no restrictions, is replete with potentiality.[3] With a trickster the abstract imaginable becomes concrete possibility. So when the Gros Ventre trickster Nix'ant, wearing an elk skull on his head, impersonates a water monster in order to grab young girls and have sex with them, he obscures the boundaries between profane behavior and the sacred world of spirits and encourages us to consider the interpenetration of the world of mythic beings and the human, mundane world.

Significant though such views are for understanding tricksters, emphasizing them, as some have done, at the expense of tricksters' other facets does not sufficiently honor their many-sidedness. Among the trickster features we must not forget is that tricksters are, in the words of Luckert, "archaic all-persons[s]."[4] Tricksters are nothing less than cartoons of our confrontations with our humanity. As tricksters wander and exercise their mythic creative powers, they also define, generally in amusing ways, the limits and nature of our humanity as we struggle through the contraries and contingencies of our experience in this world. Mircea Eliade says in another context, "what is true in eternity is not necessarily true in time."[5] Coyote's role as a marplot in the Maidu creation myth, as in other myths, reminds us that the grand design of the gods is not always of appropriately human dimensions.[6] The trickster is our oral-tradition surrogate demonstrating this truth.

Occasionally, a trickster will both amuse and touch us in his clash with the facts of our mortality. Never mind that unlike us they—immortal mortals—walk away laughing from brushes with mortality (theirs or another's) or that they somehow repeatedly resurrect themselves from various deaths to play the fool another day in another story; psychologically, they are mortal through and through. They can simultaneously be absurdly irresponsible, myopic, and pathetic in their frailty and mortality. Sometimes a trickster story kicks against earthly constraints. In the Klamath story "Coyote in Love with a Star," Coyote is quite human in his amorous tenacity, even if the desired one is beyond reasonable desire. And when the star takes him into the sky with her only to let him tumble to the earth, we recognize that he has got his comeuppance once more for reaching beyond his limits, but with that acknowledgement there is a twinge of regret that such limits must be and that we must suffer because of them.[7]

In the story Ramsey titles "The Girl Who Married a Ghost," for example, the trickster Blue Jay is killed in a prairie fire when traveling home after visiting his sister in the land of the dead. Returning among the ghosts, now as one of them, Blue Jay continues his high jinks, refusing to believe in the possibility of his own death.[8] Even as we laugh, however, we must feel a touch of pity for such blindness, which fails to accept its own mortality, but we also recognize perhaps that it is self-pity, which turns the laughter on ourselves. Finally, in "Coyote and the Shadow People" (an Orpheus-like story), Coyote—failing to retrieve his wife from the land of the dead because as always his impetuosity makes following directions and self-discipline out of the question—touches us nevertheless, for his lack of restraint grows from his very human longing for his wife.[9]

Of course tricksters are "archaic all-persons" in other ways as well. We have examined in detail how satire in tricksters affirms social order and values. Typically, as tricksters wander from place to place, they never bond themselves to socialized humanity; governed by instinct and dedicated to the self-indulgent pursuit of their own appetites as they are, they possess none of the individual self-discipline and self-awareness that sustain social order and stability. These lascivious, gluttonous, arrogant, disobedient, greedy, cruel, reckless, lazy, clever, tricky, creative, transforming, funny fellows are continually at odds with their societies because they manipulate and violate conventional moral and social expectations and realities, usually from within society itself. They are also often at odds with themselves and with reality, even with the reality that they help create. Because their antisocial, insatiable, libidinous proclivities are in all humans at all times, their foolish behavior establishes the boundaries we must not cross, and our laughter lays the fences at this frontier. Although the humor of the tales is aimed at the protagonist, it is also a warning against imitating his ridiculous excesses—not that it does much good, for we share timelessly and ineradicably some of trickster's inevitable absurdity and fall prey repeatedly to the same vices, often with consequences similar to those that befall him. As Radin concludes, "if we laugh at him, he grins at us. What happens to him happens to us."[10]

The trickster in these latter stories is another face of the same trickster Wiget describes, bringing us full circle to the question that opened chapter 1, the question that has occasioned so much Euro-American scholarship: How can it be that a creative, transforming personage—apparently of mythic stature—is simultaneously buffoon, rogue, and hero or even deity? Whether in their mythic status of power or their comic mode of impotence, tricksters' complexity makes them the very image of the imperfect world itself in all its humming, buzzing, confusing reality, "a symbol of that chaotic Everything" as Toelken and Scott call it (90).[11] According to Vizenor, the Ojibwe trickster Nanabozho "disguises himself in many living things to explain and justify through imagination the conflicts of experience in tribal life."[12]

While I disagree with many of his assumptions and conclusions, Ricketts is correct when he states that trickster stories "are sacred because they establish and explain the reality of things."[13] Tricksters are, indeed, not only creators and agents but also embodiments of reality, the All: reality experienced in finite human perception as equivocal and paradoxical, "the world as we have it," taken by American Indians for what it is.[14] This is a reality in which order, chafing though it may be, is a necessary condition of sacredness even if we do reach that order through disorder; in this world, ritual creates the stability and balance by which humans endure, while one purpose of trickster stories is to imagine order into our lives by demonstrating its absence.[15] Even before human ritual and oral traditions, tricksters were creating order. For many American Indians, what makes an object or experience sacred is its being in its ordered place, whereas that which is out of place is profane and threatens the balance of the entire universe.[16] The Navajo world and ceremonial system come to mind as a prominent example. At first glance then, it would appear that tricksters, apparent enemies of order of any sort, are automatically disqualified from participating in sacredness. But in true contrary fashion, tricksters—by virtue of their wandering, neither in an "ordered place" nor themselves orderly—are nevertheless often the creators of order, and by creating order they create the sacred.

We have seen that trickster-transformers are crucial to shaping the worlds, both natural and social, in which we live. Often, such a trickster's whims and caprices, ungoverned appetites, and psychic disorder lead to power, control, and order even if he is not aiming in that direction. But it is his higgledy-piggledy way of going about things that creates and mirrors the world we end up with, and that leads Ramsey to call the trickster—often discombobulated physically or psychically himself—a piece of do-it-yourself work.[17] Not a skilled or even a very attentive craftsman, this trickster inverts all the customary rules in his haste to realize his own designs—such as they are—to escape some danger he has brought upon himself or simply on an improvisatory whim, and ends up with a new scheme of things. We have already seen how a trickster—even in his buffoonery—might define or affirm the borders that shape and order our lives. In the same way a trickster's wandering, the spontaneous adventure of his travels—whether a physical geographical roaming, a wandering from social expectations, or a psychological wandering—establishes, clarifies, or redefines the limits. It might be recalled, for example, that the Comanche Coyote's infractions make clear what is animal, what is human, and what is supernatural in humans.[18]

Tricksters also dramatize the fact that order and disorder are not the simple, discrete phenomena we might want them to be, for they often flow into and out of each other and may even be two faces of the same reality. True, Nanabozho is a "force in the development of a pattern in the universe."[19] However, while "pattern" might mean design and design might imply order, we must remember that a crazy quilt is a design, as is the quilt pattern called "drunkard's path." Order and balance are among our significant experiences of the known world and the sacred, but sometimes they rest on shifting sands. When the painstakingly made design of a dry painting in a Navajo healing has absorbed the illness-causing powers from a patient, it is destroyed by being scattered; order creates balance and therefore health, so that now the design carries the danger of imbalance. The mystifying relationship between order and disorder—as well as other antithetical traits that tricksters embody—can be seen in the life experience of some American Indian healers. The Lakota spiritual leader Lame Deer claimed:

> A medicine man shouldn't be a saint. He should experience and feel all the ups and downs, the despair and joy, the magic and the reality, the courage and the fear, of his people. He should be able to sink as low as a bug, or soar as high as an eagle. Unless he can experience both, he is no good as a medicine man. . . . You can't get so stuck up, so inhuman that you want to be pure, your soul wrapped up in a plastic bag, all the time. You have to be God and the devil, both of them. Being a good medicine man means being right in the midst of turmoil, not shielding yourself from it. It means experiencing life in all its phases. It means not being afraid of cutting up and playing the fool now and then. That's sacred too. Nature, the Great Spirit—they are not perfect. The world couldn't stand that perfection. The spirit has a good side and a bad side. Sometimes the bad side gives me more knowledge than the good side.[20]

For the Navajos a similar association of the seemingly indiscriminate and the sacred is revealed in Gladys Reichard's depiction of the successful "singer" as one possessing admirable qualities, including intelligence, but "who, until he starts his professional training, is the Navajo idea of a wastrel. He assumes no responsibility. He resists the admonition to marry and settle down. He may work, but he is sometimes lazy, at best unsteady. He is a rover, traveling widely, becoming a professional visitor, usually at a home where there is a desirable girl or a bevy of attractive women. . . . He does not invest such property as he may gain, but spends it in dissipation, particularly gambling, although he may gain by the same means."[21] While Lame Deer and Reichard are describing humans, they are humans with special experience of the sacred; experience that one might say makes them mortal reflections of some of the trickster reality. Indeed, Reichard and Lame Deer could well be describing any number of tricksters. Clearly, in the American Indian perception of reality the disquieting and disorderly are not only integral to life but might also show the way to the sacred.[22]

The All is not, then, some immutable Platonic Ideal, and American Indian tricksters manifest this truth with a vengeance. When a trickster violates a boundary or an ordered place or moment, he is often practicing the essential trick of exposing the substance underlying appearances; that is, he reveals for us the trickiness of reality. Thus Wesucechak's self-transforming powers are consistent with the Cree perception that reality constantly changes.[23] Even the meaning of this trickster's name—"with a double face"—emphasizes the equivocal nature of reality.[24] Like the Lakota Heyoka, tricksters teach us the "'two-faced' nature of all things."[25] The trickster's identification with the constantly metamorphosing world and all of its confusions is suggested in Lincoln's identifying the trickster as a "comic 'changing' spirit who continues the shape shiftings, just as the Mother Earth herself."[26] Brown says that in addition to their moral import, trickster tales dramatize that ours is a shifting world of appearances and not real—that there are other levels of reality.[27] Finally, the Navajo Ma'i always sits by the door of the hogan during the Holy People's meetings concerning creation so that he can ally himself with either side according to his whim.[28]

As Peggy V. Beck says, "Trickster stories tell us that [the trickster's] desires . . . create the world and all the creatures in it."[29] Given the nature of tricksters' desires, what does this tell us about the world? The Kamchadels thought that the god Kutka (who corresponded to Raven) "was very foolish and that he might have arranged things much better when he was creating the world."[30] In central California stories, thought and speech are personified as cosmic creators who craft the world as they think or speak about it. But not even the sacred power of the word is safe in Coyote's world, for his actions undo or reverse these creations.[31] Is it any wonder that we find ourselves sometimes standing in utter confusion in this world? Is it surprising that our world is often paradoxical and bewildering?[32] Some Indians saw their tribal tricksters in a decidedly unfavorable light. A Winnebago member of the Peyote religion (much influenced by Christianity) referred to Wakdjunkaga by the word *Here-shguina*, the Winnebago term for Satan. The Tillamook trickster As'ai'yahal is the master of the country of death. Toelken discusses witchcraft as part of Ma'i's identity.[33]

Still, in spite of humans' perplexity in such a world, many American Indians would probably agree with the Winnebagos, who, according to Radin, saw Wakdjunkaga as representing "the reality of things, that he was a positive force, a builder, not a destroyer."[34] Wenebojo, Frances Densmore wrote, is the master of life: "the source and impersonation of the lives of all sentient things, human, faunal and floral. . . . His 'tricks' were chiefly exhibitions of his ability to outwit the enemies of life. Regarded as the master of ruses, he also possessed great wisdom about prolonging life."[35]

Contrary to current popular stereotypes, there is a decidedly anthro-pocentric element in a number of American Indian people's origin stories, including those in which a trickster is a creator. In the latter we can see another difference between the Judeo-Christian and at least some American Indian worldviews: the Judeo-Christian origin myth shows us a world originally created in perfect harmony with humans but made imperfect by humanity's Fall. Many American Indian stories, however, depict an early prehuman world that is, from a human point of view, imperfect. The trickster transforms the world so that it is more suitable for the humans who are to come or are already present. The Blackfoot origin myth, for instance, tells us that initially humans were hunted by buffalo, but Old Man taught the people how to hunt the buffalo instead. Other tricksters—like the Kiowa Sendeh and the Clacka-mas Coyote—release animals into the world so that humans have them available as food.[36] The Crow Old Man Coyote creates or causes to be created many phenomena of the human world: the sweat lodge, pem-mican, flint and stone for fire, the horse drag, the tipi, the practice of women dancing when men return from war. In brief, the material accoutrements of culture and human activities are his doing.[37]

Tricksters shape the world we live in so that it fits humans. This world has what we perceive as flaws, but they are a necessary part of reality and are essential to human experience. In a few American Indian oral traditions, the preexisting myth world or the newly created world possesses an Eden-like perfection, but a trickster's interference with the creator's efforts results in our familiar difficult world. The Coyote of the Maidu, Wintun, Yana, Pit River, and Shasta traditions opposes Earthmaker's intention to make humanity's life in this world easy and deathless.[38] His reasoning is (irony of ironies from this wag) that he wants "to make people take life seriously."[39] The trickster contradicts the creator in other ways as well. For example, he guarantees that there will be sexual intercourse, that unmarried girls will sometimes have babies, and that women will have a hard time in childbirth.[40] Similarly, the Comanche Coyote's Elder Brother Wolf creates a perfect world, but Coyote will have none of it and transforms it into a human world, or as Buller puts it, "transforms the natural order into a cultural one."[41] We do not always understand or appreciate the logic—if any—that makes such a trickster world appropriate for people, but it is the only world we have been given.

It is no coincidence that, of all the mythic figures of various tribes' oral traditions, tricksters are the ones most prominently still wandering about, experiencing the contemporary world. As a force or presence in our world, they are not relegated to a mythic past. Clearly, they embody a satisfactory image of reality. In our time tricksters generally seem to carry traditional meanings and associations, but with a difference. That Coyote is still a trickster-transformer can be seen in a Comanche story in which he establishes trade between the People and whites.[42] Of course, he is also perpetuated in his role as comic bungler and loser. Agnes Grant reports that among her Cree and Ojibwe students, and one presumes among their families, oral stories are often "modernized" so that Trickster's "song bag" is a tape recorder. Noting the popularity of country and western music and in particular Hank Snow's cover of "Your Cheating Heart," she tells of a story in which Wee-sak-ee-chak loses a contest to a Windigo (a cannibalistic monster). "[A]lways a poor loser, [the trickster] is still complaining about the unfair tactics of the Windigo, and his wailing of 'Your Cheating Heart' can be heard across the north."[43] But often in modern stories the old associations are not what are stressed. The difference comes in tricksters' confrontation of white incursions. Relatively early in Native experience with the invaders, tricksters assumed a new role.

In the nineteenth and twentieth centuries, Trickster adapted to and met the needs of Native America, most importantly showing the People how to survive in the reality that Euro-Americans have created on this continent (a reality contrary to his creation). A Winnebago/Menominee story tells of men seeking out Wenebojo's aid after the arrival of traders changes their lifestyle.[44] Among the Comanches, stories of Coyote's dealing with whites show him to be a "savior" for Comanches: "a way of escaping emotionally from the trauma of White intrusion."[45] A Brule story shows Coyote tricking a white trader who thinks he can outsmart the trickster.[46] Often a trickster's shenanigans illuminate whites' immorality. Wiget aptly points out that Trickster is just as effectual at assailing the cultural weaknesses of the European invaders as at revealing the creaks and cracks in Indian societies. For example, he discusses a Plains Cree trickster story that attacks the connection between religion and the fur trade by depicting Wisahketchak preaching to the wolves and foxes and then serving a poisoned "communion" as a way of getting pelts.[47] In a Diegueno story, Coyote carries off—and, of course, eats—chickens under the pretense of baptizing them, clearly a trenchant commentary on the conversion practices and quite likely also the predatory nature of many Catholic missions and perhaps later Protestant missionaries.[48]

More recently, the writing of many contemporary American Indians casts Trickster as savior, survivor, and satirical swindler of the white world.[49] To be sure, many poets and fictionalists present their tricksters in traditional roles. In *Storyteller* Silko tells the traditional story of the coyotes and the Stro'ro'ka ka'tsinas. Here we see a whole bevy of coyotes demonstrating the traditional trickster's foolishness. In order to get to the picnic baskets of ka'tsina dancers, the coyotes try to make a coyote chain from the top of a cliff, each coyote holding the tail of another in its mouth. The effort proceeds well until one of the coyotes farts.[50] *Elderberry Flute Song* is filled with Blue Cloud's Coyote stories—some his creations, some retellings of traditional sorts of episodes, but all with the familiar shape-shifting, deceiving, foolish, lecherous protagonist.

"Coyote/Iktomi," by S. D. Nelson (Lakota). Reproduced by permission of the artist.

Other contemporary Indian writers create new tricksters who reflect tradition. Joy Harjo's Noni is tricksterlike (with a "feminine twist") in her constant motion and freedom from time and space, her sexuality, a "creative/destructive dualism," and her shape-shifting.[51] Erdrich's Gerry Nanapush in *Love Medicine* is an Indian outlaw who, because no white prison can hold him and he repeatedly escapes, is constantly on the run. He shares with his namesake prodigious gustatory and sexual appetites. Like a trickster, he is able to satisfy his sexual longings no matter what the impediments, as when he impregnates his girlfriend during her visit to him in prison under the watchful eye of the prison security camera. Trickster also appears as Potchikoo in Erdrich's poems. Although not a traditionally named trickster, Potchikoo lives up to the reputation of his forebears. He falls in love with a cigar-store Indian maiden who eventually comes to life and becomes his wife, Josette.[52] Once, he has such ardent sex with Josette that he burns his penis to a charred twiglike thing.[53] Another time, when he is sexually aroused by the sight of breastlike rocks in mud, he ends up rubbing the stones and having sex with the mud.[54]

Nevertheless, for many writers Trickster's mission in the modern world is as a guerilla warrior and shaper in the name of American Indian survival. In Robert J. Conley's *The Way of the Priests* a trickster does not make an actual appearance; however, his influence is present when a Cherokee character escapes from Indians who have enslaved him by imitating the escape of Jisdu, the rabbit trickster, from wolves.[55] Many American Indians exhibit a heartening optimism about the survival of Native peoples: "As Native people we have always been and we will always, always, be here."[56] Trickster may well be regarded as a symbol of the courageous, adaptive survival of Native America as a whole. Silko's Toe'osh (the Laguna Coyote) manifests himself in the Laguna people themselves as they make the Trans-Western pipeline vice president, seeking right-of-way, wait all day for a conference with him and then tell him to return the next day and, another time, as they take politicians' gift hams and turkeys in return for promising their votes but then stay home on election day and laugh.[57] Coyote in Thomas King's *Green Grass, Running Water* is a comic interloper challenging the dominant culture's worldviews in various ways. Vizenor's contemporary tricksters are mixed-blood survivors.[58] In his early writings tricksters are representative of mixed bloods on whom the survival of American Indian cultures rests. They "must learn better how to balance the forces of good and evil through humor in the urban world."[59] In Ojibwe poet Kateri Damm's "Poem Without End," along with all the familiar trickiness, creativity, and scatology, Nanabush is an English professor writing unread books, a stingy landlord and noisy party-animal tenant, a singer, a female heavy-metal drummer, a trapper, a speaker of the archaic, an earthdiver, and much more.[60] And Chris LaLonde has linked the protagonist of Louis Owens's *Wolfsong* to Trickster.[61]

Not all of Trickster's appearances after contact with the Europeans have been ameliorative. Bright points out that the term "coyote" is applied by Indians in the Southwest and Mexico to "'half-breeds' or Spanish-speaking mestizos." It is also applied to "migrant labor brokers" who smuggle illegal immigrants into the southwestern United States, "sometimes to their death in the desert, if not into the hands of the U.S. immigration authorities."[62] And finally, Iktomi fills his traditional role of deceitful enemy of the Lakotas in Zitkala-Sa's "The School Days of an Indian Girl" when he "wears the mask of a U.S. Government agent responsible for enforcing the Indian Removal and Reservation policies" and the policies of acculturation.[63] Such instances are not incongruous with the trickster tradition. On the contrary, they continue to express American Indian awareness of how Trickster manifests both the light and the dark of human experience.

All in all, tricksters carry on their equivocal and paradoxical ways in the modern world. Regardless of which trickster we look at—the transformer or the announcer or the buffoon or the deceiving and deceived dupe or the dramatization of our polyvalent world—there is no doubt that he, and, of course, sometimes she, stands in the minds of American Indians as the embodiment and shaper of but also as the foil to reality and as a living, ever-present force. Perhaps for most American Indians, as for Yellowman, tricksters realize possibility and abstraction in the form of actual and concrete human experience.[64] In doing so they are essential to our encounter with the world. It is no accident that tricksters—confronting and sometimes confounding life—die but are resurrected repeatedly in time for another story. In a Maidu story, try as they will, people cannot kill Coyote, while in two Navajo stories, Coyote is intentionally resurrected by the gods.[65] It appears that willy-nilly, we must have Coyote.

Coyote Sells the Money Tree

Coyote . . . came to a peach tree. He swept the ground clean under it. He sat there and thought of tricks to play.

He got up. He looked up in the tree, wondering what to do. He finally thought of a plan. He climbed the tree. On every fork he put a piece of money. Then he came down and shook the branches. Some money fell down. You could hear it hit the ground. He picked up the money and put it in the tree again. Then he sat there.

Some people came along. They came up to Coyote. "Why do you sit there?" they asked.

"Because this tree belongs to me. Some money grows up on these branches. But I'll sell it to anyone who wants a tree like this."

"Let's see the money," said the people. "Prove that this tree bears money."

"All right," he said. He went to the tree and shook it a little. Money came falling down.

"See!" said Coyote. "It is as I said. That's why I stay here. But if anyone wants it, I'll sell it."

One man decided to buy the tree. He said, "I have to go on my journey. When I come back I'll buy it. Will it still bear money later if I buy it?"

"Why, yes. You know how fruit trees are. They bear fruit every summer. That's just how this tree is."

These people continued on their journey. Then they returned to Coyote and his tree. The man wanted to know whether it would still bear money.

Coyote had felt that it was near the time for these people to return. He had gone and put mony [sic] there again. Then when these people came back they wanted to see money fall from it again. Coyote shook the tree as before and the money came down. "See," he said, "that's the way it is always."

Then the man was convinced and wanted to buy the tree. "All right, how much to you want for it?" He offered Coyote a good price.

Coyote said, "Now this is your tree. I sold it to you. You must keep the ground clean beneath it. When the wind blows at night the money will fall down, for some of it is very ripe. And you must stay right here. I'm going on my way now."

The one who had bought the pot [another scheme of Coyote's preceding this episode] made up his mind that he was going to catch the coyote who had fooled him. He found a partner. They came to this tree and met the man who had been fooled also. This man said, "I just bought this tree from Coyote. He told me the tree would bear money and he went out this way." This man had a partner too. So the four of them went after Coyote.

Those who were trailing him came to these camps too. They met Coyote. They said, "We have come to take someone back." They didn't know they were talking to the same man.

"Wait, I'll make some medicine for you so you'll easily find the man you are looking for," Coyote told them.

He got some mountain-laurel out and pounded it. He gave this to them to eat. It was bitter but they ate it anyway. They got dizzy and drunk. The saliva ran out of their mouths. While they were drunk Coyote cut their hair in different ways. He called, "Ahau! Here are some enemies who have their hair cut in funny ways!"

Then he headed for another place. They had a good chance to catch him, but he got the best of them again.

Morris Edward Opler, *Myths and Legends of the Lipan Apache Indians*, 164–65. Originally published by J. J. Augustin, 1940; reprinted with permission of the American Folklore Society.

Saynday and Smallpox: The White Man's Gift

Saynday was coming along, and as he came he saw that all his world had changed. Where the buffalo herds used to graze, he saw white-faced cattle. The Washita River, which once ran bankful with clear water, was soggy with red mud. There were no deer or antelope in the brush or skittering across the high plains. No white tipis rose proudly against the blue sky; settlers' soddies dented the hillsides and the creek banks.

My time has come, Saynday thought to himself. The world I lived in is dead. Soon the Kiowa people will be fenced like the white man's cattle, and they cannot break out of fences because the barbed wire will tear their flesh. I can't help my people any longer by staying with them. My time has come, and I will have to go away from this changed world.

Off across the prairie, Saynday saw a dark spot coming toward him from the east, moving very slowly.

That's strange too, Saynday thought to himself. The East is the place of birth and new life. The things that come from the East come quickly; they come dancing and alive. This thing comes slowly as death to an old man. I wonder what it is?

Almost absent-mindedly, Saynday started walking eastward. As he went the spot grew larger, and after a while Saynday saw that it was a man on a horse.

The horse was black, but it had been powdered to roan with the red dust that the plows had stirred up when they slashed the open plains. Red dust spotted the man's clothing—a black suit and a high hat, like a missionary's. Red dust blurred his features, but behind the dust Saynday could see that the man's face was pitted with terrible scars.

The stranger drew rein, and sat looking at Saynday. The black roan horse lifted one sore hoof and drooped its head as if it were too weary to carry its burden any further.

"Who are you?" the stranger asked.

"I'm Saynday. I'm the Kiowas' Old Uncle Saynday. I'm the one who's always coming along."

"I never heard of you," the stranger said, "and I never heard of the Kiowas. Who are they?"

"The Kiowas are my people," Saynday said and even in that hard time he stood up proudly, like a man. "Who are you?"

"I'm Smallpox," the man answered.

"And I never heard of *you*," said Saynday. "Where do you come from and what do you do and why are you here?"

"I come from far away, across the Eastern Ocean," Smallpox answered. "I am one with the white men—they are my people as the Kiowas are yours. Sometimes I travel ahead of them, and sometimes I lurk behind. But I am always their companion and you will find me in their camps and in their houses."

"What do you do?" Saynday repeated.

"I bring death," Smallpox replied. "My breath causes children to wither like young plants in spring snow. I bring destruction. No matter how beautiful a woman is, once she has looked at me she becomes ugly as death. And to men I bring not death alone, but the destruction of their children and the blighting of their wives. The strongest warriors go down before me. No people who have looked on me will ever be the same." And he chuckled low and hideously. With his raised forearm, Smallpox pushed the dust off his face, and Saynday saw the scars that disfigured it.

For a moment Saynday shut his eyes against the sight, and then he opened them again. "Does that happen to all the people you visit?" he inquired.

"Every one of them," said Smallpox." It will happen to your Kiowa people, too. Where do they live? Take me to them, and then I will spare you, although you have seen my face. If you do not lead me to your people, I will breathe on you and you will die, no matter whose Old Uncle you are." And although he did not breathe on Saynday, Saynday smelled the reek of death that surrounded him.

"My Kiowa people are few and poor already," Saynday said, thinking fast as he talked. "They aren't worth your time and trouble."

"I have time and I don't have to take any trouble," Smallpox told him. "Even one person whom I blot out, I can count."

"Oh," said Saynday. "Some of your ways are like the Kiowas', then. You count the enemies you touch."

"I have no enemies," said Smallpox. "Man, woman, or child—humanity is all alike to me. I was brought here to kill. But, yes, I can count those I destroy. White men always count: cattle, sheep, chickens, children, the living and the dead. You say the Kiowas do the same thing?"

"Only the enemies they touch," Saynday insisted. "They never count living people—men are not cattle, any more than women and children are."

"Then how do you know the Kiowas are so few and poor?" Smallpox demanded.

"Oh, anybody can see that for himself," Saynday said. "You can look at a Kiowa camp and tell how small it is. We're not like the Pawnees.

They have great houses, half underground, in big villages by the rivers, and every house is full of people."

"I like that," Smallpox observed. "I can do my best work when people are crowded together."

"Then you'd like the Pawnees," Saynday assured him. "They're the ones that almost wiped out the Kiowas; that's why we're so few and so poor. Now we run away whenever we see a stranger coming because he might be a Pawnee."

"I suppose the Pawnees never run away," Smallpox sneered.

"They couldn't if they wanted to," Saynday replied. "The Pawnees are rich. They have piles of robes, they have lots of cooking pots and plenty of bedding—they keep all kinds of things in those underground houses of theirs. The Pawnees can't run away and leave all their wealth."

"Where did you say they live?" Smallpox asked thoughtfully.

"Oh, over there," Saynday said, jerking his chin to the north.

"And they are rich, and live in houses, with piles of robes to creep into and hide?"

"That's the Pawnees," Saynday said jauntily. He began to feel better. The deathly smell was not so strong now. "I think I'll go and visit the Pawnees first," Smallpox remarked. "Later on, perhaps, I can get back to the Kiowas."

"You do that," directed Saynday. "Go and visit the Pawnees and when you grow tired there from all the work you have to do, come back and visit my poor people. They'll do all they can for you."

"Good," said Smallpox. He picked up his reins and jerked his weary horse awake. "Tell your people when I come to be ready for me. Tell them to put out all their fires. Fire is the only thing in the whole world that I'm afraid of. It's the only thing in God's world that can destroy me."

Saynday watched Smallpox and his death horse traveling north, away from the Kiowas. Then he took out his flint and steel, and set fire to the spindly prairie grass at his feet. The winds came and picked up the fire, and carried it to make a ring of safety around the Kiowas' camps.

"Perhaps I can still be some good to my people after all," Saynday said to himself, feeling better.

And that's the way it was, and that's the way it is, to this good day.

Notes

Ojibwe Creation

This episode from the Ojibwe creation story is of a type called "earthdiver," a common sort of American Indian origin story. Nanabush is stranded in a tree because of a great deluge caused by his killing the underwater creature Michibizieu, who had killed Nanabush's wolf-nephew. He (usually) directs four animals—such as Otter, Loon, Beaver, Muskrat—to dive into the flood in order to bring up some mud, out of which he will create a new world. (As in many other American Indian cultures, the number four is sacred among the Ojibwes). The first three animals fail, but the fourth, Muskrat, is successful. In this translation Echlin allowed some awkward English word order in order to reflect the style of the original telling in Ojibwe (Echlin, personal communication). In the article from which this episode is taken, Echlin's translation is followed by a printed Ojibwe-language version using English orthography. In her discussion preceding the translation, Echlin identifies the story as an *aadisokan,* a sacred story. Nanabush, she writes, "reestablishes the link between himself and the animals by making them helpers in creation" (30). *Taiya* is apparently an untranslatable word. *Kuniginin* is "In an Ojibway context the breath which creates earth . . . also associated with sacred forms of breathing (blowing) in the Midiwiwin rites, foregrounded stylistically by the word kuniginin which is ancient and used only in myth-telling" (Echlin, "Ojibway," 30). *Manidoog* are spirits present not only in all natural phenomena but also in "life circumstances like poverty and parenthood" (Gill and Sullivan, *Dictionary,* "Manitou," 179). Alternative spellings include *manidog, manito,* and *manitou.*

INTRODUCTION

1. Chapter 4 makes clear that some stories have female tricksters as protagonists; however, in most of this book I refer to tricksters as male simply because the majority of trickster stories have male protagonists. Erdrich, *Baptism of*

Desire: Poems; Jacklight; Love Medicine; Blue Cloud, *Elderberry Flute Song: Contemporary Coyote Tales.*

2. Krupat, *Ethnocriticism,* 30.

3. Sarris, *Keeping,* 90.

4. "But what constitutes 'an Indian point of view'? By what and whose definition is a point of view 'Indian'?" Sarris, *Keeping,* 112.

5. Pelton, *The Trickster,* 18.

6. Clements, "Identity," 1–2.

7. Quoted in Clements, "Identity," 3.

8. Boas, "An Introduction," 314.

9. Ahenakew, "Cree Trickster Tales." On the other hand Ahenakew's Cree consultant might have inserted the Christian elements. Bloomfield recorded a Sweet Grass Cree origin story in which Wisahketchak (same character, different spelling), after killing Chief Fish, is told by "The Lord" that the world will be flooded. God also tells him to build a canoe and to take as passengers a male and female of each animal. Later God "descends" and tells the trickster to scrape up some earth so the waters will recede. There follows a traditional American Indian earthdiver story in which four different animals dive into the flood to retrieve mud for the creation of a new world. God later creates humans as companions for Wisahketchak (*Sacred,* 18–19).

10. Hymes, "Foreward" in Basso, *Portrait,* xi, xiii.

11. Craig Thompson, "Gender," 36, 23.

12. Moreover, no two listeners will hear the same version of a story from the same storyteller. Sands, "Narrative," 7, 13. Andrew Wiget discusses related issues in the context of American Indian tricksters in "His Life in His Tail," 92–93. Wiget's essay draws upon Babcock-Abrahams and the school of trickster thought she generated—both of which I criticize. Nevertheless, his essay is well grounded in American Indian cultures, making it both reliable and informative.

Throughout this study, I will use Dundes's definition of the term *text:* "one version of a single telling of a tale" ("Texture, Text and Context," 255).

13. Gill, *Native,* 49. The pitfalls of translating American Indian texts into English have been much discussed. For those unfamiliar with the issue, it is worth pursuit beyond my brief comments. Ruoff's discussion in *American Indian Literatures* (6–17) is a good place to begin. The essays on translation in Swann, ed., *Smoothing the Ground,* and Karl Kroeber, ed., *Traditional American Indian Literatures* are essential. See also Ramsey's defense of basing interpretations on translations in *Reading the Fire,* xvii–xviii.

14. Quoted in Ramsey, *Reading,* 48.

15. E. Grant, "He Walks in Two Worlds," 25.

16. Ramsey, *Reading,* 4.

17. Roberts, "The African," 99; Melville Jacobs, *The Content,* 249–50.

18. Levi-Strauss, "The Structural," 210.

19. We should also note that trickster stories in many American Indian cultures were commonly told in winter only: The Ojibwes, for example, have traditionally told Naanabozho stories only in the winter because in the summer that trickster might be lurking about listening. Winter is the proper time for telling these stories, for Naanabozho "is not likely to be around as a plant or a small animal" (Vizenor, *Summer,* 156).

20. Quoted in Pope, "Toward," 282.

21. "His Life," 88–89. Wiget also points out that trickster stories make use of what folklorists have called types: Bungling Host, Eye Juggler, Foolish Imitation, and so forth. For a more detailed discussion of these matters in trickster tales, readers are advised to refer to Wiget's essay.

22. Buller, "Comanche," 253.

23. Morrow, "Oral," 20.

24. Radin, *The Trickster,* 118.

25. Alfred L. Kroeber, *Gros Ventre,* 59.

26. George A. Dorsey, *The Mythology,* 20–21, 27.

27. Hulkrantz, "Religious," 554–55.

28. George A. Dorsey, *The Pawnee,* 10–11. Some other American Indian cultures also do not place trickster stories among myths—that is, true stories. For example the northern Iroquoians, whose trickster stories are borrowed from neighboring Algonquian tribes, classify them as fiction (Day and Foster, "The Northeastern," 77).

29. Toelken, "Coyote," 591.

30. Zolbrod, "Singing," 617.

31. Dennis Tedlock, "Pueblo," 222–23.

32. Melville Jacobs, *Northwest,* 14.

33. Similarly, stories commonly conclude with a formula, such as the Delaware phrase, "This is my story, an ancient one" or "I break it off," as the storyteller breaks a stick across his or her knee. Bierhorst, "Tales," 491.

34. Toelken and Scott, "Poetic," 112 n.12.

35. Ella Deloria, *Dakota,* 8.

36. Radin, *The Trickster,* 134–45.

37. Melville Jacobs, *Clackamas,* 80–106.

38. Buller, "Comanche," 250.

39. Brightman, "Tricksters," 186.

40. Watermann, "The Explanatory," 39. Readers might find it useful to review Ramsey's definition of "myth" quoted earlier in this chapter.

41. Similarly, the Navajos regard holy places like the volcanic plug called Shiprock as witnesses to the truth of myth and ritual (Toelken, "The Demands," 65).

42. Levi-Strauss, *The Savage*, 95.

43. For examples of indirection among American Indians in teaching-learning situations, see Buckley, "Doing Your Thinking," 36–52.

44. Toelken and Scott, "Poetic," 72–73. For further discussion of the indirectness and allusiveness of American Indian oral creations, see Underhill, *Papago Woman*, 46, 10–11, and Melville Jacobs, *Content and Style*, 21.

45. Allen, *The Sacred*, 241–42; Ramsey, *Reading*, 4.

46. Alfred L. Kroeber, *Gros Ventre*, 68–69.

1. ON SCHOLARS AND WANDERING

For a detailed historical summary of scholarship on world tricksters see Hynes and Doty, "Historical Overview of the Theoretical Issues."

1. Lowie, *The Crow*, 7.

2. Brinton, *Myths*. "Wenebojo," "Winabojo," "Nanabozho," "Nanibozhu," "Nanabush," "Manabozho" are all one and the same Algonquian trickster. Some of the variant forms are obviously only different spellings; others are culturally specific. In any event I use whichever spelling/variant my sources have used.

Readers will also note that I use *Trickster* when I bow to convention and refer to a general character type. I use *trickster(s)* in all other instances.

At least one more recent scholar makes an argument similar to Brinton's. In "Religious Aspects of the Wind River Shoshoni Folk Literature," Ake Hultkrantz says that the Shoshoni Coyote was once an exalted divine being (566). Interestingly, one American Indian oral tradition makes a similar claim about a trickster. By his foolish actions, the Menominee tradition says, the trickster Manabush degraded himself from his hero's status. He finally left Indian country. (See Hoffman, *The Menominee*, 161–62.) As far as I know, there is no evidence that this is a widely spread notion among American Indian oral traditions.

3. Mooney, *Myths*, 232–33.

4. Boas, "An Introduction," 10.

5. Jung, "On the Psychology," 200, 204, 209.

6. Ibid., 201–2.

7. Radin, *The Trickster*, xxiii–xxiv.

8. Ricketts, "The North," 329.

9. Ibid., 334.

10. Ibid.

11. Ibid., 349.

12. Ricketts, "The Shaman," 95.

13. Ibid., 92. One wonders, then, at Ricketts's continued devotion to his shaman argument. This more recent qualification acknowledges that tricksters are, indeed, satirical representations of all overreaching humans, not just shamans.

We should also remember many tricksters' relationship to animals. In chapter 3 I argue in more detail against this aspect of Rickett's argument.

14. Ricketts, "The Shaman," 87–88.

15. Ibid., 91.

16. Levi-Strauss, "The Structural," *Structural*, 226.

17. Diamond, "Introduction," xiii.

18. Levi-Strauss, "The Structural," *Structural*, 230. Douglas argues that the real difference between the "primitive" mind and the modern "civilized" mind is that the latter does not carry the same set of powerful symbols from one context to another; its experience is fragmented (*Purity*, 69). Hence, we might observe, the source of our difficulty in holding tricksters' many paradoxes and multi-leveled experiences in mind.

19. Babcock-Abrahams, "A Tolerated," 150.

20. Ibid.

21. Ibid., 148.

22. Ibid., 164.

23. Ibid., 185.

24. To her credit, Babcock-Abrahams addresses the problems in definition and use that terms such as *marginality* present, yet she rides the figure nevertheless (as have many after her). For a more detailed criticism of Babcock-Abrahams's use of "marginality," see my article "Living Sideways." We run into a similar problem when we apply a term such as *liminal* to tricksters, as Babcock-Abrahams and others have done. (See "A Tolerated," 150.) This term is extracted from discussions of ritual (or those aspects of some oral traditions that have reference to ritual) and then applied to nonritualistic circumstances. The concept of liminality carried to its conclusion as Victor Turner develops it in *Ritual Process* has no real bearing on First People's tricksters.

25. Babcock-Abrahams, "A Tolerated," 159–60.

26. Levi-Strauss, *The Savage*, 16–17.

27. Ramsey, *Reading*, 41. Levi-Strauss says that the bricoleur "is adept at performing a large number of tasks . . . [However, h]is universe of instruments is closed and the rules of his game are always to make do with 'whatever is at hand,' that is to say with a set of tools and materials which is always finite . . . the 'bricoleur' by inclination or necessity always remains within [the constraints imposed by a particular state of civilization]" (*Savage*, 16–19). A closed universe of instruments, a finite set of tools and materials, constrained by a particular state of civilization—these hardly seem concepts applicable to the mythic figure Ramsey is talking about. However, as I discuss in chapter 2, tricksters in their transformer roles do, indeed, often make do with what is at hand.

28. Ramsey, *Reading*, 41.

29. Ibid., 42.

30. Ibid., 39.

31. Ibid., 38.

32. Babcock-Abrahams, "A Tolerated," 166.

33. Ibid., 154.

34. Robert Frost, "Education," 334.

35. For a detailed discussion of the differences between Euro-American picaros and American Indian tricksters, see Ballinger, "Ambigere."

36. Ramsey, *Reading,* 31.

37. Doueihi, "Trickster," 288. While I agree with the general thrust of Doueihi's argument, I think that we must be careful not to deny the mythic significance tricksters often carry. Many are not all buffoon.

38. For similar assertions developed in more detail, see Doueihi, 292, 294, 297; Gill and Sullivan, "Trickster(s)," 310; and Ramsey, "Thoreau's Last Words," 53. To test these arguments, readers are invited to consider Radin's Jungian treatment of the Winnebago trickster Wakdjunkaga or the wide influence of Levi-Strauss's theories of Coyote as a mediator. For a recent example of the manhandling of trickster through application of European theory, see Clasby's "'Manabozho,' which develops an "archetypal" reading of Henry Rowe School-craft's literary version of Manabozho stories. Another clear instance of seeing tricksters with anything but Native eyes is Hubbard's "Trickster, Renewal, and Survival." Hubbard draws upon C. G. Jung, Northrup Frye, Alfred Koestler, even Lao Tzu, Chinese ideograms, and a hint of Judeo-Christian origin cosmology, and makes little reference to American Indian culture.

39. Radin, *The Trickster,* 169.

40. Douglas, *Purity,* 53.

41. Diamond, "Introduction," xii–xiii.

42. Luckert, "Coyote," 4.

43. Radin, *The Trickster,* 169.

44. Levi-Strauss, "The Structural," 441.

45. Stern, "Some Sources," 8. Interestingly, however, once these people became absorbed in the stories, all doubts seem to vanish. Experience and immediacy trump ambiguity.

46. Radin, "Trickster," 173.

47. Radin, ed., *Crashing,* 201–2.

48. Babcock-Abrahams, "A Tolerated," 148.

49. When Ojibwe listeners laughed at a trickster story, the storyteller would interrupt himself to say, "Nanibozhu is also smiling and pleased because his great exploits are admired" (Chamberlain, "Nanibozhu," 195).

50. Quoted in Bright, *A Coyote,* 20–21. However, W. W. and Dorothy Hill claimed that in Navajo stories there are two coyote roles: In the emergence

myth, Coyote is a Holy Being; in "trotting or travelling coyote" stories, he is a trickster ("Navaho Coyote Tales," 3). The Cheyennes seem to have dealt with the issue by relegating tales of low comedy and violence to *Wihio,* "whereas creation stories were told of *Heammawihio*" (Bierhorst, *The Mythology,* 14).

51. Melville Jacobs, *The Content,* 151.

52. The traditional Indo-European dualism of good/evil, hero/villain does not as a rule appear in American Indian tales (Dundes, *Morphology,* 72).

53. Yava, "Way Back," 10–11. Like the New Mexico Pueblo tribes, the Hopis believe they emerged into this world from an underworld.

54. Spencer, *Mythology,* 2, 3.

55. Babcock-Abrahams, "A Tolerated," 148.

56. Gill, *Native,* 26.

57. "We must understand that . . . American Indian views of reality are not static structures . . . but tend to incorporate the many dynamic and conflicting elements that are inseparable from the nature of human life" (Gill, *Native,* 26). A trickster's power to transform himself, the animal being only one aspect of his being (Radin, *The Trickster,* 165), reinforces our perception of him as an image of many-sidedness. In his treatment of West African tricksters, Pelton uses the term *multivalence* to convey a similar concept. He also portrays the West African trickster as "a sort of inspired handyman tacking together the bits and pieces of experience until they become what they are—a web of many-layered being" (*The Trickster,* 4). In chapter 2 I consider other aspects of tricksters' wandering.

58. Vine Deloria, *God,* 201.

59. Luckert, "Coyote," 17.

Coyote and Eagle Part.
Coyote Kills the Swallowing Monster and a Soft Basket Person

This story was told to Melville Jacobs in September 1927. He does not identify the storyteller but does identify the interpreter as Peter McGuff (Melville Jacobs, *Northwest,* 66). The "words in parentheses are implied but unexpressed in the native and are added because they seem necessary for the intelligibility of the translation." When Coyote shouts his challenges, the narrator used a pulsing basso monotone chant (Melville Jacobs, *Northwest,* 65, 66). Jacobs explains the sister-in-law reference in "How are you, sister-in-law?" as a reference to an "in-law, after the decease of the kin intermediary" (Melville Jacobs's note, *Northwest,* 66). Apparently in this case the deceased kin is the first dangerous being. Jacobs offers no explanation of what or who a Soft-basket Person was. Among some tribes of Oregon and Washington five is a sacred number. Jacobs included paragraph and sentence numbers to correspond to parts of the Indian texts.

2. A TRICKSTER BY ANY OTHER NAME

1. Wiget, "His Life," 86–87.

2. Nothing in these paragraphs should be read as meaning that I avoid broad, encompassing assertions about tricksters. When facts and circumstances warrant generalization—always a risky business—I will refer to Trickster rather than a trickster, but readers are hereby warned to keep at hand and liberally insert a well-stocked supply of qualifiers (*in many instances, usually, often, commonly,* and so forth).

3. George Wasson, "Susan." I share Wasson's discomfort with the name "trickster"; however, I have not discovered a creative and suitable substitute. "Reverend Rascal" is good but unwieldy, so for the time being I will continue to use the conventional and convenient "trickster."

4. Bright, *A Coyote,* 4.

5. Kinkade, "Native," 34, 38; Clark, *Indian,* 82; Stern, "The Trickster," 163–64.

6. Stith Thompson, *The Folktale,* 326.

7. Alfred L. Kroeber, *Yurok,* xxxi.

8. Boas, *Tsimshian,* 584.

9. George A. Dorsey, *The Pawnee,* 10–11. Probably Wolf rather than Coyote was used as the trickster's name among the Pawnees.

10. Luckert, "Coyote," 17.

11. Ricketts, "The North," 328.

12. Velie, *Four,* 131.

13. Wiget, "His Life," 90–91.

14. Gill and Sullivan, *Dictionary,* "Trickster(s)," 308.

15. Marriott and Rachlin, *Saynday's,* 1.

16. James R. Walker, *Lakota Belief,* 101, 106). As with other specific tricksters, the Spider's names vary in other Siouan tribes: Inktomi, Inktumi, Ictinike, Sitconski.

17. Hoffman, *The Menominee,* 87.

18. Barnouw, *Wisconsin,* 85.

19. George A. Dorsey and A. L. Kroeber, *Traditions,* 7. Interestingly, Nih'a[n]ca[n] also means "white man" and, at least in the late nineteenth and early twentieth centuries, was ordinarily applied to Euro-Americans. The same is true of the Cheyenne trickster Vihuk (Alfred L. Kroeber, "Cheyenne," 165).

20. Levi-Strauss, *Structural,* 224.

21. Schwartz, *The Wild,* 264; Whitaker, *The Audubon,* 537. Ma'i, the Navajo Coyote, is treated as a predator in Navajo stories (Toelken and Scott, "Poetic," 99).

22. Ryden, *God's,* 150.

23. Bright, *A Coyote,* 4.

24. Ibid., 22–23.

25. Ryden, *God's*, 22.

26. Bright, *A Coyote*, 82–83, 88.

27. Ryden, *God's*, 67, 69.

28. Ibid., 20, 78.

29. Schwartz, *The Wild*, 263; Whitaker, *The Audubon*, 537; Ryden, *God's*, 82, 201.

30. Ryden, *God's*, 203.

31. Bright, *A Coyote*, 104.

32. Ryden, *God's*, ix–x.

33. Radin, *The Trickster*, xxiv.

34. Toelken and Scott, "Poetic," 92, 103–4, 112.

35. Kroeber, *Yurok*, 69.

36. Buller, "Comanche," 247.

37. Gill and Sullivan, *Dictionary*, "Wesucechak," 334; Swanton, *Haida*, 146.

38. Chamberlain, "Nanibozhu," 210–11.

39. Hallowell, "Ojibway," 35–38.

40. Barnouw, *Wisconsin*, 160.

41. Bright, *A Coyote*, xi–xii.

42. Echlin, "Ojibway," 30.

43. Chapman, "The Belly," 16.

44. To be sure, trickster stories are often told to children as exempla, but they have adult uses and purposes as well.

45. Ramsey, *Reading*, 35. Taking a psychoanalytic approach, Ramsey says "Tricksters may be said to mediate as unstable ego-formations between Id and Superego" (*Reading*, 35). Ramsey also sees the presence of a culture hero and a buffoon in Takelma oral tradition as a resolution to the apparent ambiguity or dualism of tricksters: Doldal (Dragonfly) a "straight," virtuous transformer and hero, is doubled with a younger brother who is wholly trickster, always into mischief that Doldal must straighten out. Thus "contradictions inherent in Coyote are resolved in a kind of literary meiosis; in many Indian mythologies . . . one or more sets of twins are prominent actors, representing the fundamental duality of human life" (Ramsey, ed., *Coyote*, 262 n.18).

46. Boas, "An Introduction," 414–15.

47. Wilson, "Silver," 739.

48. Rushforth, "Oral," 31. Day," The Western," 74. Readers familiar with trickster traditions across the continent will note that there is little about northeastern tricksters in this book. By comparison with tricksters elsewhere on the continent, we have much less information about northeastern tricksters. Also, some stories are cognates of those found elsewhere on the continent. More to the present point, the character most often referred to as a northeastern trickster, Glooscap (also Gluskabe and Gluscap, along with other variants), is probably not a trickster at all. Although he is certainly a transformer, Glooscap seldom

displays other trickster traits such a buffoonery; rather, he is generally wise and even consistently benevolent toward humans. The bungling, comic trickster role is filled separately by animals such as Wolverine, Hare, and Raccoon. (See Day and Foster, "Oral," 74–75; Day, "The Western," 83; Fisher, "The Mythology," 229.)

49. Speck, *Ethnology,* 138. Discussing southeastern American Indian trickster stories is complicated by questions of potential influence from African slave trickster stories. In *Myths of the Cherokee,* Mooney concludes that it was likely slaves who adopted stories from the Indians rather than vice versa, because, he claims, Indians would have scorned receiving stories from slaves (233–24). However, in "African Tales among the North American Indians," Dundes argues that African stories were the source of at least some southeastern trickster stories. Lankford also touches upon this subject in *American Indian Legends* (229, 239–40) and "Oral Literatures of the Southeast" (88). The possible relationship and comparison of American Indian and African slave trickster stories is a subject worthy of further study but beyond the scope of this book.

50. George A. Dorsey, *The Pawnee,* 10–11.

51. Gifford, "Western," 311–26, 338–80, 359–62.

52. Lowie, *Crow,* 252, 122–310. Of course, some of this uncertainty may have been due to a source's poor knowledge of the tribe's trickster tradition.

53. Among these is the Nez Percé ethnographer Archie Phinney, who also tells us that the Nez Percé Coyote has a separate name when presented as the ribald trickster, one name obviously not being enough for this multiplex (*Nez Percé,* ix). See also Kroeber's discussion of the Yurok Wohpekunau (*Yurok,* 68–76). Also, the conservative Winnebago whom Radin quotes "was undoubtedly trying to say that Wakdjunkaga represented the reality of things, that he was a positive force, a builder, not a destroyer" (*The Trickster,* 147).

54. Gill and Sullivan, *Dictionary,* "Culture Hero(es)," 59–60.

55. Chapman, "The Belly," 6.

56. Coleman, Fragner, and Eich, *Ojibwa,* 62, 58.

57. Barnouw, *Wisconsin,* 14, 73–75; Fisher, "The Mythology," 232.

58. Velie, *Four,* 145.

59. Barnouw, *Wisconsin,* 44n.

60. Gill and Sullivan, *Dictionary,* "Silver Fox," 273; Gill and Sullivan, *Dictionary,* "Wolf," 346.

61. However, in some of these instances the sibling may be a benevolent culture hero, while the trickster is a foil or marplot to his brother's creative acts and benevolent intentions. At other times the hero is not actually a blood sibling, but he and the trickster might have a similar relationship, as in the relationship between the Comanche Coyote's Elder Brother Wolf and Coyote (see conclusion). Tricksters also appear as junior marplots associated as an oppositional force with an exemplary and powerful senior: Madumda (of the Pomos) is a

creator; Coyote is the younger brother, responsible for traveling the earth and creating humans (Loeb, "The Creator," 489–93).

62. Lowie, *Myths,* 18.

63. Velie, *Four,* 145.

64. Quoted in Ryan, *The Trickster,* 3.

65. Malotki and Lomatuway'ma, *Hopi,* 195–228. Represented by masked dancers in many Pueblo ceremonies, kachinas are Pueblo spirits who act as mediators between humans and the world of the spirits. Many are associated with natural phenomena, for example as bringers of rain or other controllers of weather; some enforce social rules; and so forth. The Korowista Kachina is associated with agricultrure, carries a stick and seeds, and wears a green-and-white manta. Historically, this kachina may have been adopted from the Keresan Pueblos of New Mexico (Shaul, "Two," 679–80).

66. Speck, *Ethnology,* 144.

67. Boas, *Tsimshian,* 618.

68. Swanton, *Haida,* 117.

69. Simpson, *The Hopi,* 13.

70. Radin, *The Trickster,* 128.

71. Phinney, *Nez Percé,* vii.

72. As always, there are exceptions. Among the Achomewi or Pit River Indians, Coyote made earth by scratching it out of nothingness (Alfred L. Kroeber, *Indian,* 179). When it came to creating humans, Jehovah and the Crow Old Man Coyote both resorted to using the material of the physical world: Jehovah's creation is made of earth (and more than incidentally, divine breath), while Old Man Coyote makes his wife, buffalo, horses, and people out of mud (Lowie, *Crow,* 16–17).

73. Swanton, *Haida,* 146.

74. Ibid., 138; Elizabeth D. Jacobs, *Nehalem,* 123; George A. Dorsey and Kroeber, *Traditions,* 17–19.

75. George A. Dorsey, *Traditions of the Caddo,* 7–13.

76. Swanton, *Haida,* 117.

77. James R. Walker, *Lakota Myth,* 45–46.

78. Clark, *Indian,* 62.

79. Coleman, Fragner, and Eich, *Ojibwe,* 62.

80. Melville Jacobs, *Sahaptin,* 213–16; Clark, *Indian,* 96–98; Erdoes and Ortiz, eds., *American Indian Trickster,* 362–65; Bright, *A Coyote,* 146–49; Melville Jacobs, *Clackamas,* 112–13.

81. Wiget, "His Life," 88.

82. Coleman, Fragner, and Eich, *Ojibwe,* 83–84.

83. Loeb, "The Creator," 475–84.

84. Bright, "Coyote's," 42.

85. Dixon, *Maidu,* 37.

86. Ibid., 46–51. See also Melville Jacobs, *The Content,* 232–33, for a discussion of announcers as plot devices in Clackamas myths.

87. Radin, *Primitive,* 347.

88. Radin, *The Trickster,* 162, 164. Loeb makes a similar point about tricksters among some California tribes when he asserts that the common transformer-trickster has been separated from the tales and deified (472).

89. Radin, *The Trickster,* 164.

90. Barnouw, *Wisconsin,* 51.

91. Hill, "Navaho," 317. But recall Toelken's statement that the Navajos see no reason to "distinguish between separate aspects" of Ma'i (quoted in Bright, *A Coyote,* 20–21).

92. Luckert, "Coyote," 9–10, 17–19; Malotki and Lomatuway'ma, *Hopi,* 195–98.

93. Hultkrantz, *The Religions,* 560–61.

94. Stern, "Trickster," 168–69.

95. Melville Jacobs, *Northwest,* 238–46.

96. Bright, *A Coyote,* xi–xii. Actually, a Supreme Being of any sort in a Euro-American sense, even if part of a tribe's belief system, may not have played a key role in most tribes' traditional mythologies (Hultkrantz, *The Religions,* 26).

97. Ricketts, "The North," 343–44.

98. Hallowell, "Ojibwe," 38–39.

99. Rice, *Lakota,* 66.

100. Stern, "Trickster," 160, 173. Transformative power helps explain some of the ostensible ambiguity about whether tricksters are human or animal.

101. Parsons, *Pueblo,* 193–94.

102. Bright, "Coyote's," 183.

103. Bright, *A Coyote,* 30. Or, less pejoratively, his wandering may simply be the consequence of his need to eat. One Crow told Lowie about the early days when people, racked with hunger, moved camp frequently, roaming about looking for food (*Crow,* 327). Considered from this perspective, tricksters' roaming and instability are not simply unruliness but are suggestive of the precariousness of existence, the uncertainty about where the next meal is coming from. This may be yet another way in which tricksters embody reality.

104. Coleman, Fragner, and Eich, *Ojibwe,* 94.

105. Thus reflecting "the rebellion of humans against their self-imposed domesticity" (Bright, *A Coyote,* 104).

106. In chapter 5, on Trickster's oral tradition and ceremonial kin, we see that the prototypical Navajo chantway hero, for example, leaves his human society and travels to sacred places where he learns a ritual from the Holy People, then returning to the Dine' to teach them the ritual.

107. Douglas, *Purity,* 128.

108. Babcock-Abrahams, "A Tolerated," 155.

Raven Steals the Moon

Swanton provides the following information about characters in the story: Marten was considered the fastest of all animals. *TaLAtg.a'dAla* was a small bird that Swanton could not identify, but the name translates as "Swift-rainbow-trout," and it was the fastest bird. *Qadadjâ'n,* the owner of the eulachon, is a mountain on the south side of Nass inlet (148). The basket referred to in paragraph seven was a basket with open weave in which fish could drain, while *lqea'mawhich* is a tall, stiff grass found near the seashore (Swanton, *Haida,* 148). The sons' throwing stick worked thus: the object to be thrown was placed on one end of a flexible stick, which was drawn back, then released (Swanton, *Haida,* 148). Swanton provides no explanation for the grandfather's actions. There are also other unexplained actions in the story that the Haida audience probably understood. Of course, there is also the possibility that the storyteller omitted information.

3. LIVING SIDEWAYS: SOCIAL RELATIONS IN TRICKSTER STORIES

1. Melville Jacobs, *The Content,* 127.

2. Luckert, "Coyote," 20.

3. Lincoln, *Indi'n,* 155, 158.

4. Babcock-Abrahams, "A Tolerated," 182–84.

5. Melendez, "The Oral," 81.

6. Babcock-Abrahams, "A Tolerated," 161.

7. Quoted by Dell Hymes in "Foreword" in Basso, *Portrait,* x.

8. Vine Deloria, *Custer,* 148–49.

9. Melville Jacobs, *The Content,* 178–79.

10. Phinney, *Nez Percé,* ix.

11. Basso, *Portrait,* 63.

12. Basso, *Portrait,* 37–38, 69.

13. Toelken, "Coyote," 591.

14. Gill, *Native,* 178.

15. Vine Deloria, *Custer,* 149.

16. Toelken, "Coyote," 591. However, trickster stories are not for children only. A story might be told to straighten out an adult as well. Moreover, Yellowman told Toelken that Ma'i is so important that his stories are told in adult contexts, such as ceremonies (Toelken and Scott, "Poetic," 80).

17. Alfred Kazin, cited in Basso, *Portrait,* 47.

18. Toelken and Scott, "Poetic," 80.

19. Skeels, "Classification," 62.

20. Radin, *The Trickster,* 152. In some tribes—but apparently not the Winnebago—ritual clowning satirized ritual (and much else besides). Why, then, would tricksters be necessary for this task?

21. "Blue Jay," *I Become,* 139.

22. Radin, *The Trickster,* 4–5, 151.

23. Ibid., 18.

24. Ibid., 152. Radin discusses other elements of Winnebago society that are satirized on pages 152–54. The story Wiget examines, discussed below, is in Radin, *The Trickster,* 22–24.

25. Wiget, "His Life," 90, 94.

26. Toelken, "The Demands," 71.

27. Radin, *Primitive,* 32, 37.

28. Cajete, *Look,* 164.

29. When considering American Indian family relationships, we must not limit our thinking to the nuclear family of father, mother, offspring (as is customary in the dominant culture). The extended family of grandparents, aunts, uncles, and so forth and clan must also be included. There may have been exceptions to the social concepts that follow. Terrell, in *American Indian Almanac,* suggests that the Yuroks lacked any notion of community, describing them as little more than "an aggregation of individuals" (478). I merely report this opinion. It is difficult to imagine such a traditional society.

30. Toelken, "The Demands," 61, 63.

31. Brown, "Becoming," 12. Pritchard, *No,* 48.

32. Toelken, "The Demands," 63.

33. Ballinger, "Coyote."

34. Chapter 4 contains a discussion of some of the stories in which we see a trickster's family.

35. Toelken, "The Demands," 63.

36. Radin, *Primitive,* 94. Rice, *Lakota,* 65.

37. Radin, *Primitive,* 50–51.

38. Ross, "Storytelling," 10.

39. My thinking on this issue is based on Douglas's discussion of kinds of social pollution (*Purity,* 122). I have omitted one—danger in the margins—for reasons I have discussed in the introduction and, as I hope this chapter makes clear, because I think it is more useful to consider tricksters in the context of community.

40. Toelken and Scott, "Poetic," 80. Much caution is warranted when considering this statement. Toelken points out that the statement was a "literal translation of the idiom; it may also mean, 'They make things simple, or easy to understand'" (Toelken and Scott, "Poetic," 114, n.35). Unfortunately, many have not approached the quotation warily but have, rather, elaborated it into further confirmation of

the romantic over-reacher approach to tricksters. Considering the context, Yellowman may have meant for us to see Ma'i's behavior as prototypical of the habitual folly and vice in human behavior.

41. Buller, "Comanche," 245.

42. Parsons, *Pueblo*, 89.

43. Clark, *Indian*, 91–95.

44. Melville Jacobs, *Northwest*, 213–16.

45. Melville Jacobs, *Clackamas*, 19–20.

46. Boas, *Tsimshian*, 619.

47. Brown, "Becoming," 10. Many would agree with Brown that the American Indian sense of family relatedness extends to all things—natural phenomena and animals as well as humans. Lincoln writes, for example, that American Indian "aesthetics turn on a sense of tribe, that is, an extended family that reciprocates among people, places, history, flora, fauna, spirits and gods" (*Native*, 42). Toelken, however, argues that such "dreamy conclusions" are not applicable to the Navajos. Beyond the family, he argues, "relational ideas are applied as ritual metaphors, not as loving extensions of the family circle" ("The Demands," 70).

48. George A. Dorsey, *Traditions of the Caddo*, 10–11.

49. Lowie, *Crow*, 128.

50. Lowie, *Myths*, 30. Joking relatives are those relatives, determined by tribal kin customs, who act as a person's moral censors by trying to shame a person publicly when his or her behavior is objectionable. There is, of course, more than a little irony in the fact that it is a trickster who creates this social control.

51. Melville Jacobs, *Northwest*, 188–90.

52. Talking about descriptive names by which Navajos might refer to a person who is not present, Toelken includes an example of life following art. He refers to the descriptive name of a "woman of prodigious sexual appetites: Woman Whose Genitals Are Always Hungry" ("The Demands," 61).

53. There are a few exceptions to such behavior in tricksters. See Deward E. Walker's discussion of the Nez Percé Coyote's few cooperative arrangements in *Nez Percé*, 213 ff. and 218.

54. Radin, *The Trickster*, 6, 54.

55. Speaking of the Ojibwe trickster Wenebojo, Barnouw reminds us that social "living involves giving and taking of advice, while independence is expressed in rejecting it" (*Wisconsin*, 56–57).

56. Ibid.

57. Melville Jacobs, *The Content*, 32. We see further evidence of conflict between reality and the ideal or between community and individual values and desires in Ojibwe trickster stories, in which "independence is valued. Wenebojo is happiest when he is all alone" (Barnouw, *Wisconsin*, 244). Ideally, Barnouw hypothesizes, an Ojibwe man was independent, self-controlled, and generous.

However, there was also within this society a strong pressure to achieve that probably led to an unspoken desire to be dependent, uncontrolled, and selfish. "Perhaps that was why Wenebojo's 'foolishness' was regarded with sympathy. One could appreciate the trickster's self-centeredness and greed" (246).

58. Radin, *The Trickster,* 8, 18.

59. One version of this story can be found in Ramsey, *Reading,* 44–45.

60. Radin, *The Trickster,* 41.

61. Coleman, Fragner, and Eich, *Ojibwa,* 56; Radin, *The Trickster,* 4.

62. However, because kinship implies obligations of support, tricksters often address others in kinship terms even when there is in fact no kinship, thereby hoping to benefit from the ostensible relationship.

63. Jahner, "Wilderness Mentors," 430.

64. Lowie, *Crow,* 122.

65. Cruikshank and Sydney, "How," 143.

66. Vine Deloria, *God,* 201, 81.

67. Melville Jacobs, "Humor," 189.

68. Melville Jacobs, *The Content,* 22–23.

69. These are folklorists' names, of course, not American Indian ones. Bungling Host and Foolish Imitation tales are so common in American Indian oral traditions that even a bibliographical sampling would be an unnecessary burden in these notes. Stith Thompson's *Tales of the North American Indians* (299, 301) identifies extensive sources.

70. Benedict, *Zuni,* 307–8.

71. Zuni People, *The Zunis,* 102–4.

72. Cushing, *Zuni,* 203–14.

73. Douglas, *Purity,* 112.

74. Karl Kroeber, "Poem," 112.

75. Similarly, Vine Deloria points out that "while religious experiences may be individual in specific events, the impact of them is generally quickly felt by respective groups of men. . . . [Religion] is probably more a national or tribal affair then either an individual or universal affair" (*God,* 293).

76. Ricketts, "The North," 338; Ramsey, "*Reading,*" 33.

77. There are a few stories in which a trickster imitates successfully. In a Crow story Old Man Coyote successfully hosts Crow, a creature much like Coyote in his living habits and character, but not other qualities (Lowie, *Myths,* 38–39). Blue Jay successfully gathers mud and twigs for food—substances that already exist—in imitation of Beaver (Boas, *Chinook,* 180). In both cases the trickster's accomplishment—in terms of spiritual power—is illusory, for in neither instance has he stepped beyond his innate habits or abilities to achieve special powers.

78. Radin, *Primitive,* 64.

79. Buller, "Comanche," 248.

80. Radin, *The Trickster,* 36–37.

81. Melville Jacobs conjectured that the Chinook Coyote's behavior may be attributable to the domineering role of Chinook headmen in relation to their families (especially younger brothers) and to other villagers. In this status-conscious and competitive society, people might have felt that headmen were like the trickster (*The Content,* 23–24). Radin comments on the Winnebago trickster as chief and object of satire (*The Trickster,* 153).

82. Commonly these stories end with the trickster's being absent from his family so long that they starve to death. (See George A. Dorsey, *Mythology,* 280–81, for an example.)

83. George A. Dorsey, *The Pawnee,* 457–58, and *Mythology,* 277.

84. Luckert, "Coyote," 10.

85. Erdoes and Ortiz, eds., *American Indian Myths,* 347–52.

86. Occasionally, a story in which a trickster's sexuality is prominent in his social manipulations has an ameliorative ending. For example, in a Winnebago story Wakdjunkaga's extraordinarily long penis is bitten off and chewed up by a chipmunk. Wakdjunkaga turns the pieces into various objects for the benefit of humans: pond-lily, lily-of-the-lake, potatoes, turnips, artichokes, ground-beans, and so forth (Radin, *The Trickster,* 39).

87. George A. Dorsey and Kroeber, *Traditions,* 55–56.

88. Dixon, *Maidu,* 89.

89. Malotki, *Gullible,* 22–31, 43–55.

90. Melville Jacobs, *Clackamas,* 134, 167.

91. Stories in which a trickster marries his daughter are relatively common. See George A. Dorsey and Kroeber (*Traditions,* 82) and Hill ("Navaho," 335) for bibliographical information on a few versions.

92. Douglas recognizes the role that ritual—as public confirmation—plays in legitimizing relationships when she writes that social rituals create reality that would not exist without them (*Purity,* 62).

93. Dooling, ed., *The Sons,* 39.

94. Ibid., 39–41.

95. Ibid., 118. South Wind, the Nehalem trickster, also creates strife to suit his own ends. Needing a knife to cut up a whale, he manipulates Flint and Copper so that they fight each other. As they fight, pieces of flint fall. Southwind picks up the flint and then reveals his plot to them (Elizabeth Jacobs, *Nehalem,* 124). Dooling, *The Sons,* 94–96.

96. Dooling, *The Sons,* 119–22.

97. Ibid., 108.

98. Rice, *Lakota,* 83.

99. Ibid., 88.

100. Ibid., 83–84.

101. James R. Walker, *Lakota Belief,* 128.

102. George A. Dorsey, *The Pawnee,* 482.

103. Allen, *The Sacred,* 162.

104. Ramsey, *Reading,* 36–37.

Iktomi Takes Back a Gift

The rolling-stone episode is told throughout the Plains Indian tribes. This version is a Rosebud Sioux story. In a Pawnee version it is a knife that Coyote gives to a rock. For Pawnee children the story is a warning that they must never take back gifts made to a tree, a stone, or anything else, for that could lead to their dying (George A. Dorsey, *The Pawnee,* 506). "Tunka, Inyan, the Rock, is the oldest divinity in the Lakota cosmology. Everything dies; only the rock is forever" (Erdoes and Ortiz, *American Indian Trickster,* 114).

4. COYOTE, HE/SHE WAS GOING THERE: SEX AND GENDER IN TRICKSTER STORIES

1. Senier, "A Zuni," 223.

2. "The final question may [be] whether it is appropriate at all to draw broad conclusions about the functions of these story's gendered figures in their cultures" (Senier, "A Zuni," 224). See also my summary of Craig Thompson's discussion in the introduction to this book.

3. Melville Jacobs, *The Content,* 141.

4. Ibid., 121.

5. Barnouw, *Wisconsin,* 117.

6. Day, "The Western," 77.

7. Stern, "Some," 137. As Klamaths were exposed to and adopted Euro-American attitudes, such details have often been omitted or concealed (Stern, "Trickster," 168).

8. Lincoln, "MELUS," 75–76.

9. Other trickster stories that are not so sexually oriented make socially focused observations on male tricksters' behavior. It is probably in the ribald tales, however, that gender plays the most obvious role.

10. Alfred L. Kroeber, *Yurok,* 311.

11. Wiget, *Native,* 16–17. Also well equipped, the Athapascan Coyote carries his penis flung over his shoulder (Erdoes and Ortiz, *American Indian Trickster,* 71). There is one story in which the fact that trickster's penis has a will of its own is manifested in anomalous fashion. Erdoes and Ortiz retell a Gros Ventre story in which Nix'ant's penis proves to be a more responsible citizen than its owner by warning girls about the trickster's designs on them, telling others that he is a liar, and so forth (*American Indian Trickster,* 160–61).

12. Lowie, *Myths,* 43.

13. Lowie, *Crow,* 56. Stories of sexual intercourse between humans and animals and their resulting offspring are much more than salaciousness. They reaffirm our relationship to the world of nonhuman persons. Some remind us of the obligations we owe such relatives. For example, see the Blackfoot story "The Piqued Buffalo-wife," reprinted in Feldman's *The Storytelling Stone,* 217–20. In this story a young man (not a trickster) takes advantage of a buffalo cow stuck in a wallow. After she gives birth to his son, they all live together for a time until the man strikes his wife. The remainder of the story recounts his fatal efforts to recover his wife.

14. Bright, *A Coyote,* 70–72; Ramsey, *Reading,* 44–45.

15. Of course, little is straightforward and unambiguous when we are talking about Tricksters. According to the conventional wisdom in Trickster studies, the bawdy stories are, on another level, a vicarious romp in the forbidden. Further, while the stories may unveil lurking threats of social disintegration and chaos, Trickster's doings—by ripping through the barbed wire of human moral proscriptions and artificial moral categories—also reveal how Trickster exercises creative, even sacred, powers. Out there beyond our social frontier, Trickster makes all things possible and creates reality. This aspect of trickster stories has been amply discussed by Babcock, Ramsey, Toelken, Wiget, et al. I touch on this theme in the conclusion. For more detailed discussions, see the above writers.

16. Deward E. Walker, *Nez Percé,* 206.

17. Clark, *Indian,* 113.

18. Deward E. Walker, *Nez Percé,* 207–8.

19. See the discussion of the Upper Cowlitz story of Soft Basket Woman's vaginal teeth in chapter 3. A Kwakiutl story tells of Coyote's similarly defeating Death-Bringing Woman and her vaginal dentata (Erdoes and Ortiz, *American Indian Myths,* 362–65). Two other versions are in Erdoes and Ortiz, *American Indian Myths,* 283–85, and Melville Jacobs, *Sahaptin,* 188–90. There are nontrickster versions of such episodes as well. Other stories in which Coyote has sex with dangerous females—a butterfly and mussel-shell killers—are included in Deward E. Walker, *Nez Percé,* 25–29.

20. Ramsey, *Coyote,* 52.

21. Niethammer, *Daughters,* 37–38.

22. Hoffman, *The Menominee,* 173–75.

23. Lowie, *Crow,* 124.

24. Kroeber, *Yurok,* 304.

25. George A. Dorsey and Kroeber, *Traditions,* 73–74.

26. Parsons, *Tewa,* 242–46.

27. Kidwell, "The Power," 114.

28. Ibid., 116.

29. Barnouw, *Wisconsin,* 106.

30. Norman, *The Wishing,* 165. I am aware of the criticism of Norman's Swampy Cree trickster stories by Nichols ("'The Wishingbone Cycle,'" 157–78, and Brightman ("Tricksters," 179–203). They are largely concerned, however, with the source of the stories and the nature of the translations, not with the authenticity of the stories themselves.

31. Norman, *The Wishing,* 165.

32. Deward E. Walker, *Nez Percé,* 206, 221.

33. Ibid., 85–88, 211.

34. Wiget, "His Life," 89.

35. Ibid. Wiget further observes, "Female trickster figures are known in American Indian traditional literatures, and their occurrence does not seem to depend on the sex of the storyteller or audience or even particular contexts. Thus, at least in some societies, a female trickster was a commonly understood, unexceptional figure, whose character is contrasted with that of the male. Among the Arizona Tewa, for instance, Coyote Woman is all treachery and malevolence and lacks the pathetic qualities of the male figure that ameliorate our judgment of him" (89). Wiget overstates the case here. The Coyote Woman in the Tewa story is neither more nor less treacherous and malevolent than many male Coyotes. And if the male Coyote possesses "pathetic qualities that ameliorate our judgment of him," such an evaluation can be made only after examining a range of trickster stories. Given as large a body of female trickster stories, we might well make similar assertions about them.

36. Parsons, "Pueblo," 227–28.

37. That indigenous storytellers allow gender to influence their performance is evidenced elsewhere as well as in trickster stories. See Morrow and Mather, "Two Tellings," and McClellan, Johns, and Wedge, "The Girl," 129.

38. Parsons, *Tewa,* 291; Malotki and Lomatuway'ma, *Hopi,* 77.

39. The use of male or female tricksters according to the culture's lineal traditions is not invariable. To be accurate, even between two closely related matrilineal societies such as the Arizona Tewas and the Hopis there may be gender differences in the tricksters of the same or similar episodes (Parsons, *Tewa,* 282; Malotki and Lomatuway'ma, *Hopi,* 91). In different versions of one story with either a male or female protagonist, a Coyote's desire to have children as pretty as Deer's makes him/her gullible enough to burn or suffocate his/her own children when he/she is tricked into putting them in a fire. In a Hopi version of this story, it is the spots of Antelope's children that Coyote wants to imitate (Malotki and Lomatuway'ma, *Hopi,* 27). A Navajo variant can be found in Parsons, "Navaho," 371. A Hopi version with a male Coyote combines Coyote's gullible admiration of Turkey's children with a variation on the Bungling Host episode (Voth, *The Traditions,* 199–201). And even within the same tradition, the same episode told by different persons might have not only differences in narrative details but

differences in the trickster's sex. Thus, a Zuni story in which Coyote repeatedly forgets a song just learned has a male protagonist in the version Dennis Tedlock published in *Finding the Center,* 98–101.

40. Lowie, *Myths,* 28–30. In a secondary creative role she also originates moccasins, leggings, tanned robes, and methods of preparing pemmican. In one story she debates another woman about how things should be arranged on earth and in Crow society, insisting that life should not be made too easy for the People (Lowie, *Crow,* 132).

41. Malotki and Lomatuway'ma, *Hopi,* 55.

42. A Lipan Apache version of this story has a male Coyote as its protagonist (Opler, *Myths,* 165–66). This Coyote is more obviously a trickster, and the story is consistent with what we expect of a trickster.

43. Schlegel, "Three," 169–71; Dozier, *The Pueblo,* 137; Honigman, "Hopi," 50.

44. Kessler, *Women,* 112.

45. "[T]his legitimate predator-trickster of the hunter era is out of tune with the lifestyle of sedentary planters, such as the Hopi Indians. Hopi Coyote tales therefore tend to reduce, more straightforwardly than their Navajo counterparts, the Coyote person to the level of a laughable fool" (Malotki and Lomatuway'ma, *Hopi,* vi). We should also note that men were traditionally the hunters among the Hopis.

46. Parsons, *Tewa,* 161, 283.

47. Malotki and Lomatuway'ma, *Hopi,* 93.

48. Voth, *Traditions,* 196–97, 201–2.

49. Allen, *The Sacred,* 82.

50. Bataille and Sands, *Native,* 19–20; Kessler, *Women,* 111.

51. Among the New Mexico Pueblos a kiva is a partially subterranean ceremonial chamber; among the Hopis, the room is above ground.

52. Malotki and Lomatuway'ma, *Hopi,* 161–77.

53. Actually, the latter term refers to all "alternatively gendered people of either sex" (Lang, "Various," 100). My discussion focuses on the person traditionally called a *berdache.* The most comprehensive treatment of this social role is Williams's *The Spirit and The Flesh.* Because the term *berdache* carries inappropriate connotations (such as slave), I shall use either the term Two Spirit or a tribal name for this gender. The Lakota term is *winkte;* the Arapaho term is *hax-u'xan;* Crow, *baté;* Navajo, *nádleehé;* Shoshoni, *tainna wa'ippi.* Callender and Kochems provide a table identifying American Indian cultures that acknowledged Two Spirits ("The North," 445).

54. Callender and Kochems, "The North," 455; Maltz and Archambault, "Gender," 230.

55. Sharp, "Asymmetric," 68; Lang, "Various," 103.

56. Callender and Kochems, "The North," 451.

57. Ibid., 454–55.

58. Lang, "Various," 104–5.

59. Williams, *The Spirit,* 101.

60. Ibid., 27.

61. Gill and Sullivan, *Dictionary,* "White Faces," 337; Callender and Kochems, "The North," 448–49. Thayer suggests that because the Two Spirit's "power was from outside the ordinary realm, and was located within the sacred realm of the vision quest-guardian-spirit complex," gender behavior that might otherwise have been considered outside of the norm was accepted ("The Berdache," 292).

62. Alfred L. Kroeber, *Arapaho,* 19.

63. Lang, "Various," 103–4; Williams, *The Spirit,* 32.

64. Thayer, "The Berdache," 290.

65. Gill and Sullivan, *Dictionary,* "Gender Crossing," 99.

66. Thayer, "The Berdache," 290, 293, 292. Among the Lakotas, *winktes* were feared as well as respected because of the supernatural origin of their skills (Gill and Sullivan, *Dictionary,* "Gender Crossing," 98; Gill and Sullivan, *Dictionary,* "Winkte," 342). Do we see evidence of Arapaho ambivalence in the name *haxuxana[n]*, which Kroeber says means "rotten bone" (*Arapaho,* 19)? It is also interesting to recall again that Old Woman Coyote—in a contrary mood—was responsible for the creation of the Crow *batés.* Apparently, husbands of Two Spirits faced some difficulties as well. Callender and Kochems report that among Plains tribes a husband might be ridiculed for taking a wife who could both hunt and keep house, the implication being that the husband was too lazy or unable to hunt ("The North," 448). Not all cultures were accepting and tolerant of Two Spirited people—for example, the Iroquois, the Apaches, the Comanches, and the Tohono O'odams (Williams, *The Spirit,* 39). Similarly, not all people in nations that once accepted Two Spirits still accept this tradition. Little Thunder claims that Two Spirits are no longer honored in Lakota communities (Little Thunder, "I Am," 204–9).

67. Thayer, "The Berdache," 290. The protective, restorative role widows and orphans often play in American Indian stories might be noted. For example, see the story of Bloodclot Boy in Parsons's "Kiowa Tales," 62. Like the orphans of oral tradition, *winktes* might have been marginal in a social sense but still loaded with potential for power. In fact, many might argue that they received their power from their marginality, a concept Babcock and Pelton have explained ("A Tolerated Margin of Mess" and *The Trickster in West Africa*).

68. Callender and Kochems, "The North," 451, 453.

69. Thayer, "The Berdache," 289.

70. Erdoes and Ortiz, *American Indian Trickster,* 133. Doing something in a different way, "just for a change," is certainly consistent with tricksters' characters. They are never satisfied with what they have or who they are.

71. Is this detail a parody related to the stories in which trickster's feces are his advisors and are sometimes referred to by a relational name?

72. Erdoes and Ortiz, *American Indian Trickster*, 133–35.

73. It should also be recalled that some American Indians came to identify Trickster with Satan (Radin, *Crashing Thunder*, 201–2; Stern, "The Trickster," 168–69.

74. Williams, *The Spirit*, 96–97.

75. Alfred L. Kroeber, *Arapaho*, 19.

76. Ibid.

77. Other versions can be found in Ramsey, *Coyote*, 23–24, and Deward E. Walker, *Nez Percé*, 97.

78. Radin, *The Trickster*, 22–24.

79. Ibid., 57.

80. Wiget, "His Life," 90.

81. Ibid.

82. Ibid.

Bluejay and the Well-Behaved Maiden

Among many tribes, menstruating women were considered a danger in that their power could affect hunting, crops, and even men's spiritual power. A variety of taboos was associated with menstruating women. Among them, sexual intercourse was generally proscribed. Often, a young woman menstruating for the first time was placed in isolation in a special shelter, and in many tribes a woman went into isolation each time she menstruated.

5. BLOOD KIN: TRICKSTER, HERO, CLOWN

1. Radin, *The Trickster*, xxiii–xxiv.

2. Dennis Tedlock, *Finding*, 259–62. I have reproduced the typography by which Tedlock wanted to capture the rhythms and emphases of Zuni narrative poetry. He discusses his approach to translation in the introduction to *Finding the Center* as well as in "On the Translation."

3. Ramsey, *Reading*, 25.

4. Dundes, *The Morphology*, 66.

5. Makarius, "The Crime," 671. Babcock-Abrahams makes the same argument ("The Tolerated," 164).

6. Also spelled *Midewiwin* and known as the Grand Medicine Society, this society prepares practitioners for healing and using herbs to provide long life.

7. Makarius, "Crime," 670.

8. This word is the plural of *manido*, an alternative spelling of *manitou*.

9. Makarius, "Crime," 665.

10. Ibid.

11. Gill, *Native,* 26.

12. Buckley, "Doing," 48.

13. Spencer develops in much more detail the points about plot, character, and values that are summarized here in *Mythology,* chapter 2, "Plot Construction and Value Themes."

14. Spencer, *Mythology,* 19, 25.

15. Ibid., 20.

16. Ibid., 25.

17. Ibid., 27.

18. Luckert, "Coyote," 10.

19. Spencer, *Mythology,* 59.

20. Ibid., 80.

21. Quoted in Hultkrantz, *The Religions,* 39.

22. Dixon, *Maidu,* 46–51.

23. de Angulo and Freeland, "Miwok," 250.

24. Gill and Sullivan, *Dictionary,* "Sunawavi," 293.

25. Stith Thompson, *Tales,* 15–16.

26. See Stith Thompson, *Tales* (392) for bibliographical information regarding variants of this story type.

27. In many societies twins were regarded as possessing supernatural powers and could be indicators of either good or bad fortune. In societies that believed the latter, the twin who was thought to embody evil was killed, perhaps by exposure, or adopted by another family (Hultkrantz, *The Religions,* 42).

28. Marriott and Rachlin, eds., *American,* 102–15.

29. This becomes the first Kiowa ring-target game, a game in which boys would try to throw a stick or an arrow through a rolling ring.

30. Sometimes the twin heroes have sacred forbears, as in the Sia brothers who are born to Ko'chinako, virgin daughter of Spider Woman and Father Sun. Their adventurous careers, however, are like those of other twin brothers. For example, they disobey their mother repeatedly and travel to places where they kill giant enemies of various sorts (Stevenson, *The Sia,* 43–57).

31. Marriott and Rachlin, *American Indian,* 113–14. On a journey searching for his two grandsons, who took two different trails, Old Man Coyote runs back and forth between trails so that one or the other of his grandsons will not think he likes the other more. When he throws a stick into the air, it falls, cleaving him in two. His two halves look at each other and say, "I am you and you are I. Now we can both go after my grandsons" (de Angulo and Freeland, "Miwok," 249).

32. Marriott and Rachlin, *American,* 115.

33. Benedict, *Zuni,* 58–61.

34. Ibid., 54–55; Parsons, "The Origin," 155–58. The Flint Society priests say nothing about killing a woman with whom one has had sex. We should not be

put off by what we would see as sexist implications here. This story teaches ceremonialism, not gender relations.

35. Barnouw, *Wisconsin*, 74–75.

36. Coleman, Fragner, and Eich, *Ojibwa*, 87.

37. Makarius, "The Crime," 672.

38. Reichard, *Navaho*, 183.

39. Alexander, *The World's*, 214–19; Coleman, Fragner, and Eich, *Ojibwa*, 68. The Lakota Iktome sometimes plays a role in magic: "A design representing iktome, the tricky spider-man, would not ordinarily be used by a medicine man, but by somebody who wanted to perform some magic, a heyoka perhaps. This spider design could be used like a love charm. With this powerful design one could take the souls of a boy and a girl and tie them together. Then they couldn't help finding each other, falling in love. You don't have to believe this, but it really works" (Lame Deer and Erdoes, *Lame Deer*, 180).

40. Quoted in Barbara Tedlock, *The Beautiful*, 131.

41. Quoted in Ibid., 131.

42. Velie, *Four*, 133.

43. Vine Deloria, *Custer*, 148–49.

44. Lincoln, *Indi'n*, 38.

45. Cited in Toelken and Scott," Poetic," 87.

46. Barbara Tedlock, "The Clown's Way," 106.

47. "Indian ceremony as 'comic' pattern is seldom linear escape or structural transformation or social liberation, but more a celebrative acceptance of what-is, a curve back home." The Heyoka "tradition points toward a sacred sense of comic mediation in all things worldly and spiritual . . . teaches traditional Lakotas the 'contrary,' or 'two-faced' nature of all things. . . . Tribe transcends the terminal first person, the existential 'hero' as clown in communal terms at best. The comic mistake is a valuable teaching. Every trickster tale in North America turns on this point" (Lincoln, *Indi'n*, 31, 62, 86). "American Indian religion has a place for laughter, the laughter that goes with a sudden opening or dislocation in the Universe" (Barbara Tedlock, "Clown's," 115).

48. Makarius, "Clowns," 46; Velie, *Four*, 133.

49. Blackbird, *History*. Reviewing the names given to the Algonquian Trickster, Chamberlain examines their etymological meanings and suggests that the idea of "clown," "deceiver," "tormentor" may be suggested in the names but says that nothing definite is known regarding the name's origins ("Nanibozhu," 193–94).

50. Makarius, "Clowns," 45; Gill, *Native*, 327. A Heyoka—a contrary or clown—was free from the restrictions of social rules and taboos and could, therefore, "freely critique established custom," as well as "draw attention to deviancy by burlesquing actions and deeds not acceptable to the society" (Fast Wolf, "Wakinyan," 433).

51. Makarius, "Clowns," 64n.

52. Ibid., 45–46.

53. Ibid., 53.

54. Ibid., 61.

55. Ibid., 60.

56. Dixon, "Maidu," 39. Makarius, "Clowns," 46.

57. Dooling, *The Sons*, xix, 40. James R. Walker gives another account of the Heyoka character. The Heyokas are opposite Nature and are among the Wakan beings that are not spirits; rather, they are of this world with power over men. Iktomi is also among these and, like the Heyoka, is *wakan* for evil (*Lakota Belief*, 71–72, 140).

58. Stevenson, *The Sia*, 33.

59. Yava, "Way," 8–13. Yava is a descendant of those Tewa people who moved near the Hopi pueblos in order to escape the Spanish as they reestablished themselves in the Southwest following the Pueblo Revolt. He has been educated in both the Tewa and Hopi cultures (8).

60. Yava, "Way," 12.

61. Sekaquaptewa, "One," 14–15. Gill, too, discusses the clowns as manifestations of the obstacles humans meet within themselves as they try to fulfill their humanity (*Native*, 77). Yava writes about Tewa clowns that "they sort of represent people as they were when they came from the underworld. They are funny looking and they don't understand good manners. . . . By their actions they remind everyone how important it is to be decent and respectful and harmonious in their way of living" (13). This parallels part of Ramsey's analysis of tricksters: "As mirrors of a hypothesized primitive mind and condition, then, as well as of infantile minds, tricksters would seem to function as sources of a kind of tribal historical perspective. As if to say: 'here's how uncouth and infantile it was around here at the beginning'" (*Reading*, 38).

62. Barbara Tedlock, "Boundaries," 127.

63. Ibid., 134, 127.

64. Yava, "Way," 12.

65. Lincoln, *Indi'n*, 15.

66. Hunter, "A MELUS," 84; see also Yava, "Way," 13, and Makarius, "Clowns," 60.

67. Yava, "Way," 13; Gill, *Native*, 76, 26.

68. Rice, *Lakota*, 59.

69. Gill, *Native*, 76.

70. Ibid.

71. Barbara Tedlock, "Clown's," 115.

72. Ibid., 111.

73. Ibid., 108.

74. Toelken and Scott, "Poetic," 89.

75. Ibid.

76. Barbara Tedlock, "Boundaries," 138.

77. "Although the clown, by causing people to laugh at shamans and other religious authorities, might appear to weaken the very fabric of society's religion, he may actually revitalize it by revealing higher truths" (Barbara Tedlock, "Clown's," 109).

78. Ibid., 110.

Wenebojo in the Whale and the Fight with His Brother

Alec Martin told this story at Court Oreilles to Robert Ritzenthaler in 1942. Prosper Guibord interpreted. A megis shell is a small shell thought to have mystic power that is used in the *Mide'wi'win,* a religious curing society.

CONCLUSION: THE WORLD AS IT IS

1. Wiget, *Native,* 20.

2. Toelken and Scott, "Poetic," 80–81. However, see chapter 3, n.40.

3. Douglas, *Purity,* 94.

4. Luckert, "Coyote," 7.

5. Eliade, *The Quest,* 167.

6. Loeb, "The Creator," 467–93.

7. Ramsey, *Coyote,* 210.

8. Ibid., 161–65.

9. Ibid., 33–37.

10. Radin, *The Trickster,* 169.

11. Toelken and Scott, "Poetic," 90.

12. Vizenor, *Summer,* 155.

13. Ricketts, "The North," 344.

14. Ramsey, *Reading,* 41.

15. Toelken and Scott, "Poetic," 90.

16. Levi-Strauss, *Savage,* 10.

17. Ramsey, *Reading,* 41.

18. Buller, "Comanche," 247.

19. Coleman, Fragner, and Eich, *Ojibwa,* 62.

20. Lame Deer and Erdoes, *Lame Deer,* 68.

21. Reichard, *Navaho,* xxix.

22. Gill, *Native,* 36.

23. Gill and Sullivan, *Dictionary,* "Wesucechak," 334; Brown, "Becoming," 60–61.

24. Hultkrantz, *The Religions,* 38n.

25. Lincoln, *Indi'n,* 62.

26. Ibid., 22.

27. Brown, "Becoming," 60–61.

28. Gill and Sullivan, *Dictionary,* "Ma?ii," 178.

29. Beck, "In the Company," 22.

30. Boas, "An Introduction," 411, 413.

31. Gill, *Native,* 39–40.

32. Sometimes, however, we are spared "the world according to Coyote," as in the Navajo origin myth, when Coyote tried to beat First Man in making a miniature model of the earth, which apparently would determine the pattern of life on the actual earth. Little Wind warned First Man that because Coyote's model was bound to be distorted, its realization would be disastrous to man (Reichard, *Navaho,* 196–97).

33. Radin, *The Trickster,* 148–50; Boas, "Notes," 11; Toelken, "Life," 396–97.

34. Radin, *The Trickster,* 147.

35. Densmore, *Chippewa,* 97.

36. On the other hand, the prophecy of Tenskwatawa explained the absence of game animals in more recent times as a consequence of Manabozho's calling them from the forest and shutting them underground (Spicer, *A Short,* 266–67).

37. Lowie, *Myth,* 20, 27–28.

38. Dixon, *Maidu,* 37.

39. Bright, "Coyote's," 48.

40. Dixon, *Maidu,* 46–51.

41. Buller, "Comanche," 245.

42. Ibid., 257.

43. Agnes Grant, "*The Way,*" 140.

44. Even more immediately dramatic in this respect is the fact that some American Indians thought the Shawnee prophet Tenskwatawa (who brought messages of survival from the Master of Life) was an incarnation of Wenebojo (Gill and Sullivan, *Dictionary,* "Winabojo," 340–41; Gill and Sullivan, *Dictionary,* "Tenskwatawa," 301).

45. Buller, "Comanche," 257.

46. Erdoes and Ortiz, *American Indian Myths,* 342.

47. Wiget, "His Life," 90–91.

48. Bright, *A Coyote,* 91.

49. Interestingly, stories about interaction between whites and a trickster generally star Coyote, occasionally Iktomi. Lakota Artist S. D. Nelson has created a composite Trickster, Coyote/Iktomi, whose features are more heroic than comic—a fitting representation perhaps, at least in his modern incarnation as champion of Indian America. See illustration on 144.

50. Silko, *Storyteller,* 229–34.

51. Holmes, "This," 47–60.

52. Erdrich, *Jacklight*, 75.
53. Erdrich, *Baptism*, 54–55.
54. Erdrich, *Jacklight*, 77.
55. Conley, *The Way*, 190–91, 204–9.
56. Pensineau, "We," 26.
57. Silko, *Storyteller*, 238–39.
58. Vizenor, *Earthdivers*, ix.
59. Vizenor, *Wordarrows*, 30.
60. Damm, "Poem," 86–87.
61. Lalonde, "Trickster," 29.
62. Bright, *A Coyote*, 91.
63. Susag, "Zitkala-Sa," 12.
64. Toelken and Scott, "Poetic," 80–81.
65. Dixon, *Maidu*, 6–8; Haile, *Navajo*, 13.

Coyote Sells the Money Tree

The story does not explicitly identify Coyote's victims as whites; however, it seems a reasonable inference that they are whites. Indians often noted whites' love of wealth in the form of money. It is well known among whites that "money doesn't grow on trees," but the fact that the people forget their own proverb demonstrates how easily they are blinded by the prospect of achieving wealth without having to work for it. Finally, their suspicious demand for proof seems consistent with white attitudes.

"The Lipan never used mountain-laurel as a narcotic. They knew of its effect, nevertheless, as this detail shows" (Opler, *Myths*, 164–65).

Saynday and Smallpox: The White Man's Gift

Saynday is an alternative spelling of *Sendeh*. Both refer to the Kiowa trickster. Marriott and Rachlin date this story to the late nineteenth century (*Saynday's*, 125). The story was told to Alice Marriott by Frank Givens (Eagle Plume). The decimation of whole tribes by smallpox, as well as other European diseases, is well documented. Saynday's reference to counting the enemies one touches is an allusion to the practice of "counting coup," for which warriors gained credit by having touched an enemy (not necessarily killing him) during battle. The Kiowas and Pawnees were enemies.

Bibliography

Abrams, David M., and Brian Sutton-Smith. "The Development of the Trickster in Children's Narrative." *Journal of American Folklore* 90 (1977): 29–47.

Ahenakew, E. "Cree Trickster Tales." *Journal of American Folklore* 42 (1929): 309–53.

Alexander, Hartly Burr. *The World's Rim: Great Mysteries of the North American Indian.* Lincoln: University of Nebraska Press, 1953.

Allen, Paula Gunn. *The Sacred Hoop: Recovering the Feminine in American Indian Traditions.* Beacon: Boston, 1986.

Babcock-Abrahams, Barbara. "Liberty's a Whore: Inversion, Marginalia and Picaresque Narrative." In *The Reversible World: A Symbolic Inversion in Art and Society,* edited by Barbara Babcock-Abrahams, 95–116. Ithaca: Cornell University Press, 1978.

———. "A Tolerated Margin of Mess: The Trickster and His Tales Reconsidered." *Journal of Folklore Institute* 11 (1975): 147–48.

Ballinger, Franchot. "Ambigere: The Euro-American Picaro and the Native American Trickster." *MELUS* 17, no. 1 (1991–92): 21–39.

———. "Coyote Was Going There; Met Anansi the Spider; Thought He Looked Kind of Familiar: Native American and African Tricksters." Paper presented at the Modern Language Association Annual Meeting, December 1986.

———. "Living Sideways: Social Themes and Social Relationships in Native American Trickster Tales." *American Indian Quarterly* 13, no. 1 (1989): 15–30.

———. "Sacred Reversals: Tricksters in Gerald Vizenor's *Earthdivers: Tribal Narratives on Mixed Descent.*" *The American Indian Quarterly* 9, no. 1 (Winter 1985): 55–59.

Barnouw, Victor. *Wisconsin Chippewa Myths and Tales and Their Relation to Chippewa Life*. Madison: University of Wisconsin Press, 1977.

Basso, Keith. *Portrait of "the Whiteman": Linguistic Play and Cultural Symbols among the Western Apache*. Cambridge, England: Cambridge University Press, 1979.

Bataille, Gretchen M., and Kathleen Mullen Sands. *Native American Women in a Changing World: Their Lives As They Told Them*. Lincoln: University of Nebraska Press, 1984.

Beck, Peggy. V. "In the Company of Laughter." *Parabola: The Magazine of Myth and Tradition* 11, no. 3 (1986): 18–25.

Beier, Ulli. *Yoruba Myths*. Cambridge, England: Cambridge University Press, 1980.

Benedict, Ruth. *Zuni Mythology*. 2 vols. Columbia Contributions to Anthropology, no. 21. New York: Columbia University Press, 1935.

Bierhorst, John. *The Mythology of North America*. New York: William Morrow, 1985.

———. "Tales of the Delaware Trickster." In *Coming to Light*, edited by Brian Swann, 489–502. Vintage: New York, 1994.

Blackbird, Andrew J. *History of the Ottawa and Chippewa Indians of Michigan; A Grammar of Their Language, and Personal and Family History of the Author*. 1887. Petoskey, Mich.: Little Traverse Regional Historical Society, n.d.

Bloomfield, L. *Sacred Stories of the Sweet Grass Cree*. National Museum of Canada Bulletin, no. 60, Anthropological Series, vol. 11. Ottawa: National Museum of Canada, 1930.

Blue Cloud, Peter. *Elderberry Flute Song: Contemporary Coyote Tales*. Trumansburg, N.Y.: The Crossing Press, 1982.

"Blue Jay." In *I Become Part of It: Sacred Dimensions in Native American Life*, edited by D. M. Dooling and Paul Jordan-Smith, 139–49. New York: Parabola Books, 1991.

Boas, Franz. *Bella Bella Texts*. Columbia Contributions to Anthropology, no. 5. New York: Columbia University Press, 1928.

———. *Chinook Texts*. Bureau of American Ethnology Bulletin, no. 20. Washington, D.C.: GPO, 1894.

———. "An Introduction to James Teit's, 'The Traditions of the Thompson Indians of British Columbia.'" *Race, Language and Culture*, 407–24. New York: Macmillan, 1940.

———. "Notes on the Tillamook." University of California Publications in Archaeology and Ethnography, no. 20. Berkeley: University of California, 1923.

———. "Traditions of the Tillamook Indians." *Journal of American Folklore* 11 (1898): 23–38, 133–50.

———. *Tsimshian Mythology.* 31st Annual Report of the Bureau of American Ethnology. Washington, D.C.: GPO, 1916.

Bowers, Neal, and Charles L. P. Silet. "An Interview with Gerald Vizenor." *MELUS* 8, no. 1 (1981): 41–49.

Brandon, S. G. F. "Trickster." *A Dictionary of Comparative Religion.* New York: Charles Scribners' Sons, 1970.

Bright, William. *A Coyote Reader.* Berkeley: University of California Press, 1993.

———. "Coyote's Journey." *American Indian Culture and Research Journal* 4, no. 1–2 (1980): 21–48.

———. "The Natural History of Old Man Coyote." In *Recovering the Word: Essays on Native American Literature,* edited by Brian Swann and Arnold Krupat, 339–87. Los Angeles: University of California Press, 1987.

———. "Oral Literature of California and the Intermountain Region." In *Dictionary of Native American Literature,* edited by Andrew Wiget, 47–51. New York: Garland, 1994.

Brightman, Robert. "Tricksters and Ethnopoetics." *International Journal of American Linguistics* 55, no. 2 (1989): 179–203.

Brinton, Daniel. *The Lenape and Their Legends.* Brinton's Library of Aboriginal Literature no. 5. Philadelphia: D. G. Brinton, 1885.

———. *Myths of the New World.* New York: Rudolf Steiner, 1976.

Brown, John Epes. "Becoming Part of It." In *I Become Part of It: Sacred Dimensions in Native American Life,* edited by D. M. Dooling and Paul Jordan-Smith, 9–20. New York: Parabola Books, 1991.

Bruchac, Joseph, ed. *Returning the Gift: Poetry and Prose from the First North American Native Writers' Festival.* Tucson: University of Arizona Press, 1994.

Buckley, Thomas. "Doing Your Thinking." In *I Become Part of It: Sacred Dimensions in Native American Life,* edited by D. M. Dooling and Paul Jordan-Smith, 36–52. New York: Parabola Books, 1991.

Buller, Galen. "Comanche and Coyote, the Culture Maker." In *Smoothing the Ground: Essays in Native American Literature,* edited by Brian Swann, 245–58. Berkeley: University of California Press, 1983.

Cajete, Gregory. *Look to the Mountaintop: An Ecology of Indigenous Education.* Durango, Colo.: Kivaki, 1994.

Callender, Charles, and Lee M. Kochems. "The North American Berdache." *Current Anthropology* 24, no. 4 (1983): 443–70.

Carroll, Michael Press. "Levi-Strauss, Freud, and the Trickster: A New Perspective upon an Old Problem." *American Ethnologist* 8, no. 2 (1981): 301–13.

Chamberlain, Alexander F. "Nanibozhu Amongst the Otchipwe, Mississag, and Other Alkongian Tribes." *Journal of American Folklore* 4 (1891): 192–213.

Chapman, Mary. "'The Belly of This Story': Storytelling and Symbolic Birth in Native American Fiction." *Studies in American Indian Literature* 7, no. 2 (1995): 3–16.

Clark, Ella E. *Indian Legends of the Pacific Northwest.* Berkeley: University of California Press, 1953.

Clasby, Nancy Tenfelde. "'Manabozho': A Native American Resurrection Myth." *Studies in Short Fiction* 30, no. 4 (1993). http://search.epnet.com/ direct.asp?an=9404180425&db=aph.

Classen, Cheryl, and Rosemary A. Joyce. *Women in Prehistory: North America and Mesoamerica.* Philadelphia: University of Pennsylvania Press, 1997.

Clements, William. "'Identity' and 'Difference' in the Translation of Native American Oral Literatures: A Zuni Case Study." *Studies in American Indian Literatures* 3, no. 3 (1991): 1–13.

Coleman, Sister Bernard, Ellen Fragner, and Estelle Eich. *Ojibwa Myths and Legends.* Minneapolis: Ross and Haines, 1962.

Conley Robert J. *The Way of the Priests.* New York: Bantam, 1994.

Cruikshank, Julie, and Angela Sydney. "How the World Began." In *Coming to Light,* edited by Brian Swann, 138–50. New York: Vintage, 1994.

Cushing, Frank. *Zuni Folk Tales.* New York: Putnam's Sons, 1901.

Damm, Kateri. "Poem without End." In *Returning the Gift: Poetry and Prose from the First North American Native Writers' Festival,* edited by Joseph Bruchac, 86–87. Tucson: University of Arizona Press, 1994.

Davis, Mary B. *Native America in the Twentieth Century: An Encyclopedia.* Garland Reference Library of Social Science, vol. 452. New York: Garland, 1996.

Day, Gordon M. "The Western Abenaki Transformer," *Journal of the Folklore Institute* 13 (1976): 74–89.

———, and Michael K. Foster. "Oral Literature of the Northeastern Algonquians and the Northern Iroquoians." In *Dictionary of Native American Literature,* edited by Andrew Wiget, 73–82. New York: Garland, 1994.

de Angulo, J., and L. A. Freeland. "Miwok and Pomo Myths." *Journal of American Folklore* 41 (1928): 232–52.

Delgadillo, Theresa. "Gender as Work in Laguna Coyote Tales." *Studies in American Indian Literatures* 7, no. 1 (1995): 3–24.

Deloria, Ella. *Dakota Texts.* New York: AMS, 1974.

Deloria, Vine. *Custer Died For Your Sins: An Indian Manifesto.* New York: Avon, 1969.

———. *God is Red.* New York: Grosset and Dunlap, 1973.

Densmore, Frances. *Chippewa Customs.* Bureau of American Ethnology Bulletin, no. 86. Washington, D.C.: GPO, 1929.

Dewdney, Selwyn, and Kenneth E. Kidd. *Indian Rock Paintings of the Great Lakes.* 2nd ed. Toronto: University of Toronto Press, 1967.

Diamond, Stanley. "Introductory Essay: Job and the Trickster." In *The Trickster: A Study in American Indian Mythology*, by Paul Radin, xi–xxii. New York: Schocken Books, 1972.

Dixon, Roland B. *Maidu Myths*. Bulletin of the American Museum of Natural History, no. 17. Washington, D.C.: Museum of American Natural History, 1902.

———. "Some Coyote Stories from the Maidu Indians." *Journal of American Folklore* 13 (1900): 269–70.

Dooling, D. O., ed. *The Sons of the Wind*. San Francisco: Parabola, 1992.

———. "The Wisdom of the Contrary: A Conversation with John Epes Brown." *Parabola* 4, no. 1 (February 1979): 54–65.

Dorothea M., Susan. "Zitkala-Sa (Gertrude Simmons Bonnin): A Powerful Literary Voice." *Studies in American Indian Literature* 5, no. 4 (1993): 3–24.

Dorsey, George A. *The Mythology of the Witchita*. Washington, D.C.: Publications of the Carnegie Institution, no. 24. Carnegie Institution of Washington, 1904.

———. *The Pawnee: Mythology*. Part I. Publications of the Carnegie Institution, no. 59. Washington, D.C.: Carnegie Institute of Washington, 1906.

———. *Traditions of the Caddo*. Publications of the Carnegie Institution, no. 41. Washington, D.C.: Carnegie Institute of Washington, 1905.

———. "The Two Boys Who Slew the Monsters and Became Stars." *Journal of American Folklore* 17 (1904): 153–60.

Dorsey, George Amos, and A. L. Kroeber. *Traditions of the Arapahoe*. Field Columbian Museum Publication, no. 81, Anthropological Series, vol. 5. Chicago: Field Museum of Natural History, 1903.

Dorsey, James Owen. "Nanibozhu in Siouan Mythology." *Journal of American Folklore* 5 (1892): 293–304.

Doueihi, Ann. "Trickster: On Inhabiting the Space Between Discourse and Story." *Soundings: An Interdisciplinary Journal* 67, no. 3 (1984): 283–311.

Douglas, Mary. *Purity and Danger: An Analysis of Concepts of Pollution and Taboo*. New York: Praeger, 1966.

Dozier, Edward. *The Pueblo Indians of North America*. New York: Holt, 1970.

Dundes, Alan. "African Tales among the North American Indians." *Southern Folklore Quarterly* 29 (1965): 207–19.

———. "The Making and Breaking of Friendship as a Structural Frame in African Folk-tales." In *Structural Analysis of Oral Traditions*, edited by Pierre and Elli Miranda, 171–85. Philadelphia: University of Pennsylvania Press, 1981.

———. *The Morphology of North American Indian Folktales*. Folklore Fellows Communications, no. 195. Helsinki: Suomalainen Tiedeakatemia, 1964.

———. "Texture, Text and Context." *Southern Folklore Quarterly* 28 (1966): 251–65.

Dunsmore, Roger. *Earth's Mind: Essays in Native Literature.* Albuquerque: University of New Mexico Press, 1997.

Echlin, Kim. "Ojibway Creation." *Studies in American Indian Literatures* 8, no. 2 (1984): 29–35.

———. Personal communication to author, 24 April 2003.

Eliade, Mircea. *The Quest: History and Meaning in Religion.* Chicago: University of Chicago Press, 1969.

Erdoes, Richard, and Alfonso Ortiz, eds. *American Indian Myths and Legends.* New York: Pantheon, 1984.

———, eds. *American Indian Trickster Tales.* Viking: New York, 1998.

Erdrich, Louise. *Baptism of Desire: Poems.* Harper: New York, 1989.

———. *Jacklight.* New York: Holt, Rinehart and Winston, 1984.

———. *Love Medicine.* Bantam: New York, 1985.

Evan, Antone, and Jane McGary. "Raven." In *Coming to Light,* edited by Brian Swann, 97–106. New York: Vintage, 1994.

Fast Wolf, Calvin W. "Wakinyan and Wakinyan Wicaktepi." In *Coming to Light,* edited by Brian Swann, 432–40. New York: Vintage, 1994.

Feldman, Susan. *The Storytelling Stone: Myths and Tales of the American Indian.* Dell: New York, 1965.

Finnegan, Ruth. *Oral Literature in Africa.* Oxford, England: Clarendon Press, 1970.

Fisher, Margaret W. "The Mythology of the Northern and Northeastern Algonkians in Reference to Algonkian Mythology as a Whole." In *Man in Northeastern North America,* edited by Frederick Johnson, 226–62. Papers of the Robert S. Peabody Foundation for Archaeology, vol. 3. Andover: Phillips Academy, 1946.

Frost, Robert. "Education by Poetry: A Meditative Monologue." In *Robert Frost: Poetry and Prose,* edited by Edward Connery Latham and Lawrence Thompson, 329–40. New York: Holt, Rinehart and Winston, 1972.

Ghezzi, Ridie Wilson. "Nanabush Stories from the Ojibwe." In *Coming to Light,* edited by Brian Swann, 443–63. New York: Vintage, 1994.

Gifford, Edward W. "Western Mono Myths." *Journal of American Folklore* 36 (1923): 301–67.

Gill, Sam D. *Mother Earth: An American Story.* Chicago: University of Chicago Press, 1987.

———. *Native American Religion: An Introduction.* Belmont, Calif.: Wadsworth, 1982.

———, and Irene F. Sullivan. *Dictionary of Native American Mythology.* New York: Oxford University Press, 1992.

Glover, William B. "A History of the Caddo Indians." *Louisiana Historical Quarterly* 18, no. 4 (October 1935): http://ops.tamu.edu/x075bb/caddo/ Indians.html.

Goldman, Irving. "Boas on the Kwakiutl: The Ethnographic Tradition." *Theory and Practice: Essays Presented to Gene Weltfish,* edited by Stanley Diamond, 331–45. The Hague: Mouton, 1980.

Grant, Agnes. *"The Way to Rainy Mountain* in a Community-Based Oral Narratives Course for Cree and Ojibway Students." In *Approaches to Teaching Momaday's The Way to Rainy Mountain,* edited by Kenneth M. Roemer, 138–44. New York: Modern Language Association, 1988.

Grant, E. "He Walks in Two Worlds: A Visit with Maurice Kenny." *Studies in American Indian Literature* 7, no. 3 (1995): 17–27.

Grinnell, George Bird. *Blackfoot Indian Stories.* New York: Charles Scribners' Sons, 1915.

Haile, Berard. *Navahoe Coyote Tales: The Curly to' A heeli'inii Version.* Lincoln: University of Nebraska Press, 1984.

Hallowell, Irving A. "Ojibway Ontology, Behavior and World View." In *Culture in History: Essays in Honor of Paul Radin,* edited by Stanley Diamond, 19–52. New York: Columbia University Press, 1960.

Harrington, John Press. "Karuk Indian Myths." Bureau of American Ethnology Bulletin, no. 107. Washington, D.C.: Smithsonian Institute, 1932.

Hieb, Louis A. "Meaning and Mismeaning: Toward an Understanding of the Ritual Clowns." In *New Perspectives on the Pueblos,* edited by Alfonso Ortiz, 163–95. Albuquerque: University of New Mexico Press, 1972.

Hill, W. W., and Dorothy Hill. "Navaho Coyote Tales and Their Position in the Southern Athabaskan Group." *Journal of American Folklore* 58 (1945): 317–43.

Hoffman, Walter J. *The Menominee Indians.* 14th Annual Report of the Bureau of American Ethnology, pt. 1. Washington, D.C.: Smithsonian Institute, 1896.

Holmes, Kristine. "'This Woman Can Cross Any Line': Feminist Tricksters in the Works of Nora Naranjo-Morse and Joy Harjo." *Studies in American Indian Literatures* 7, no. 1 (95): 45–63.

Honigman, John J. "Hopi Womenpower" *Human Behavior* 3 (1974): 49–50.

———. "North America." In *Psychological Anthropology,* edited by F. L. Hsu, 121–66. Homewood, Ill.: Dorsey, 1961.

Hubbard, Patick. "Trickster, Renewal and Survival." *American Indian Culture and Research Journal* 4, no. 4 (1980): 113–24.

Hultkrantz, Ake. *The Religions of the American Indians.* Translated by Monica Setterwall. Berkeley: University of California Press, 1967.

———. "Religious Aspects of the Wind River Shoshoni Folk Literature." In *Culture in History: Essays in Honor of Paul Radin,* edited by Stanley Diamond, 552–59. New York: Columbia University Press, 1960.

Hunter, Carol: "A MELUS Interview: Wendy Rose." *MELUS* 10, no. 3 (1983): 67–87.

Huntsman, Jeffrey F. "Traditional Native American Literature: The Translation Dilemma." In *Smoothing the Ground: Essays on Native American Oral Literature,* edited by Brian Swann, 87–97. Berkeley: University of California Press, 1983.

Hymes, Dell. "Coyote, Master of Death, True to Life." In *Coming to Light,* edited by Brian Swann, 286–306. New York: Vintage, 1994.

———. Foreword to *Portrait of "the Whiteman": Linguistic Play and Cultural Symbols Among the Western Apache,* by Keith Basso. Cambridge, England: Cambridge University Press, 1979.

———. *"In vain I tried to tell you": Essays in Native American Ethnopoetics.* Philadelphia: University of Pennsylvania Press, 1981.

Hynes, William J., and William Doty. "The Historical Overview of Theoretical Issues: The Problem of the Trickster." In *Mythical Trickster Figures: Contours, Contexts, and Criticisms,* edited by William J. Hynes and William G. Doty, 13–22. Tuscaloosa: University of Alabama Press, 1993.

———, and William Doty, eds. *Mythical Trickster Figures: Contours, Contexts, and Criticisms.* Tuscaloosa: University of Alabama Press, 1993.

Jacobs, Elizabeth D. *Nehalem Tillamook Tales.* Edited by Melville Jacobs. Eugene: University of Oregon Press, 1959.

Jacobs, Melville. *Clackamas Chinook Texts.* Part I. Indiana University Research Center in Anthropology, Folklore and Linguistics, no. 8. Bloomington: Indiana University Press, 1958.

———. *The Content and Style of an Oral Literature: Clackamas Myths and Tales.* New York: Wenner-Gren Foundation, 1959.

———. "Humor and Social Structure in an Oral Literature." In *Culture in History: Essays in Honor of Paul Radin,* edited by Stanley Diamond, 181–89. New York: Columbia University Press, 1960.

———. *Northwest Sahaptin Texts.* Part 1. Columbia Contributions to Anthropology, no. 19. New York: Columbia University Press, 1934.

Jacobs, Sue-Ellen, Wesley Thomas, and Sabine Lang, eds. *Two-Spirit People: Native American Gender Identity, Sexuality, and Spirituality.* Urbana: University of Illinois Press, 1997.

Jahner, Elaine. "Wilderness Mentors." In *Coming to Light,* edited by Brian Swann, 423–31. New York: Vintage, 1994.

Johnston, Basil. *The Manitous: The Supernatural World of the Ojibway.* New York: Harper, 1995.

Jung, C. G. "On the Psychology of the Trickster Figure." Translated by R. F. C. Hull. In *The Trickster: A Study in American Indian Mythology,* edited by Paul Radin, 195–211. New York: Schocken Books, 1972.

Kendall, Martha B, ed. *Coyote Stories II.* IJAL-NATS Monograph, no. 6. Chicago: University of Chicago Press, 1980.

Kessler, Evelyn S. *Women: An Anthropological View.* New York: Holt, Rinehart and Winston, 1976.

Kidwell, Clara Sue. "The Power of Women in Three American Indian Societies." *The Journal of Ethnic Studies* 6, no. 3 (1978): 113–21.

King, Thomas. *Green Grass, Running Water.* New York: Bantam, 1993.

Kinkade, M. Dale. "Native Oral Literature of the Northwest Coast and the Plateau." In *Dictionary of Native American Literature,* edited by Andrew Wiget, 33–45. New York: Garland, 1994.

Klein, Laura F., and Lillian A. Ackerman, eds. *Women and Power in Native North America.* Norman: University of Oklahoma Press, 1995.

Kluckhohn, Clyde. "Navaho Categories." In *Culture in History: Essays in Honor of Paul Radin,* edited by Stanley Diamond, 65–98. New York: Columbia University Press, 1960.

Kroeber, Alfred L. *The Arapaho.* Lincoln: University of Nebraska Press, 1983.

———. "Cheyenne Tales." *Journal of American Folklore* 12 (1900): 161–90.

———. *Gros Ventre Myths and Tales.* Anthropological Papers of the American Museum of Natural History, no. 1. Museum of Natural History: New York, 1970.

———. *Indian Myths of South Central California.* University of California Publications, vol. 4, no. 4. Berkeley: University of California Press, 1906–7.

———. *The Religon of the Indians of California.* University of California Publications, American Archaeology and Ethnology. vol 4, no. 6. Berkeley: University of California Press, 1907. http://www.sacred-texts.com/nam/ ca/ric.htm.

———. "Ute Tales." *Journal of American Folklore* 14 (1901): 252–85.

———. *Yurok Myths.* Berkeley: University of California Press, 1978.

Kroeber, Karl. "Deconstructionist Criticism and American Indian Literature." *Boundary* 27, no. 3 (1979): 73–89.

———. "Poem, Dream, and the Consuming of Culture," *Georgia Review* 32, no. 2 (1978): 266–80.

———, ed. *Traditonal American Indian Literatures: Texts and Interpretations.* Lincoln: University of Nebraska Press, 1981.

Krupat, Arnold. *Ethnocriticism: Ethnography, History, Literature.* Berkeley: University of California Press, 1992.

———. *For Those Who Come After: A Study of Native American Autobiography.* Berkeley: University of California Press, 1985.

Lalonde, Chris. "Trickster, Trickster Discourse, and Identity in Louis Owens' *Wolfsong.*" *Studies in American Indian Literatures* 7, no. 1 (1995): 27–42.

Lamadrid, Enrique R. "The Picaro in the Literature of New Mexico." *MELUS* 20, no. 2 (1995): 15–34.

Lame Deer, John (Fire), and Richard Erdoes. *Lame Deer: Seeker of Visions.* New York: Washington Square, 1976.

Lang, Sabine. "Various Kinds of Two-Spirit People: Gender Variance and Homo-
     sexuality in Native American Communities." In *Two-Spirit People: Native
     American Gender Identity, Sexuality, and Spirituality,* edited by Sue-Ellen
     Jacobs, Wesley Thomas, and Sabine Lang, 100–18. Urbana: University of
     Illinois Press, 1997.

Lankford, George E. *Native American Legends: Southeastern Legends, Tales from
     the Natchez, Caddo, Biloxi, Chickasaw, and Other Nations.* American
     Folklore Series. Little Rock: August House, 1987.

———. "Oral Literature of the Southeast." In *Dictionary of Native American
     Literature,* edited by Andrew Wiget, 83–89. New York: Garland, 1994.

Lasley, Mary. "Sac and Fox Tales." *Journal of American Folklore* 15 (1902):
     170–78.

Lee, Francis, and James Bruchac, eds. *Reclaiming the Vision Past, Present and
     Future: Native Voices for the Eighth Generation.* New York: Greenfield
     Review Press, 1996.

Levi-Strauss, Claude. "Four Winnebago Myths: A Structural Sketch." In *Culture
     in History: Essays in Honor of Paul Radin,* edited by Stanley Diamond,
     351–62. New York: Columbia University Press, 1960.

———. *The Savage Mind.* Chicago: University of Chicago Press, 1973.

———. "The Structural Study of Myth." *Journal of American Folklore* 68 (1955):
     428–44.

———. "The Structural Study of Myth." *Structural Anthropology,* translated by
     Claire Jacobson and Brooke Grundfest Schoepf, 206–31. New York: Basic
     Books, 1963.

Lincoln, Kenneth. *Indi'n Humor: Bicultural Play in Native America.* New York:
     Oxford University Press, 1993.

———. "MELUS Interview: Hanay Geiogamah." *MELUS* 16, no. 3 (1989–90):
     69–81.

———. *Native American Renaissance.* Berkeley: University of California Press,
     1983.

Little Thunder, Beverly. "I Am a Lakota Womyn." In *Two-Spirit People: Native
     American Gender Identity, Sexuality, and Spirituality,* edited by Sue-Ellen
     Jacobs, Wesley Thomas, and Sabine Lang, 204–9. Urbana: University of
     Illinois Press, 1997.

Loeb, E. M. "The Creator Concept among the Indians of North Central Califor-
     nia." *American Anthropologist* 28 (1926): 463–93.

Lopez, Barry. *Giving Birth to Thunder, Sleeping with His Daughter: Coyote Builds
     North America.* Kansas City: Sheed, Andrews and McMeel, 1977.

Lowie, Robert. *The Crow Indians.* New York: Farrar and Rinehart, 1935.

———. "The Hero-Trickster Discussion." *Journal of American Folklore* 22 (1909):
     431–33.

———. *Myths and Traditions of the Crow Indians.* American Museum of Natural History, no. 25. New York: American Museum of Natural History, 1918.

Luckert, Karl. "Coyote in Navajo and Hopi Tales." In Berard Haile, *Navajo Coyote Tales: The Curly to' A heeli'inii Version.* American Tribal Religions, vol. 8, edited by Karl W. Luckert, 3–19. Lincoln: University of Nebraska Press, 1984.

McClellan, Catherine, Maria Johns, and Dora Austin Wedge. "The Girl Who Married a Bear." In *Coming to Light,* edited by Brian Swann, 124–37. New York: Vintage: 1994.

McDermott, Laura. "Folklore of the Flathead Indians of Idaho: Adventures of Coyote." *Journal of American Folklore* 55 (1901): 240–51.

McNickle, D'Arcy. *Native American Tribalism: Indian Survivals and Renewals.* New York: Oxford University Press, 1973.

Makarius, Laura. "The Crime of Manibozho." *American Anthropologist* 75 (1973): 663–75.

———. "Ritual Clowns and Symbolic Behavior." *Diogenes* 69 (1970): 44–73.

Malotki, Ekkehart. *Gullible Coyote: Una'ihu, A Bilingual Collection of Hopi Coyote Stories.* Tucson: University of Arizona Press, 1985.

———, and Michael Lomatuway'ma. *Hopi Trickster Tales: Istutuwutsi.* Lincoln: University of Nebraska Press, 1984.

Maltz, Daniel, and Jo Allyn Archambault. "Gender and Power in Native North America." In *Women and Power in Native North America,* edited by Laura F. Klein and Lillian A. Ackerman, 230–49. Norman: University of Oklahoma Press, 1995.

Mander, Jerry. *In the Absence of the Sacred: The Failure of Technology and the Survival of the Indian Nations.* San Francisco: Sierra Club Books, 1991.

Marriott, Alice. *Saynday's People: The Kiowa Indians and the Stories They Told.* Lincoln: University of Nebraska Press, 1963.

———, and Carol K. Rachlin, eds. *American Indian Mythology.* New York: New American Library, 1968.

Mattina, Anthony. "Blue Jay and His Brother-in-Law." In *Coming to Light,* edited by Brian Swann, 332–45. New York: Vintage, 1994.

———. *The Colville Narrative of Peter J. Seymour (Kʷikʷit'as and Peter J. Seymour's Man-Eater Stories: A Colville Trilogy).* N.p., n.d.

———. "North American Indian Mythography: Editing Texts for the Printed Page." In *Recovering the Word: Essays on Native American Literature,* edited by Brian Swann and Arnold Krupat, 129–48. Los Angeles: University of California Press, 1987.

Melendez, Theresa. "The Oral Tradition and the Study of American Literature." In *Redefining American Literary History,* edited by A. Lavonne Brown Ruoff and Jerry W. Ward, 75–82. New York: MLA, 1990.

Millman, Lawrence. "Wolverine: An Innu Trickster." In *Coming to Light,* edited by Brian Swann, 208–21. New York: Vintage, 1994.

Mooney, James. *Myths of the Cherokee.* 19th Annual Report of the Bureau of American Ethnology, 1897–98, pt. 1. Washington, D.C.: GPO, 1900.

Moore, David L. "Decolonizing Criticism: Reading Dialectics and Dialogics in Native American Literatures." *Studies in American Indian Literature* 6, no. 4 (1994): 7–33.

Morrow, Phyllis. "Oral Literature of the Alaskan Arctic." In *Dictionary of Native American Literature,* edited by Andrew Wiget, 19–26. New York: Garland, 1994.

———, and Elsie Mather. "Two Tellings of the Story of Uterneq: 'The Woman Who Returned From the Dead.'" In *Coming to Light,* edited by Brian Swann, 37–56. New York: Vintage, 1994.

Nichols, John D. "'The Wishingbone Cycle': A Cree Ossian?" *International Journal of American Linguistics* 55 (April 1989): 155–78.

Niethammer, Carolyn. *Daughters of the Earth: The Lives and Legends of American Indian Women.* New York: Collier, 1977.

Norman, Howard A. *The Wishing Bone Cycle: Narrative Poems from the Swampy Cree Indians.* 2nd ed. Santa Barbara: Ross-Erikson, 1982.

Opler, Morris Edward. *Myths and Legends of the Lipan Apache Indians.* New York: J. J. Augustin, 1940.

Ortiz, Simon J. *Woven Stone.* Tucson: University of Arizona Press, 1992.

Owen, Mary A. *Folklore of the Musquaki Indians of North America.* Publication of the Folklore Society, no. 51. London: Folklore Society, 1904.

Parsons, Elsie Clews. *Kiowa Tales.* Memoirs of the American Folklore Society, no. 22. New York: American Folklore Society, 1929.

———. "Micmac Folklore." *Journal of American Folklore* 38 (1925): 55–133.

———. "Navaho Folk Tales." *Journal of American Folklore* 36 (1923): 368–75.

———. "The Origin Myth of Zuni." *Journal of American Folklore* 36 (1929): 135–62.

———. "Pueblo Folk-tales, Probably of Spanish Provenience." *Journal of American Folklore* 31 (1918): 216–55.

———. *Pueblo Indian Religion.* 2 vols. Chicago: University of Chicago Press, 1939.

———. *Tewa Tales.* New York: American Folklore Society, 1926.

Paulme, Denise. "The Impossible Imitation in African Trickster Tales." *Forms of Folklore in Africa,* edited by Bernth Lindfors, 64–103. Austin: University of Texas Press, 1977.

Pelton, Robert. *The Trickster in West Africa: A Study of Mythic Irony and Sacred Delight.* Berkeley: University of California Press, 1980.

Pensineau, Migizi. "We Have Always Been Here." *Native Americas* 19, nos. 3–4 (2002): 26.

Phinney, Archie. *Nez Percé Texts.* Columbia University Contributions to Anthropology, no. 25. New York: Columbia University Press, 1934.

Pope, Polly. "Toward a Structural Analysis of North American Trickster Tales." *Southern Folklore Quarterly* 31 (1967): 274–86.

Pritchard, Evan T. *No Word for Time: The Way of the Algonquin People.* San Francisco: Council Oak Books, 1997.

Provost, Kara. "Becoming Afrekete: The Trickster in the Work of Audre Lord." *MELUS* 20, no. 4 (1995): 45–59.

Pulitano, Elvira. "Telling Stories through the Stage: A Conversation with William Yellow Robe." *Studies in American Indian Literature* 10, no. 1 (1981): 19–44.

Radin, Paul. *Primitive Man as a Philosopher.* New York: Appleton, 1927.

———. *The Trickster: A Study in American Indian Mythology.* New York: Schocken Books, 1972.

———, ed. *Crashing Thunder: The Autobiography of an American Indian.* Lincoln: University of Nebraska Press, 1983.

Ramsey, Jarold. *Reading the Fire: Essays in the Traditional Literatures of the Far West.* Lincoln: University of Nebraska Press, 1983.

———. "Thoreau's Last Words—And America's First Literatures." In *Redefining American Literary History,* edited by A. Lavonne Brown Ruoff and Jerry W. Ward, 52–61. New York: Modern Language Association, 1990.

———. "The White Man in Native Oral Tradition." In *Dictionary of Native American Literature,* edited by Andrew Wiget, 139–42. New York: Garland Publishing, 1994.

———, ed. *Coyote Was Going There: Indian Literatures of the Far West.* Lincoln: University of Nebraska Press, 1983.

Red Earth, Michael. "Traditional Influences on a Contemporary Gay-Identified Sisseton Dakota." In *Two-Spirit People: Native American Gender Identity, Sexuality, and Spirituality,* edited by Sue-Ellen Jacobs, Wesley Thomas, and Sabine Lang, 210–16. Urbana: University Illinois Press, 1997.

Reichard, Gladys. *Navaho Religion: A Study in Symbolism.* 2 vols. Bollingen Series, no. 18. New York: Pantheon, 1950.

Rice, Julian. *Lakota Storytelling: Black Elk, Ella Deloria, and Frank Fools Crow.* Series 21, Regional Studies no. 3. New York: Peter Lang, 1989.

Ricketts, MacLinscott. "The North American Indian Trickster." *History of Religions* 5, no.2 (1966): 323–50.

———."The Shaman and the Trickster." In *Mythical Trickster Figures: Contours, Contexts, and Criticisms,* edited by William J. Hynes and William Doty, 87–105. Tuscaloosa: University of Alabama Press, 1993.

Roberts, John W. "The African American Animal Trickster as Hero." In *Redefining American Literary History,* edited by A. Lavonne Brown Ruoff and Jerry W. Ward, 97–114. New York: Modern Language Association, 1990.

Róheim, Geza. "Culture Hero and Trickster in North American Mythology." In *Indian Tribes of Aboriginal America,* edited by Sol Tax, 190–94. Selected Papers of the 24th International Congress of Americanists. Chicago, 1952.

Rose, Wendy. "Trickster: 1977." *The Remembered Earth: An Anthology of Native American Literature,* edited by Geary Hobson, 384. Albuquerque: University of New Mexico Press, 1979.

Ross, A. C. "Storytelling." In *Reclaiming the Vision, Past, Present and Future: Native Voices for the Eighth Generation,* edited by Lee Francis and James Bruchac, 9–10. New York: Greenfield Review Press, 1996.

Ruoff, A. LaVonne Brown. *American Indian Literatures: An Introduction, Bibliographic Review, and Selected Bibliography.* New York: Modern Language Association, 1990.

———, and Jerry W. Ward, eds. *Redefining American Literary History.* New York: Modern Language Association, 1990.

Rushforth, Scott. "Oral Literature of the Subarctic Athapaskans." In *Dictionary of Native American Literature,* edited by Andrew Wiget, 27–32. New York: Garland, 1994.

Russell, Frank. "Myths of the Jicarilla Apache." *Journal of American Folklore* 11 (1898): 253–71.

Ryan, Allan J. *The Trickster Shift: Humor and Irony in Contemporary Native Art.* Toronto: UCB Press, 1999.

Ryden, Hope. *God's Dog: A Celebration of the North American Coyote.* New York: Lyons Press, 1979.

Sanders, Thomas E., and Walter W. Peek. *Literature of the American Indian.* Beverly Hills, Calif.: Glenco Press, 1973.

Sands, Kathleen M. "Narrative Resistance: Native American Collaborative Autobiography." *Studies in American Indian Literature* 10, no. 1 (1998): 1–18.

Sarris, Greg. *Keeping Slug Woman Alive: A Holistic Approach to American Indian Texts.* Berkeley: University of California Press, 1993.

Schlegel, Alice. "The Socialization of the Hopi Girl." *Ethnology* 12 (1937): 449–62.

———. "Three Styles of Domestic Authority: A Cross-Cultural Study." In *Being Female: Reproduction, Power and Change,* edited by Dana Raphael, 165–76. The Hague: Mouton, 1975.

Schmerler, Henrietta. "Trickster Marries His Daughter." *Journal of American Folklore* 44 (1931): 196–207.

Schoolcraft, Henry Rowe. *Algic Researches, Comprising Inquiries Respecting the Menial Characteristics of the North American Indians.* Indian Tales and Legends, First Series. New York: Harper, 1839.

————. "Manabozho." In *Schoolcraft's Indian Legends,* edited by Mentor L. Williams, 65–83. East Lansing: Michigan State University Press, 1956.

Schwartz, Charles W., and Elizabeth R. Schwartz. *The Wild Mammals of Missouri.* Rev. ed. Columbia: University of Missouri Press and Missouri Department of Conservation, 1981.

Sekaquaptewa, Emory. "One More Smile for a Hopi Clown." *The South Corner of Time: Hopi, Navajo, Papago, Yaqui Tribal Literature,* edited by Larry Evers, 14–17. Tucson: University of Arizona Press, 1980.

Senier, Siobahn. "A Zuni Raconteur Dons the Junco Shirt." *American Literature* 66 (1994): 223–38.

Seumptewa, Evelyn, with C. F. Vogelin and F. M. Vogelin. "Wren and Coyote." In *Coyote Stories II,* edited by Martha B. Kendall, 104–10. IJAL-NATS Monograph, no. 6. Chicago: University of Chicago Press, 1980.

Sharp, Henry S. "Asymmetric Equals: Women and Men among the Chipewyan." In *Women and Power in Native North America,* edited by Laura F. Klein and Lillian A. Ackerman, 46–74. Norman: University of Oklahoma Press, 1995.

Shaul, David Leedom. "Two Hopi Songpoems." In *Coming to Light,* edited by Brian Swann, 679–89. New York: Vintage, 1994.

Silko, Leslie Marmon. *Storyteller.* New York: Seaver, 1981.

Simpson, Ruth DeEtte. *The Hopi Indians.* Southwest Museum Leaflets, no. 25. Los Angeles: Southwest Museum, 1953.

Sims, Leo. *Sun Chief: The Autobiography of a Hopi Indian.* New Haven: Yale University Press, 1942.

Skeels, Dell. "A Classification of Humor in Nez Percé Mythology." *Journal of American Folklore* 67 (1954): 57–64.

Snyder, Eloise, ed. *The Study of Women: Enlarging Perspectives of Social Reality.* New York: Harper and Row, 1979.

Snyder, Gary. "A Berry Feast." *Evergreen Review* 2 (1957): 110–14. Reprinted in Gary Snyder, *The Back Country,* 13–16. New York: New Directions, 1968.

Speck, Frank G. *Ethnology of the Yuchi Indians.* University of Pennsylvania Anthropological Publications of the University Museum, no. 1. Philadelphia: University Museum, 1909.

Spencer, Katherine. *Mythology and Values: An Analysis of the Navaho Chantway Myths.* Philadelphia: American Folklore Society, 1957.

Spicer, Edward H. *A Short History of the Indians of the United States.* New York: D. Van Nostrand, 1969.

Spinden, Herbert J. "Myths of the Nez Percé Indians." *Journal of American Folklore* 21 (1908): 13–23, 149–57.

Spindler, George D., and Louise S. "American Indian Personality Types and Their Sociocultural Roots." *The Annals of the American Academy of Political and Social Science* 311 (May 1957): 145–57.

Stern, Theodore. "Some Sources of Variability in Klamath Mytholology." *Journal of American Folklore* 69 (1956): 1–12, 135–46, 377–86.

———. "The Trickster in Klamath Mythology." *Western Folklore* 12, no. 3 (1953): 158–74.

Stevenson, Matilda Cox. *The Sia*. 11th Annual Report of the Bureau of American Ethnology. Washington, D.C.: GPO, 1894.

Susag, Dorothea M. "Zitkala-Sa (Gertrude Simmons Bonnin): A Powerful Literary Voice." *Studies in American Indian Literatures* 5, no. 4 (1993): 3–24.

Swann, Brian, ed. *Coming to Light*. Vintage: New York, 1994.

———, ed. *Smoothing the Ground: Essays on Native American Oral Literature*. Berkeley: University of California Press, 1983.

———, and Arnold Krupat, eds. *Recovering the Word: Essays on Native American Literature*. Los Angeles: University of California Press, 1987.

Swanton, John R. *Haida Texts and Myths*. 29th Annual Report of the Bureau of American Ethnology. Washington, D.C.: GPO, 1905.

Tedlock, Barbara. *The Beautiful and the Dangerous*. New York: Penguin, 1992.

———. "Boundaries of Belief." *I Become Part of It: Sacred Dimensions in Native American Life*, edited by D. M. Dooling and Paul Jordan-Smith, 124–38. New York: Parabola Books, 1991.

———. "The Clown's Way." In *Teachings from the American Earth: Indian Religion and Philosophy*, edited by Barbara and Dennis Tedlock, 105–18. New York: Liveright, 1975.

———, and Dennis Tedlock. *Teachings from the American Earth: Indian Religion and Philosophy*. New York: Liveright, 1975.

Tedlock, Dennis. "Pueblo Literature: Style and Verisimilitude." In *New Perspectives on the Pueblo*, edited by Alfonso Ortiz, 219–42. Albuquerque: University of New Mexico Press, 1972.

———. "On the Translation of Style in Oral Narrative." *Journal of American Folklore* 84 (1971): 114–33.

———, trans. *Finding the Center: Narrative Poetry of the Zuni Indians*. New York: Dial, 1972.

Teit, James. *Traditions of the Thompson River Indians*. Memoirs of the American Folklore Society, no. 6. Boston: Houghton-Mifflin, 1898.

Terrell, John Upton. *American Indian Almanac: The Authoritative Reference and Chronicle*. New York: Thomas Y. Crowell, 1974.

Thayer, James Steele. "The Berdache of the Northern Plains: A Socioreligious Perspective." *Journal of Anthropological Research* 36 (1980): 287–93.

Thompson, Craig. "Gender Representation in Two Clackamas Myths." *Studies in American Indian Literatures* 3, no. 1 (1991): 19–39.

Thompson, Stith. *The Folktale*. New York: Dryden Press, 1946.

———. *Tales of the North American Indians.* Bloomington: Indiana University Press, 1971.

Tinker, George. "Spirituality, Native American Personhood, Sovereignty and Solidarity." In *Native and Christian: Indigenous Voice on Religious Identity in the United States and Canada,* edited by James Treat, 116–31. Routledge: New York, 1996.

To'dích'ii'nii Binalí Biye (Timothy Benally, Sr.). "Hane', Ma'ii Jooldloshí: Stories about Coyote, the One Who Trots." In *Coming to Light,* edited by Brian Swann, 601–13. New York, 1994.

Toelken, Barre. "Coyote, Skunk, and the Prairie Dogs." In *Coming to Light,* edited by Brian Swann, 590–600. New York: Vintage, 1994.

———. "The Demands of Harmony." In *I Become Part of It: Sacred Dimensions in Native American Life,* edited by D. M. Dooling and Paul Jordan-Smith, 59–71. New York: Parabola Books, 1991.

———. "Life and Death in the Navajo Coyote Tales." In *Recovering the Word: Essays on Native American Literature,* edited by Brian Swann and Arnold Krupat, 388–401. Los Angeles: University of California Press, 1987.

———, and Tacheeni Scott. "Poetic Retranslation and the 'Pretty Language' of Yellowman." In *Traditional American Indian Literatures: Texts and Interpretations,* edited by Karl Kroeber, 65–116. Lincoln: University of Nebraska Press, 1981.

Turner, Victor. *The Ritual Process: Structure and Anti-Structure.* Chicago: Aldine, 1969.

Underhill, Ruth. *The Autobiography of a Papago Woman.* American Anthropological Association Memoirs, vol. 46. Menasha, Wisc.: American Anthropological Association, 1936.

Velie, Alan R. *Four American Indian Literary Masters: N. Scott Momaday, James Welch, Leslie Marmon Silko, and Gerald Vizenor.* Norman: University of Oklahoma Press, 1982.

Vizenor, Gerald. *Darkness in Saint Louis Bearheart.* St. Paul, Minn.: Truck Press, 1978.

———. *Earthdivers: Tribal Narratives on Mixed Descent.* Minneapolis: University of Minnesota Press, 1981.

———. *Summer in the Spring: Ojibwe Lyric Poems and Tribal Stories.* Minneapolis: Nodine Press, 1981.

———. *Wordarrows: Indians and Whites in the New Fur Trade.* Minneapolis: University of Minnesota Press, 1978.

Voth, Henry. *The Traditions of the Hopi.* Anthropological Series, no. 8. Chicago Field Columbian Museum, 1905.

Walker, Deward E., in collaboration with Daniel N. Matthews. *Nez Percé Coyote Tales: The Myth Cycle.* Norman: University of Oklahoma Press, 1998.

Walker, James R. *Lakota Belief and Ritual,* edited by Raymond DeMallie and Elaine A. Jahner. Lincoln: University of Nebraska Press, 1980.

———. *Lakota Myth,* edited by Elaine A. Jahner. Lincoln: University of Nebraska Press, 1983.

Walle, Alf. H. "The Morphology and Social Dynamics of an American Indian Folktale." *Kentucky Folklore Record* 24 (1978): 74–80.

Wasson, George. "Susan Wasson Wolgamott Story." Personal e-mail to author, 9 May 2003.

Wasson, Will. "How Salmon Got Greasy Eyes." *Parabola* 4, no. 1 (1990): 66–69.

Watermann, T. T. "The Explanatory Element in the Folktales of the North American Indians." *Journal of American Folklore* 27 (1914): 1–55.

Whitaker, John O. *The Audubon Society Field Guide to North American Mammals.* New York: Alfred A. Knopf, 1980.

Whitbourne, Christine. "Moral Ambiguity in the Picaresque Novel Spanish Tradition." In *Knaves and Swindlers: Essays on the Picaresque Novel in Europe,* edited by Christine Whitebourne, 1–24. London: Oxford University Press, 1974.

———, ed. *Knaves and Swindlers: Essays on the Picaresque Novel in Europe.* London: Oxford University Press, 1974.

Whitehead, Harriet. "The Bow and the Burden Strap: A New Look at Institutionalized Homosexuality in Native North America." In *Sexual Meanings: The Cultural Construction of Gender and Sexuality,* edited by Sherry B. Ortner and Harriet Whitehead, 85–112. Cambridge, England: Cambridge University Press, 1981.

Wiget, Andrew. "His Life in His Tail: The Native American Trickster and the Literature of Possibility." In *Redefining American Literary History,* edited by A. LaVonne Brown Ruoff and Jerry W. Ward, 83–96. New York: Modern Language Association, 1990.

———. *Native American Literature.* Boston: Twayne, 1985.

———. "Telling the Tale: A Performance Analysis of a Hopi Story." In *Recovering the Word: Essays on Native American Literature,* edited by Brian Swann and Arnold Krupat, 297–336. Los Angeles: University of California Press, 1987.

———, ed. *Dictionary of Native American Literature.* Garland Reference Library of the Humanities, vol. 1815. New York: Garland, 1994.

Williams, Walter L. *The Spirit and the Flesh: Sexual Diversity in American Indian Culture.* Boston: Beacon, 1992.

Wilson, Darryl Babe. "Silver Gray Fox Creates Another World." In *Coming to Light,* edited by Brian Swann, 737–48. New York: Vintage, 1994.

"The Wisdom of the Contrary: A Conversation with Joseph Epes Brown." *Parabola* 4, no. 1 (1990): 54–65.

Wissler, Clark. "Some Dakota Myths." *Journal of American Folklore* 20 (1907): 121, 195.

Wright, Barton. *Clowns of the Hopi: Tradition Keepers and Delight Makers.* Flagstaff, Ariz.: Northland, 1994.

Yava, Albert. "Way Back in the Distant Past." In *The South Corner of Time: Hopi, Navajo, Papago, Yaqui Tribal Literature,* edited by Larry Evers, 8–13. Tucson: University of Arizona Press, 1980.

Yes I Am Not Iktomi, directed by Charles Nauman. Nauman Film Production, 1999. Videocassette.

Zitkala-Sa. *Old Indian Legends.* Lincoln: University of Nebraska Press, 1985.

———. *Old Indian Legends.* http;//etext.lib.virginia.edu/toc/modeng/public/ZitLege.html.

Zolbrod, Paul. "Singing Up the Mountain." In *Coming to Light,* edited by Brian Swann, 614–23. New York: Vintage, 1994.

Zuni People. *The Zunis: Self-Portrayals,* translated by Alvina Quam. New York: New American Library, 1972.

Index

CPSIA information can be obtained at www.ICGtesting.com
Printed in the USA
LVOW12s2346150315

430682LV00001B/9/P

9 780806 137964